C000261455

DRAGONS AND ALL BLACKS

WALES V.
NEW ZEALAND
– 1953 AND A
CENTURY OF
RIVALRY

DRAGONS ALL BLACKS

Huw Richards
Forewords by Bob Stuart and Bleddyn Williams

MAINSTREAM
PUBLISHING
EDINBURGH AND LONDON

First published in Great Britain in 2004 by
MAINSTREAM PUBLISHING COMPANY (EDINBURGH) LTD
7 Albany Street
Edinburgh EH1 3UG

ISBN 1 84018 928 2

A catalogue record for this book is available from the British Library

Typeset in Frutiger and Garamond
Printed and bound in Great Britain by
Creative Print and Design, Wales

To my parents, Stan and Sheila Richards, who were married in 1953, and to my goddaughter, Sydney Christina Wittstock McDonald, born during the writing of this book.

CONTENTS

ACKNOWLEDGEMENTS

This book had its origins in a conversation and a dialogue. The conversation was with historian David Kynaston, author of *WG's Birthday Party*, a vivid portrait of late Victorian cricket via a reconstruction of the 1898 Gentlemen–Players match. Discussion turned to which rugby match might prove comparably rewarding. David nominated Obolensky's match – England's victory over the All Blacks in 1936. I cited the passage of time (the conversation was in 1991) and explained that great match though it undoubtedly was, an English victory was not quite sufficient to inspire the commitment needed to write a book. A Welsh win over New Zealand, on the other hand . . .

The dialogue is with my longest-standing New Zealand friend Jamie Belich, now Professor of History at the University of Auckland, concerning the rugby relationship between our two nations, begun when we were both postgraduate students at Nuffield College, Oxford, and continued whenever the opportunity has arisen since.

The essential element in researching the book was the participation of the surviving players. I must plead guilty to occasional professional cynicism about the alleged camaraderie of rugby. The surviving players from the 1953 Wales v. All Blacks match showed me exactly what it really meant with their warm, willing reception of a writer who wished to delve into their memories. In particular thanks are due to Richard and Elsie

White, who prolonged a stay in Auckland for another day in order to save me the long journey to Gisborne, and to Bill McCaw, who gave an interview only a few days after the death of his wife. John Tanner, Brian Fitzpatrick and Gareth Griffiths put up with being interviewed twice, while Bill Clark, Gwyn Rowlands, Bob Scott and Bob Stuart have all been prepared to enter into further correspondence. Thanks therefore to Brian Fitzpatrick, John Tanner, Richard and Elsie White, Allan Elsom, Bill McCaw, Peter Eastgate, Bill and Billa Clark, Bob Stuart, Bob and Irene Scott, Keith Davis, Kevin Skinner, Snow White, Stoker Williams, Gwyn Rowlands, Cliff Morgan, John and Pegi Gwilliam, the late Dai Davies and Glyn Davies. Thanks also to the late Sir Terry McLean, Don Cameron and Warwick Roger for giving freely of their memories of 1953 and Ron Waldron for talking about the trio of Neath forwards who played for Wales.

None of this would have been possible without locating the players first. Bob Howitt's enormous knowledge of old All Blacks and unstinting generosity with his time, expertise and contacts made the New Zealand end of the book practicable, while Arwyn Owen, Rob Cole, Bleddyn Williams, Colin Bosley and Paul Beken were similarly helpful in tracking down Welsh survivors.

Other research was carried on at the National Newspaper Library, Colindale; the New Zealand Rugby Museum, Palmerston North; the British Library; the Bodleian library, Oxford; Swansea City Library; and Auckland University Library. Thanks are also due to the British and New Zealand National Sound Archives/Nga Taonga Korero for rushing through the copying and delivery of a recording of the entire match commentary which was both grippingly fascinating and an invaluable research tool. The Patio de la Cartuja in Seville provided an ideal environment for the bulk of the writing.

Once the manuscript was completed, Gareth Williams, Huw Bowen and David Scott gave up large amounts of time and mental energy to reading and offering invariably apposite suggestions as to how it might be improved. Kate Green, in spite of not having the slightest interest in rugby, proofread the manuscript. I owe all of them a debt for generosity far beyond the normal demands of friendship.

Thanks are also due to colleagues at the *Financial Times* and FT.com – David Owen, Tom O'Sullivan, Adam James, Charles Morris and Peter

ACKNOWLEDGEMENTS

Chapman – for humouring the eccentric and time-consuming enthusiasm of their rugby writer, while Peter Berlin and Pete Wyckoff of the *International Herald Tribune* were similarly tolerant of this project's impact on their cricket coverage. Other rugby writers – notably Tim Glover, Rob Kitson, Ian Malin, Julian Guyer and Chris Hewett – were similarly helpful and encouraging. Martin Flanagan of the *Melbourne Age* offered invaluable advice, based on his own outstanding study of the 1970 Australian Rules Grand Final, on writing at length about old matches, while John Jenkins provided enormous assistance from his unmatched knowledge of the detail and statistics of Welsh rugby (and other) history.

Thanks for assistance taking a range of forms are due also to Peter Stead, Gareth Williams, Huw Bowen, Dick Holt, Tony Collins, Peter Lush and Dave Farrar, Graham Thomas, David Parry-Jones, David Scott, John Mehaffey, Greg Ryan, Len Richardson, Lloyd Jones, Grahame and Briony Thorne, Mary Scott, Oma Nepia, Bob Luxford and everybody at the Rugby Museum of New Zealand, Bryan Waddle, Dean McLachlan, Peter Sellers, Phil Minshull, Jamie and Margaret Belich, Mike Price, Steve Lewis, Alan Evans, Kamran Abbasi, Helen Elwell, Rob Steen, Steve Pinder, Eva Melly, Jane and Roy Elvin, Mark McDonald and Melinda Wittstock, Paul Geradine, John Nicol, Phil Melling, Brian Matthews, Paul Melly, Neil Levis and Jill James.

Thanks for the assistance with photos to Jen Little of Empics, Bob Luxford, Coxie and Marc Weakley, and to the late Sir Terry McLean for permission to quote from his book on the tour.

Particular thinks are due to Ashley Drake, whose confidence in and enthusiasm for this project as its initial publisher were immensely important. It is a matter of considerable personal regret that circumstances should have prevented his bringing the project to fruition, and of great gratitude that he should have enabled its placement with Mainstream, where Bill Campbell, Graeme Blaikie, Ailsa Bathgate, Becky Pickard and Lizzie Cameron have all demonstrated how the company has attained so prominent a place in British sports, and general, publishing.

Huw Richards
Walthamstow, London
July 2003 and June 2004

FOREWORD

by Bob Stuart

The 1953–54 All Blacks last year held their fourth reunion in honour of the fiftieth anniversary of their 'Grand Tour'. It included the UK unions, France, Canada and the USA, comprised 36 matches and extended just in excess of five months.

It was wonderful to have 19 of the team together after 50 years and the following paragraph from the foreword to the reunion programme sums up the core team spirit:

'The fact that the surviving players of the Fourth All Blacks are still eager to come together for a fourth reunion speaks volumes for the pride and character that was generated among the side. The fact that several widows of players who have passed on are keen to join in the reunion adds a special flavour to the celebrations.'

Tour memories took pride of place – 'great moments' were recalled in some detail. It would be natural to assume that any one 'great moment' would be an historical rugby victory. On the contrary, one such moment focused on the loss in the final few minutes to a great Welsh team at Cardiff Arms Park on 19 December 1953.

This historic match has been the subject of many books and analysed from every perspective – but refuses to be consigned to the bin of rugby history.

Huw Richards has revisited the match in this book, and I am sure it reflects his in-depth research with objectivity, fairness and a surprising degree of freshness.

In particular, he captures the unique rugby fellowship that has endured in a very meaningful fashion for fifty years between the two teams. He captures, too, the atmosphere of that great match at Cardiff. The mass rendering by 60,000 Welsh people of 'Land of My Fathers' is an awe-inspiring experience impossible to equal anywhere.

This is a book which, I am confident, will bring great pleasure to all rugby generations.

Bob Stuart,
Wellington

FOREWORD

by Bleddyn Williams

Many of the happiest memories from a lifetime watching and playing rugby have concerned New Zealand. I first saw the All Blacks as a 12 year old in 1935, proudly watching my brother Gwyn, himself only 17, play against them for Cardiff.

To watch New Zealand play was memorable in itself. To play against them, against the Kiwis in 1945, for the Lions on tour in 1950 and against Bob Stuart's All Blacks in 1953, was a privilege. To lead club and country against them, and to win both matches, is fortune given to very few and means that 1953 ranks very high indeed among my memories. I am particularly proud that we achieved what we did without a coach. We had nobody to tell us how to play against New Zealand. We had to work it out for ourselves, based on the memories some of us brought back from the 1950 Lions tour and our own observations of the All Blacks' earlier matches. In the Welsh match, we had also to cope with a period when we were reduced to 14 men, when Gareth Griffiths dislocated his shoulder, and had to battle for survival until he bravely came back on to the field.

Perhaps even more important than those memories are the friendships, lasting to this day, that came out of those matches. The surviving Cardiff players – there are now seven of us – meet every year on the anniversary of our match against the All Blacks. The fiftieth anniversary, in 2003, fell on the eve of the World Cup final in Sydney.

Those friendships extend to New Zealand – to people like Snow White, who propped against Cardiff; Ron Hemi, the hooker on the 1953 tour, who is sadly no longer with us; and Fred Allen of the Kiwi team. They reflect the wider friendship between Wales and New Zealand, based on shared memories and a mutual passion for rugby.

The sad part is that Wales's rugby has not kept up with New Zealand's. Of course, they have had the great advantage of the influx of islanders into New Zealand, bringing huge amounts of rugby talent. Their back division in 2003 was perhaps the best I have ever seen, an extraordinary combination of enormously gifted players. To play against the All Blacks is still rugby's supreme challenge, one we in Wales sadly rarely rise to.

We no longer seem to produce great fly-halfs, or a sufficient number of players who combine physical power with ball-playing skills. Until we do, we will struggle. I am, of course, happy that our achievements of 1953 are remembered, and that they are recounted in this book, but would have been shocked beyond belief had anyone suggested at the time that we would still be waiting for another Wales victory after more than 50 years. Proud as I am of being Wales's last winning captain against New Zealand, it is a distinction that I would very much like to lose.

Bleddyn Williams,
Cardiff

PROLOGUE

Saturday, 19 December 1953, 4 p.m.

Five minutes to go. Wales 8, New Zealand 8. The 57,000 crowd packed into Cardiff Arms Park had been subdued earlier as the New Zealanders dominated. Now, though, they were transformed along with their team. Wales, who had equalised only a few minutes earlier with a contentious penalty, pressed for victory.

Wales right-winger Ken Jones threw into a lineout in front of the double-decker North Stand between New Zealand's 10-yard and 25-yard lines. 'Up she goes,' said radio commentator Winston McCarthy, his words heard simultaneously via crackling short-wave radio reception on the other side of the world in New Zealand, where it was the early hours of Sunday morning.

Wales won possession, which was worked rapidly back to scrum-half Rex Willis. He dive-passed to his outside-half, the mercurially darting Cliff Morgan, already under pressure from his marker Bill Clark, a lanky, whippet-fast flanker, as he moved fast to his left. Morgan dummied and, as the crowd's roar mounted, chipped a cross-kick left-footed towards the opposite touchline, aiming for left-winger Gwyn Rowlands.

All Blacks winger Allan Elsom was there first, just inside the 25 and a few yards from the touchline, slightly ahead of Rowlands. The tall, powerful Elsom gathered but was tackled immediately by the

Welshman. Down went the ball and as the two wingers scrambled for possession the battle was joined by New Zealand centre John Tanner and his opposite number Gareth Griffiths. It was won, though, by a fast-moving late arrival, the Welsh flanker Clem Thomas, a forceful, powerfully built figure wearing the number 15. Thomas gathered and his momentum took him towards the left touchline, closely pursued by Elsom. Just as Thomas looked certain to career into touch he turned, almost on the line, shrugging off the New Zealand winger's attempt to grasp him around the shoulders.

Still there seemed no space. 'For a moment everything stood still,' wrote the New Zealand journalist Terry McLean. Then Thomas, 'like a man in a slow-motion film', raised the ball above his head before dropping his hands and kicking right-footed across the field, completing the movement just before the New Zealand full-back Bob Scott could smother it.

Cleanly struck, it soared across the pitch just inside the New Zealand 25. Waiting on the right were two men left isolated as other players had been drawn towards the scuffle on the left. Jones, an Olympic sprinter, and his New Zealand marker Ron Jarden. The fastest men on either side, the two best wingers in the world. A try seemed certain, but at which end? The ball struck the Arms Park turf and bounded high between the two fast-converging figures . . .

CHAPTER 1

THE RED AND THE BLACK:

Rugby's Special Relationship

Jones, Jarden and the 28 players reduced to spectatorship as the wings closed in on Thomas's cross-kick were 1953's participants in rugby union's special relationship – an intense, sometimes fractious, but affectionate and mutually admiring rivalry between two small countries from opposite ends of the earth who shared a national passion for the game. Both countries had other important relationships. New Zealand's contest with South Africa was to reach such a pitch of passion in 1956 that, said one historian, 'the whole country was worked up to the point where reason seemed to have fled'. Wales's local rivalries, particularly that with England, were refuelled annually by the Five Nations championship.

The extent, though, to which this one mattered is summed up by two men present at their first Wales v. New Zealand match on 19 December 1953. The journalist Terry McLean, 40, had just begun a career as New Zealand's most faithful chronicler of this (and every other) rivalry, an invariable presence at every meeting for the next 30 years. As the representative of the New Zealand Press Association, he sat in the press box in the South Stand alongside J.B.G. Thomas of the Cardiff *Western Mail*, feeding page after page of yellow foolscap copy paper through a typewriter 'liberated' from the New Zealand Army at the end of his war service as he sent a running report back to his employers in Wellington. Years later, McLean was to write: 'Of all New Zealand's relationships in sport, none had been quite so precious as that, in rugby, with Wales.'

Among the crowd was Clive Rowlands, a 15-year-old schoolboy from Upper Cwmtwrch in the Swansea Valley. Next time Wales played New Zealand, in 1963, he would be Wales's scrum-half and captain. Six years after that, he was to be the coach on Wales's first ever tour of New Zealand, and in 1987 he would manage the Welsh team who finished third in the first Rugby Union World Cup, also in New Zealand. He would also become president of the Welsh Rugby Union. Arriving in New Zealand as Wales's coach, he was to say: 'The greatest thing a Welsh rugby man can do is to play against the All Blacks.'

It was 65 years to the day since Welsh and New Zealand teams first met on the rugby field. On 19 December 1888, Llanelli entertained the New Zealand Natives, who were approaching the midway point of an extraordinary year-long odyssey encompassing 115 matches – including 8 of Australian Rules football – in New Zealand, Australia and Britain. A predominantly Maori team, their forerunning echoed Australian aborigine cricketers who had toured England 20 years earlier, also well in advance of a full national team.

Their pioneering was not limited to arriving first. They played in all black, with a large silver fern on their shirts. Five years later, one of their number, Tom Ellison – a man of parts, both the first Maori admitted to the legal profession and author of *The Art of Rugby Football*, the first New Zealand coaching manual – was the proposer of black with the silver fern as the national colours. In the same year, Ellison led the New Zealand Rugby Union's first official touring team to Australia.

As the Natives' team historian Greg Ryan has pointed out, they were the only touring team to face the full strength of British rugby before the rugby league schism of 1895 left union, in England at least, 'a shadow of its former self during the first quarter of the twentieth century'. They also, Ryan notes, 'set a familiar pattern for later New Zealand visitors by losing to the Welsh', falling to Llanelli by 3–0 and Wales, in the international at Swansea, by 5–0. Victories over Swansea and Newport followed, but their final match brought a 4–1 loss and 'rough treatment by the crowd' at Cardiff. Playing all five games in ten days was in keeping with a ludicrously arduous schedule that fitted seventy-four matches into just under six months in Britain.

One Welshman, William Thomas, a Cambridge blue who had attended Llandovery College, was a member of the first British touring team to visit New Zealand in 1888 and there were eight in the squad who visited in 1904 and lost 9–3 to the All Blacks in Auckland. There is little doubt, though, that the true foundation date of the special relationship was 1905.

The first meeting between Wales and New Zealand, at Cardiff Arms Park on 16 December 1905, was, as the title of Welsh historian Gareth Williams's book *1905 and All That* implies, rugby's answer to the Battle of Hastings – a crucial formative moment. It was recognised as such at the time. New Zealand journalist C.C. Reade wrote on the morning of the match: 'The world's championship in rugby will be decided in Cardiff today.' For the first time, the best team in Britain – Wales was in the middle of its first Golden Age – was to meet a challenger from overseas, a New Zealand team that had laid waste the best of British rugby with 27 consecutive victories. In a unique and almost certainly unrepeatable set of circumstances, it matched two nations in search of an identity. Its outcome would provide a legend of foundation for both.

It is hardly surprising that New Zealand was still seeking an identity. It had broken from the rest of British-ruled Australasia only five years earlier, rejecting membership of the new Australian Federation. Dominion status was still two years away. The Maori wars were still a living memory. The new nation had shown the taste for political innovation which persists to this day. It was the first country to introduce women's suffrage in 1893, following with state labour arbitration in 1894 and old age pensions in 1898. It was a dynamic, fast-growing society, its annual population growth of 23 per 1,000 between 1881 and 1921 the highest recorded for any country in this period. Yet in other ways it was deeply conservative. Far from striving to separate itself from a colonial past, it remained self-consciously, at times ostentatiously, British.

New Zealand's population would never match politicians' claims that it was '98.5 per cent British' – nor, historian James Belich points out, could that of Britain. Yet that the claim was made was revealing. Belich argues that early twentieth-century New Zealand was 'recolonial' – politically independent but tied economically to Britain through overwhelming dependence on exports of dairy products and meat, and ideologically through a self-image as 'Better Britain', healthier and happier than the home country but still inextricably connected. Labour leader Walter Nash may have been speaking in part for himself when he told the departing 1953 All Blacks that they were 'leaving home to go home' – Nash was born in Kidderminster – but he summed up New Zealand attitudes for much of the twentieth century. Immigration rules discriminated in favour of the British and (from 1922) Irish.

That explosive population growth was from a narrow base – New Zealand had roughly one million people in 1905. Small nations struggle to make their mark on the world. Uruguayan football coach Ondino Viera once said: 'Other countries have their history. Uruguay has football.' Belich points out: 'There are only two spheres in which New Zealand has been a superpower. One is the export of protein. The other is sport.' New Zealand rugby, he asserts: 'ranks in socio-cultural resonance with soccer in Latin America and cockfighting in Bali'.

How a game devised for public schoolboys prospered so in this settler society remains a subject for debate. Jock Phillips has suggested that emphasis on physical strength fitted the values and occupations of a frontier society where hard physical work was the norm. It also happened to fit in very well with New Zealand's distinctive take on Britishness. Belich argues that rugby is peculiarly British – cricket is essentially English and soccer universal – and asks rhetorically: 'What better way to be Better Britain than by being better than Britain at the most British of games?'

New Zealanders proved to be good not only at playing but also at thinking about rugby – bringing to an elementally brutal game the sophistication and ingenuity that the supposedly primitive Maori had brought to warfare. New Zealand's first recorded match, at Nelson College at the north end of the South Island, did not take place until 1870. Within less than a decade, forwards – still a milling, undifferentiated mass in the British game – were starting to take on specialised roles.

This specialisation enabled New Zealand's great tactical innovation, the seven-man pack – complete with two-man front row – with the eighth man detached as supplementary half-back or 'rover'. George Dixon, manager of the 1905 team, was to explain: 'A man continually practised in one position will perform the work of that position better than another who plays here one moment and there the next. Seven men, properly packed, are quite the equal in pushing power of eight of equal individual weight, and the facilities for obtaining possession and quick heeling are infinitely greater.' The New Zealanders, packing in a 2–3–2 formation, formed a wedge driving inwards to create pressure on the opposing hooker, while British teams, packing 3–2–3, merely pushed straight ahead.

The 'rover' – the position of 1905 team captain Dave Gallaher – was, reckons one historian, 'the most controversial position in rugby history'. The rover put the ball into the scrum, while the scrum-half waited behind for it to emerge, allowing attacks to be launched much more rapidly. The controversy was over his positioning. Rhys Gabe, centre for Wales in 1905, explained: 'When the opposition heeled, he performed the function of a scrum-half, but when New Zealand obtained possession, he remained still and was legally offside, being in front of the ball and not in a scrummage. Moreover he was guilty of passive obstruction, for the opposing scrum-half was obliged to run round him.'

The basic text of New Zealand's rethinking and remaking of the game was *The Complete Footballer on the New Zealand System*, published by Gallaher and his vice-captain Billy Stead on their return home. Gareth Williams has written of this 322-page tome that: 'Their penetrating discussion of the game – lines of running, angles of packing, miss moves, compiling statistics on different phases of play – brought a startlingly new technical discussion to rugby literature, raising it to a level of sophistication previously unheard of and rarely exceeded since.'

The All Blacks wrought greater havoc on Britain than any visitors since the Vikings. Devon, a powerful county side, were demolished 55–4 in the opening match of the tour. The tourists won all 23 matches in England, scoring 721 points against 15. England, who did not help their cause with a bizarre selection including eight new caps and five three-quarters, were beaten 15–0, as were Ireland. Scotland declined to award caps against such unknown opposition and demanded a £200 guarantee rather than a share of the gate money for the international match at Inverleith. This generated a monumental fit of pique when the

All Blacks walked off with a four-figure profit from a bumper gate, but at least the Scots produced the first worthwhile resistance by a British national team before losing 12–7. It was not until the New Zealanders went to Wales at the end of their tour that they met opponents of comparable talent and cunning.

Wales was also in search of an identity. This might seem strange for an ancient nation with its own language, but that nationhood was short on the signifiers most countries take for granted. Conquest by the English crown in the thirteenth century and formal administrative absorption, in what looks suspiciously like oedipal revenge on a father born in Pembroke, by Henry VIII's Acts of Union, meant that it lacked institutions such as a parliament, a capital city or even the legal and education systems which underpin Scotland's sense of self. As journalist John Morgan pointed out in 1961, 'Selecting the rugby team is the nearest Wales gets to self-government.' The 1888 *Encyclopaedia Britannica* entry 'For Wales, see England' richly deserves its notoriety but reflected both administrative reality and the frustrations felt to this day by the Welsh traveller abroad who feels constrained to explain that, no, he isn't English and the apparently aberrant spelling of his name has a perfectly logical explanation.

Recent history had further confused the matter. Wales too had grown explosively, transforming itself – in places literally – out of recognition. In 1905, there were approximately two and a quarter million people in Wales – up more than 50 per cent in a little over 30 years. The population would grow by more than 400,000 in the first decade of the twentieth century. The balance of that population was changing. All of the growth was concentrated in the industralised south – Glamorgan, Monmouthshire and East Carmarthenshire. Coal and tinplate were both to reach their historic peak of employment and output immediately before the First World War.

In contrast to the other Celtic nations, Welsh experience has been marked more by immigration than emigration. While many of the people attracted to the industrial regions were Welsh, displaced from the rural counties, more came from outside, particularly the west country and other bordering areas of England. Incomers included the Hancock family, who furnished Cardiff with both beer and the invention of the four-man three-quarter line in the 1880s and Wales's

1905 captain Gwyn Nicholls, described by Gareth Williams as 'a west countryman by birth, but Welsh by adoption, inclination and location'.

This new fast-growing Wales of the southern coastal plane and valleys was urban, industrial and predominantly English-speaking. The proportion of Welsh speakers in Wales dropped below 50 per cent around the turn of the century. By 1913 there were 234,000 coal miners, around one-third of the total Welsh workforce. Fast-growing Cardiff was described by a French visitor in 1905 as '*ce petit Chicago*'. This was not a world amenable to traditional signifiers of identity such as the Welsh language.

While soccer predominated in the north, it arrived late in South Wales. Cricket was there before either code of football. The Arms Park and St Helen's, Swansea, were cricket fields before they ever saw a rugby ball and, as in New Zealand, most major rugby grounds also staged the summer game. Cricket, though, continued to insist on social stratification, with its separation of amateurs and professionals. Wales, like New Zealand, tends to impatience of pretension, deference and conventional social distinction. An exclusive game elsewhere in Britain, rugby adapted to local circumstances to become inclusive in Wales. It was, as Gwyn Alf Williams put it, 'the only field on which it was possible to be simultaneously Welsh and a gentleman (normally a difficult undertaking), where doctor and lawyer could ruck happily together, shoulder to shoulder with miner'.

Not every Welshman enjoyed rugby football. As late as 1901, the *Western Mail*, showing a characteristic grasp of the national psyche, argued that the majority of the population were: 'Too puritanical. They look upon sport as degrading and football especially is to them an abomination.' In 1893, one Michael Craven, speaking in Swansea, complained – not without some justification – that rugby was the 'twin sister of the drinking system'. The last of the great religious revivals, led by Evan Roberts in 1904–05, claimed 100,000 converts including Jenkin Thomas, who shocked a congregation that had not previously associated Kenfig Hill RFC with diabolic possession by proclaiming, 'I used to play full-back for the devil, but now I am forward for God.'

There was little doubt, though, who had the better tunes. Kenneth Morgan wrote of the Edwardian Welsh that '[they] may well have been a musical nation, perhaps a religious one as well. Beyond doubt they were, and have remained, a sporting nation with a fierce commitment to national success.' Rugby, with six Triple Crowns and only seven defeats in forty-three internationals between 1900 and 1911, was the unmatched source of such success.

How good a match it was on 16 December 1905 is open to debate. Matches of this magnitude, considered merely as spectacles, tend to disappoint. Dixon recalled: 'It was not a great game . . . Keen, strenuous and intensely exciting, *yes*. Brilliant, *no*.' Yet it transfixed a crowd estimated at 47,000, 'the biggest rugby assembly hitherto'. To the *Lyttelton Times* reporter it was 'an Homeric contest of skill, endurance, pace and sheer brute strength – the hardest, keenest struggle I can ever remember'. Townsend Collins, 'Dromio' of the *South Wales Argus*, would recall it as one of the three toughest matches he saw in more than half a century of rugby reporting.

Whatever doubts Wales had about the 'rover' – and Dixon reports that the crowd 'showed a degree of bitterness' towards Gallaher – it was quite prepared to adopt New Zealand's weapon in order to slay it. Wales, too, played with seven forwards and a 'rover' – Cliff Pritchard of Pontypool. It had also, unprecedentedly, staged two practice sessions before the match.

For 25 minutes, Wales's scrum-half Dicky Owen ignored Pritchard. Then Wales were awarded a scrum in midfield about midway between the New Zealand 25 and halfway. Wales won the scrum and Owen, with outside-half Percy Bush, centre Nicholls and wing Willie Llewellyn outside him, broke to the right, dragging the New Zealand cover with him. He then reversed direction with a pass to Pritchard, running to the left of the scrum. Owen was to recall 'realising that, barring accidents, a try was almost certain'. Pritchard swerved to the left and passed to centre Rhys Gabe, who sent wing Teddy Morgan in from 20 yards. The try was a triumph both of pre-planning – plotted at the second practice session – and of the ingenuity and skill needed to devise and implement such a plan.

There was no further score, but it is neither Morgan, the scorer, nor Owen, the progenitor, who is remembered from this match. In the final few minutes, New Zealand centre Bob Deans, at 6 ft tall and 13 st. 4 lb christened the 'Goliath of the backs' by the Welsh press, was brought down at the Welsh line after a run of about 30 yards. The Scottish referee, John Dallas, ruled that he had not scored. End of matter, in one, narrow sense. Only the beginning in another.

Deans, who died only three years later, was to state that he had grounded the ball six inches over the line, but that Welshmen had dragged him back and moved the ball before the referee arrived on the scene. New Zealanders have made much of a written 'confession' by Teddy Morgan to 1924 All Blacks captain Cliff Porter that, as the man who had made the tackle, he knew Deans had scored.

Welsh opinion is more impressed by Rhys Gabe, who said he was the tackler. In a broadcast in 1935, the substance of which he reproduced in the 1953 match programme, he remembered that Deans had attempted to struggle forward rather than simply grounding the ball, and asked why he needed to do this if he had scored. He recalled asking Deans this question when the New Zealander claimed after the match that he had scored, and that 'there was no answer'. David Parry-Jones, in his biography of Nicholls, cites a rare neutral opinion – a spectator from Yorkshire who felt that it was not a try. Others have suggested that the incident may have owed more to subsequent newspaper hype than real doubt over the referee's decision. J.J. Stewart, an eminently fair-minded New Zealand analyst, points out that Gallaher and Stead make no mention of it in their account.

As Gabe was also to write: 'The longer this incident recedes into antiquity, the more nebulous becomes the truth about it.' That, of course, is much of its importance – that like many great debates it defies resolution. It meant that both countries took something from their meeting in 1905. Wales had the affirmation of victory over a uniquely challenging rival. New Zealand had a sense of injustice and of martyrdom, accentuated by Deans' early death. McLean described it as: 'The greatest event in the history of New Zealand rugby because it provided a basis, a starting point, a seed of nationalism upon which all aspects of the game were to depend in succeeding years.'

As such, it has mattered more to the losers. Almost every one of the 1953 All Blacks recalled knowing of the Deans incident from an early age. Brian Fitzpatrick, second five-eighth at Cardiff in 1953, recalls: 'I was brought up on stories of the "disaster of 1905" and the other All Black teams who followed them.' When New Zealand broadcaster Peter

Sellers, exultant at New Zealand's 13–0 lead over Wales at half-time in the Christchurch Test of 1969, proclaimed to the press box: 'I've been waiting for 64 years for this day', nobody required any further explanation, even though he was considerably less than 64 years old. It was, to historian Keith Sinclair, 'the Gallipoli of New Zealand sport'. While Cliff Morgan remembered the Deans story as 'a close third behind the Lord's Prayer and the Welsh National Anthem in my early education', this was a minority experience in Wales.

Deans' was not the only hard-luck story to emerge from the 1905 All Blacks visit to Wales. Cardiff might have beaten them but for an aberration by Bush, who, very much like Toulouse's Clement Poitrenaud in the Heineken Cup Final 99 years later, delayed a routine in-goal touch-down only to be betrayed by a rogue bounce and the opportunism of All Black George Nicholson. Swansea were denied by an extraordinary drop-goal from Billy Wallace, kicked 40 yards into a swirling wind – under 1905 scoring values worth four points to three from a try by Swansea 'rover' Frank Scrine. One Welsh writer, John Billot, has asked if the 1905 All Blacks were really that good, arguing that one defeat and two near-defeats in five matches with only six tries to four against is not, by New Zealand standards, a remarkable record. Against that it must be remembered that they were right at the end of an immensely demanding tour – Gabe found them 'keyed-up and ill at ease' when visiting them at their hotel. Dicky Owen, a shrewd and demanding judge, reckoned them, 'By far the best team I ever played against – or am ever likely to. They were veritable giants.'

Differences in style and emphasis that went beyond scrummage formation were also emerging. Gallaher and Stead did not rate the teamwork of the Welsh much higher than that of the other home nations but were impressed by their talent and imagination. British critics were unanimous in acclaiming the seamless combination of the New Zealand 15. It is possible to overemphasise this contrast. New Zealand has produced ample rugby genius, while the best Welsh teams have combined as smoothly as All Blacks. Nicholls was to write: 'In an ideal Welsh game, you really see fifteen great chess masters working in partnership and without consultation, each man knowing instinctively not only the best thing to be done, but that all the other fellows know it also, and are falling, or have fallen, into their places accordingly.' This has never been quite the clash of South Sea Stalinism and anarcho-Celticism that the more extreme stereotypes would have us believe.

Yet as with most stereotypes there is an element of truth. As Gerald Davies, the most perceptive of great players, has written, Wales and New Zealand differ 'only in the way they imagine the game'. The key word in the Nicholls quotation is 'instinctively'. Welsh rugby has always prized the instinctive creator and the diminutive deceiver, the individual capable of the unexpected. It is a matter of tastes, of aesthetics and – for a country whose formative rugby challenge was finding an answer to the fact that their English and Scottish opponents were generally prosperous and well fed, and therefore larger and stronger – a matter of practicality. The 5 ft 3 in. tall Owen would have been no match for most opponents in trials of strength, but more than compensated with ingenuity and imagination. Observers from more austere rugby cultures, New Zealand included, have argued that this taste is sometimes indulged at the expense of efficiency.

New Zealand has normally played a more collective and calculated game that British critics have been wont to decry as mechanical or joyless. McLean's is the definitive rejoinder: 'To get 15 men of a team into positions where they are efficiently performing the needed tasks of handling, passing, running and backing-up is not a mechanical exercise – it is a sublime art.'

What they had in common was already more important. Gareth Williams' description of rugby as 'a pre-eminent expression of Welsh consciousness, a signifier of Welsh nationhood' applies equally to New Zealand. To pinpoint exactly when this became true is as impossible as establishing exactly where Deans did ground the ball, but the best guess for both countries is on or around 16 December 1905 – each consciousness informed by acute awareness of the other, both as the other country most passionate about the game and as joint custodian of its greatest *cause célèbre*.

Little matter that, had any world championship taken a tangible form, it would have been stripped from Wales by the first Springboks a year later, nor that the next meeting between the full strength of Wales and New Zealand would not be until 1924. Indeed, infrequency of contact may have contributed to the strength of the affinity. The relationship between Wales and New Zealand was conducted to a marked degree through the agency of rugby.

New Zealanders were not yet the great travellers they would become. As late as 1953, the reminiscences and observations of those who returned home after a spell in the UK were considered worth a few paragraphs even in a big-city paper like the Auckland *New Zealand Herald*. Wartime servicemen apart, All Black teams were the only New Zealanders the average Welshman was likely to encounter.

There were Welshmen in New Zealand. During the 1924 All Black tour, New Zealand's great first five-eighth Bert Cooke was fêted at Llanelli, his parents' home before they emigrated in the 1890s. Cooke's ancestry was reflected in his play – in 1953 the veteran New Zealand expert Norm McKenzie likened him to Cliff Morgan. Peter Jones, the youthful 1953 tourist who was to win a permanent place in New Zealand mythology three years later with a spectacular long-range try against the Springboks, had a Welsh father. Terry McLean told with a smile the story of his father waiting for the result of the 1905 match with a Welsh workmate who swore that he was now a New Zealander. When the score arrived, he reverted to older loyalties and disappeared into town on an epic bender. Two of Wales's chosen back row in 1953, John Gwilliam and Glyn Davies, had relatives in New Zealand.

Yet we know little, beyond anecdote, of the New Zealand Welsh. The *World Bibliographical Series* volume on New Zealand lists ethnographic studies of the Irish, Jews, Danes, Italians, Dutch, Chinese, Pacific Islanders, Asians, Indians and Yugoslavs. Belich cites work on the Scots, Irish and Norwegians. There is little or nothing on the Welsh. Researchers are hampered by the fact that they were invariably aggregated with the English for statistical purposes, so we don't even know how many they were. What is clear is that they were heavily outnumbered by the other British nations – drawing on the estimates by Canadian scholar Donald Akenson, Belich suggests that around 2 per cent of white New Zealanders between 1860 and 1950 were Welsh, compared to around 50 per cent English, 21–24 per cent Scots and 16–18 per cent Irish.

This could paradoxically have deepened New Zealand's affection for the Welsh. For the average New Zealander, be they English, Scottish or Irish, other large ethnic groups took the tangible form of the bloke down the road who disagreed with you about politics and went to a different church. The Welsh, by contrast, will have been for the most part an imagined community – this strange, rather fantastic society 12,000 miles away in which people loved rugby just as much as New Zealanders did. Distance really may have let enchantment.

While the second All Blacks did not visit Britain until 1924, there were visitors in the interim: the New Zealand Army team of 1919. The First World War was another vital formative experience for New Zealand nationhood. There was no doubt that New Zealand would participate – as it would again in 1939, when Prime Minister Michael Savage would say, 'Where Britain goes, we go', and automatically declared war alongside Britain. Even so, Sinclair suggests that the 100,000 men – around 9 per cent of the population – sent to the war were the 'first identifiable New Zealanders' because they had the chance to learn what made them different from the British, Canadians and Australians they fought alongside. Self-knowledge came at a high price – 17,000 died and a further 41,000 were wounded.

Even at this casualty rate, there were sufficient survivors in Britain in 1919 for a New Zealand Army team to be entered in the King's Cup, alongside the British Army, Australian Expeditionary Force, South African Forces, Canadian Expeditionary Forces and RAF. They duly won this proto-World Cup, beating the British Army – known as the 'Mother Country' – in the final, and also beat the French Army. These matches were part of a 38-game programme spread across Britain and France, including 13 games in Wales. The Welsh national team led by Glyn Stephens of Neath, whose son Rees would play for Wales against the All Blacks in 1953, were beaten 6–3 at Swansea. The Army team had scoreless draws with Cardiff and the Newport suburban club Pill Harriers, enormously powerful during this period, and lost 4–3 to a Monmouthshire side led by 45-year-old George Boots, who had played against the 1905 All Blacks for Newport.

The 1924 All Blacks left for Britain under strict instructions 'not to lose to Wales'. They did not – nor did they lose to anyone else, winning all 30 matches. They encountered Wales at its lowest point before the 1990s, its rugby reflecting the state of industrial communities which would lose more than 300,000 people – cancelling out the Edwardian boom – between 1921 and 1935. Between 1920 and 1933, 127,000 jobs – almost half of the workforce – were lost in the coal industry, while pay was cut savagely for those who remained. The Welsh Rugby Union's annual income was halved. Seventy Welsh internationals cashed in their skills by signing for rugby league clubs between 1919 and 1939. Historian Tony Collins has found records of a further 300 non-international participants in this huge migration of talent.

The Wales team reflected this demoralisation. Reform of the selection process to replace a 13-man district-based committee with a small group immediately nicknamed the 'Big Five' did nothing to lessen what Dai Smith and Gareth Williams term, 'a genius for bizarre and inscrutable choices'. Albert Jenkins of Llanelli, the outstanding player and personality of the decade, won only fourteen caps spread across eight years. Cambridge University and Swansea wing Rowe Harding would recall: 'Even as late as 1928 it had not filtered into Welsh rugby that there should be specialisation in forward play. I remember very well that the Welsh pack once scrummaged against six Cardiff city policemen and failed to get the ball once in six put-ins. That pack had gone into the scrum on the basis of first up, first down. In other words the first forward to arrive was the first into the scrum.'

To make things worse, England, Ireland and Scotland were all in periods of great strength – England in particular was developing much more sophisticated forward play under the leadership of Wavell Wakefield, who readily acknowledged his debt to New Zealand examples, while Scotland's 1925 team was the best in its history, winning its first Grand Slam and scoring 17 tries, a prodigious total by the standards of the time, in doing so. Wales won only seven matches, five of them against the still inconsiderable French, out of twenty-six between 1923 and 1928.

New Zealand rugby's cultural importance by 1924 was reflected in Deputy Prime Minister Gordon Coates' attempt to intervene in the selection of the team. Its confidence was shown in the firm manner in which Coates was rebuffed. This team is forever associated with the remarkable George Nepia, a 19-year-old five-eighth who was chosen as a full-back, and played every game on the tour. It announced itself in Wales with a 39–3 defeat of Swansea, leading one reporter to warn that, 'panic must be avoided at all costs'. It is arguable whether it was. The newly installed 'Big Five', impressed by the All Blacks' one close call in

Wales – a late 10–8 victory over Newport – and suffering from the misapprehension that New Zealand's 'five-eighth' was a wing-forward rather than a back, picked Newport veteran Jack Wetter as a third half-back in response. Wetter, unsuited in any case to the job asked of him, was injured early in the international, played at Swansea. The All Black victory margin of 19–0 represented, it was noted, a point for every year since 1905. Wales would not suffer a greater defeat anywhere until 1964, and at home until 1980.

Wales was to be robbed of a further chance to see Nepia the player. A certainty for the 1927 Maori tour of Britain, he was ruled out by a hoax telegram to the selectors saying he was unavailable. Neverthless, he was as revered in Wales as in New Zealand. Cliff Morgan described meeting him as 'like having an audience with the Pope'. Returning to Swansea in 1982 along with the Maori touring team of that year, Nepia, who declared accurately that little about the St Helen's ground had altered in 58 years, received a standing ovation from the entire crowd.

The single asterisk against 'the Invincibles' is that they did not play the strongest team in Britain that season – Scotland. This was none of their doing, since the SRU continued its 19-year sulk over the financial outcome of the 1905 match by refusing to play on the flimsily legalistic grounds that the invitation to tour had been issued by the Rugby Football Union rather than the International Board. Scotland's best-ever team was denied the chance of its own version of 1905 and nearly 80 years on it is still waiting for its first victory over the All Blacks.

There was substantial Welsh involvement in the best-remembered incident of the tour, the sending-off of lock Cyril Brownlie against England – the first, and until 1967 only, dismissal in international rugby. The referee, Albert Freethy, was a Welshman, while the other protagonist in the vital incident was England lock Reg Edwards, a Newport player never again selected for an international. The sending-off, Nepia was to recall, 'for a time knocked us completely off our perch'. Yet forced to play for 72 minutes with 14 men against the toughest opposition of the tour, New Zealand won 22–11.

Opponents like Rowe Harding and England's Len Corbett reiterated a common theme in British analysis of New Zealand rugby players – doubting that they were individually more talented than their British counterparts, but accepting that their teamwork, particularly between backs and forwards, and ability to take advantage of opposition errors were infinitely superior. Not the least remarkable aspect of their success was that they struggled consistently for possession. New Zealand had persisted with the seven-man scrum plus 'rover'. British (if not Welsh) teams had learnt the lessons of 1905 and now scrummaged well enough to take advantage of their numerical advantage. Carwyn James and John Reason suggest that New Zealand's habitual rugby pragmatism was outweighed by a variety of ancestor worship and an unwillingness to abandon the system perfected by the team of 1905 and Gallaher, who had died on the Western Front in 1917. The Invincibles might also have argued with some conviction that their playing record was a vindication of their methods.

Even so, the seven-man scrum's days were numbered. In 1928, the All Blacks visited South Africa for the second instalment of New Zealand's other great rivalry, started in 1921. The South Africans had dumped the traditional 3–2–3 scrum in favour of a 3–4–1 formation. Graeme Barrow explains: 'With the flanks pushing inwards on the props as well as frontwards, the scrum had a wedge effect rather like the New Zealand 2–3–2 foundation, only on a broader front.' New Zealand were massacred in the scrums, lost the First Test 17–0, an unprecedented margin of defeat not exceeded until 1999, and were forced to adopt 3–4–1 themselves in self-preservation. Their more mobile forwards and brilliant backs secured a share of the four-Test series.

Two years later, the British Lions visited New Zealand. On the field, Ivor Jones of Llanelli, unable to command a regular Wales place, convinced many New Zealanders that he was the greatest forward ever to visit. Off it, Lions manager James Baxter, one of nature's gunboat diplomats and a member of the lawmaking International Board, condemned the 'rover' straightforwardly as a 'cheat' – robust language in an era when the word 'unsporting' would come close to causing an Anglo-Australian diplomatic breach during the 'Bodyline' cricket tour of 1932–33. In 1932, the rover was legislated out of existence when the International Board ruled that in future the front row should be three-strong.

So, while New Zealand was on the up socially and economically when the next All Blacks came to Britain in 1935 – it had just elected its first Labour government, which would create a pioneering Welfare State a decade in advance of its British counterpart, while an American economist would conclude in 1939 that it had the highest real-terms standard of living in the world – its rugby was in one of its rare periods of recession, still adjusting to the outlawing of its distinctive formation.

Wales still had its problems – the devastation of the valleys coalfields had continued apace since 1924. The west, though, had not suffered as grievously, while the products of schools rugby – the Welsh Secondary Schools Rugby Union was founded in 1923 – and universities, with a talented generation of backs winning Oxford and Cambridge blues, had produced an upturn. There was no new Golden Age, but after the misery of the 1920s, Wales had marginally the best record of any home nation in the 1930s, the most evenly contested decade in British and Irish rugby history. It won its first Five Nations Championship for nine years in 1931, then two years later finally won at Twickenham, England's home ground since 1910.

The third All Blacks of 1935 were not, by any standards except those of their two predecessors, unsuccessful. They won 24 of their 28 matches in Britain and Ireland. The first loss came in West Wales in late September, against a Swansea team fielding two Gowerton Grammar School boys, Haydn Tanner and Willie Davies, at half-back. The All Blacks were so outscrummaged that Swansea frequently opted for scrums in preference to lineouts, Tanner's breaking from the base of the scrum created the space for Davies' ghosting runs and Claude Davey, a 'demoniac . . . volcanic force' at centre scored two first-half tries as Swansea won 11–3. The All Whites were the first club side, and second only to the British Lions among all teams, to complete victories over New Zealand, South Africa and Australia. All Black captain Jack Manchester unsuccessfully appealed to journalists: 'Don't tell them back home we were beaten by schoolboys.'

Shock abated over the next three months as the All Blacks were undefeated in their next 20 matches, though drawing 3–3 with Ulster and winning by only single-point margins against Glasgow and Edinburgh, Combined Services, and Oxford University. Their more prestigious matches were won comfortably, with Ireland beaten 17–9 and Scotland 18–8, while Llanelli (16–8), Cardiff (20–5) and Newport (17–5) were seen off in nine late October days. Gwyn Williams, a 17-

year-old back-row forward and first of eight Taffs Well brothers to play for Cardiff, was watched by his 12-year-old brother Bleddyn, who remembers: 'I was hugely impressed. It was my first association with the All Blacks.' It was not to be his last.

Four of Swansea's victors, including Davey, chosen as captain, and international debutant Tanner, were in the Wales team who played the tourists at Cardiff on 21 December 1935. After playing it tight before half-time, when New Zealand led 3–0, Wales unleashed the jinking of outside-half Cliff Jones and the powerful running of his fellow Cambridge blue, the centre Wilf Wooller, exiled to the wing before the break. Two tries in six minutes resulted. First Jones chipped ahead for Davey to gather and score, then Wooller charged down the middle, kicked past full-back Mike Gilbert and was beaten by the bounce, only for wing Geoffrey Rees-Jones to follow up and score. New Zealand responded with an opportunistic drop-goal by Gilbert, followed by a second try from wing Nelson Ball to lead 12–10. When Swansea and Royal Navy hooker Don Tarr was carried off with what turned out to be a broken neck – his life was saved by referee Cyril Gadney's insistence that he be lowered face-down on to the stretcher – with 10 minutes to go, the 14 Welshmen who remained looked defeated.

But, Wooller was to recall: 'We could feel the will of the vast crowd urging us on. It was a sustained roar of excitement and encouragement.' With four minutes to go, Jones put Wooller into space: 'I paused and ran across behind Davey and turned upfield to find myself clear and in the open. On the All Black 25, I found a covering defence on my left, Gilbert ahead, up went the ball again. It dropped dead in front of me and bounced perpendicularly back over my head. As I skidded into the straw, I heard the roar of all roars. Rees-Jones, following up, had scored.'

Most accounts suggest that this epic piece of déjà vu was no more than Wales deserved for greater imagination in attack, and resilience when reduced to 14 men. An alternative analysis is supplied by the Welsh writer John Billot: 'Three kicks. Three lucky bounces. Three tries.' It would be 1969 before Wales again scored against New Zealand from a handling movement.

There was considerably less doubt about the All Blacks third defeat – a 13–0 loss to England that would be their only home nations defeat .

outside Wales until 1973 and is remembered for the two tries by Russian-born wing Alexander Obolensky, the most romantically unlikely figure in English rugby history even before he became the first international to die in the Second World War, less than five years later.

The 1935 All Blacks were popular in Wales – a New Zealand cynic could retort that well they might have been. Eighteen years later, J.B.G. Thomas of the *Western Mail* would write of the arriving 1953 team: 'Welshmen want them to play as they did in 1935. They want to see them indulge in their swift, combined passing movements which leave the keenest of defences bewildered.' They were less fondly remembered at home, accused of over-indulgence in black-tie dinners, although McLean, whose elder brother Hugh was a member of the team, was surely nearer the mark when he diagnosed a lack of 'pushing power' among the forwards. New Zealand gloom was deepened by a further defeat, this time at home, by South Africa in 1937.

The Second World War was not as traumatic for New Zealand as its predecessor, but made impact enough. Around 200,000 men were mobilised from a population of 1.6 million, of whom 40,000 were to be killed, wounded or taken prisoner. There was a foreign invasion, although not the one feared: 'New Zealand expected 100,000 Japanese. Instead it got 100,000 Americans,' notes Belich. New Zealanders were particularly prominent in the Royal Air Force and in military operations in the Mediterranean – and forces from Italy formed the core of the 1945–46 New Zealand Armed Forces team, popularly known as the Kiwis.

The New Zealand Division were known as effective rather than punctiliously obedient soldiers, but followed the instruction of their commander Bernard Freyberg – that they should play bright, attacking rugby regardless of the possible outcome – to the letter. Playing in line with their captain Charles Saxton's dictum that 'Rugby is 14 men combining to put the 15th into the clear', they were, according to Billot, a team with 'audience appeal surpassing all the New Zealand teams who followed them to Wales'.

Full-back Bob Scott, who remembers the tour as an experience to match any in one of the great All Black careers, recalled of spectators at the first match at Swansea that 'they didn't seem to care; all they worried about was the quality of rugby' as the Kiwis won 22–6 against a team including Tanner and two other survivors of 1935. Not all Welsh crowds were quite as sporting. Later experience would convince Scott that, 'Of all the rugby places, Wales is the place you must take the greatest care of the partisan voice; and of all the places in Wales, Cardiff is where the partisan cry has been raised to a science.' They beat Cardiff on Christmas Day, then played Wales on the first Saturday of 1946 in front of a crowd restricted to 27,000 by the bomb which in 1941 had wrecked the double-decker North Stand and damaged the terraces. In the absence of Tanner, unable to get leave from the army, Wales were led by the 22-year-old Bleddyn Williams, while the pack included Rees Stephens of Neath, son of their 1919 captain.

The Kiwis' 11–3 victory was highlighted by an extraordinary long-range try from the outsize winger Jim Sherratt – to be christened '*Le Grand Cheval*' by the French. Commentator Winston McCarthy, whose voice forms the soundtrack for postwar New Zealand much as his contemporary John Arlott evokes cricket for the British, remembered: 'He took the ball in his hands, at top speed, when it was shin high. That was on the ten-yard line and five yards from touch. Then came one of the most thrilling runs of all time. Looking neither to right or left, but with his eyes glued on the goal-line 65 yards ahead, he set sail with the weight of his 14 colleagues on his shoulders. Lloyd-Davies went after him, so did Graham Hale; the nearest Kiwi was Smith, the others just stood where they were and cheered and yelled encouragement to the big winger. As he got to the corner Sherratt swung in towards the posts to touch down for a try that must rank with the greatest ever.'

It was reported that listeners in the early hours back in New Zealand ran into the streets in their excitement. It was then, McLean notes sardonically, that, 'Wales discovered that, anyway, this was not a true international.' Unlike their predecessors of 1919, the Welsh team were not awarded caps.

The Kiwis sealed their popularity, in East Wales at least, by following their predecessors of 26 years earlier in losing their final match to Monmouthshire. Outside-half Hedley Rowland's trio of interception tries in the 15–0 victory allegedly cost him international recognition by selectors who wanted him to moderate a risk-taking style of play, but remains the only hat-trick scored by a Welshman against a representative New Zealand team.

Their influence was enormous in Wales and New Zealand. Bleddyn Williams recalls: 'They set a precedent with their style of play that we tried to follow.' The All Black prop Kevin Skinner says: 'They were important to us in New Zealand, providing a lot of inspiration to get going properly again after the war.' Sixteen of the thiry-one Kiwis were to become All Blacks. Yet their influence was to be comparatively shortlived. Only one, Scott, would return seven years later with the 1953 All Blacks and that after a spell out of top-class rugby. Rugby careers in those days were shorter, and several of the team had lost their best years to war.

The dominant postwar power, setting the tone in New Zealand rugby, was Skinner's own team, Otago. It held the Ranfurly Shield – New Zealand's provincial championship played on a challenge basis – from 1947 to 1950, holding on even when it had 11 players in the All Black squad touring South Africa. McCarthy described their style, devised by coach Vic Cavanagh, as, 'almost perfect forward play'. Ideally adapted to the muddy grounds of a South Island winter, it was based around the ruck – inviting tackles, then when the ball went to ground, driving quickly in unison over the ball (and anyone on the ground) and then, in McCarthy's words, 'start all over again until the defences were breached'. Since they were also very powerful in scrum and lineout, opponents were denied possession, sucked into the rucks and battered physically.

The main limit on Kiwi influence, though, was the impact of the 1949 tour of South Africa. The team chosen was acclaimed on its departure as the best ever to leave New Zealand. This view was not wholly ill-founded. Bob Scott recalls it as, 'one of the best-balanced teams I ever played in'. The front row, with Kevin Skinner and Johnny Simpson propping Has Catley, is still rated one of New Zealand's finest. Yet this team went down to shattering defeat, losing all four Test matches.

Any number of pleas in mitigation might have been offered. The squad had been chosen at the end of the previous season, leaving six months for those selected to lose both form and condition. New Zealand, as was its shameful practice until 1960, acceded to South Africa's demand that it exclude Maori players. So Kiwi centre J.B. Smith, acclaimed by Bleddyn Williams as 'the best centre I ever played against', half-back Vince Bevan and other outstanding players were left behind. The All Blacks faced a demanding travel schedule, with long train journeys across South Africa. Skinner recalls: 'We spent an awful lot of time on trains and buses, including a lot of overnight journeys. That takes it out of you over time.' At one point they spent eight nights out of eleven on trains. It was poorly coached. Cavanagh was widely expected to be coach, but lost out to Alec McDonald, one of the selectors. He was regarded with suitable reverence as one of the 1905 Originals, but remained rooted in the era of the 2–3–2 scrummage. New Zealand undoubtedly suffered at the hands of South African referees. Losing in spite of scoring more tries is an occasional hazard of rugby. It is, however, all but unknown for a team to do it three times in four matches. New Zealand scored four tries to three during the series, but conceded ten penalty goals to two. Skinner has no doubt: 'If we'd had neutral referees, we could have won the series.' The resentment this caused in New Zealand underpinned national frenzy when the Springboks paid their return visit in 1956.

Kickable penalties are not, however, random events. They reflect pressure. Scott, much criticised in New Zealand for a number of misses during the series, still argues forcefully in his own defence, pointing out: 'Nearly all of my attempts were from long range,' while his opposite number, the Springbok prop Okey Geffin, was taking most of his kicks in or around the All Black 25. Scott, a ferocious competitor but coolly objective analyst, would admit in his memoirs that the better team won. South Africa, while not the most attractive team in the world, were exceptionally accomplished in certain ways. One was scrummaging. Skinner recalls: 'Every scrum in every match was like a Test match. They were all good at it.'

The All Blacks were in trouble from the start of the tour, when they were outscrummaged by South African Universities. In mid-tour, they had a much-publicised training session with Springbok coach Danie Craven, who instructed them in the techniques used by their opponents. Skinner remembers that he and two or three other of his teammates were not particularly amused. Craven inevitably extracted the maximum publicity from New Zealand's humiliation and, Skinner recalls: 'By then we were getting to grips with them and starting to get on top. We didn't need the session.'

Most important of all, though, was the destruction wrought by Hennie Muller, an extraordinarily fast, skilled and ruthless back-rower. The rules of the time placed no limit on the length of the lineout. Muller stood opposite the New Zealand five-eighths and ran at them aggressively whenever they won the ball. J.J. Stewart summed up the implications – that instead of simply worrying about their opposite numbers, midfield backs now faced a player 'Whose every intention was to arrive onto him at the same time as the ball, to tackle him in the hardest way humanly possible and to initiate a ruck over him, or toe the ball ahead once it had spilled from his hands, or to pick up the ball and run with it or pass it. And this player was never more than one to three yards away.' Skinner remembers: 'Every kid in South Africa wanted to be like Hennie Muller. He was allowed to get away with murder, but he was an extraordinary player and we simply didn't have anyone with those skills in our side.' A back division with a fair leavening of Kiwis understandably struggled.

At the same time as the All Blacks were suffering in South Africa, a second squad, including several of the betrayed Maoris and promising players such as Canterbury back-rower Bob Stuart and Poverty Bay lock Richard 'Tiny' White, was entertaining Australia. This team was also given full Test status, and lost both matches. New Zealand was traumatised. Terry McLean remembered: 'You can hardly imagine the depths of despair at the results in 1949.'

This was, McLean has written: 'The great watershed of international rugby. On the rearward slope lay the great backs and back-plays . . . On the forward slope lay intense forward effort, domination of ground by touch-kicking and deliberate stifling of back-line initiative by the posting of loose-forwards operating from cruelly advantageous positions.' The influence of South African formations and tactics was grafted on to that of Otago. Kevin Skinner remembers: 'All of a sudden, back row was a popular position and you had quick, clever young players like Bill McCaw and Bill Clark coming through.'

In fact, Otago's power was on the wane – Cavanagh quit in 1950 after being snubbed for national recognition – and its rival Canterbury had worked out how to counter the ruck. Bob Stuart remembers: 'It was vulnerable only in its predictability. The only way to counter it was to arrive at the breakdown first and, if at all possible, drive. If Otago forwards were there first you should not get sucked in. Otago rarely went forward, but always sent the ball back and you could counter this by getting your players very quickly into defensive position.' In 1950, Canterbury took the Shield from Otago using these tactics. They were, Stuart says: 'Simply a major refinement of the Otago technical approach, but a significant tactical change'. Canterbury-style driving would become the tactical hallmark of New Zealand teams throughout the 1950s and beyond.

Otago were still good enough to administer a comprehensively demoralising thrashing to the 1950 British Lions. Rees Stephens, one of the British forwards, was so impressed that he forever afterwards regarded them as the best team, All Blacks and Springboks included, he ever played against. The Lions were, in Bob Scott's words, 'the Kiwi tour in reverse', with an outstanding back division in which Irish outside-half Jack Kyle combined with Bleddyn Williams, Ken Jones and prodigious 18-year-old Welsh full-back Lewis Jones in some brilliant attacking play. Ken Jones's try in the fourth Test at Auckland was to be recalled in McLean's *Great Days in New Zealand Rugby* as, 'The Greatest Try Ever'. Of New Zealand, Scott would recall that: 'Our attack did not begin with sufficient speed and variety' and that 'Had their forwards done no better than hold ours, they would have beaten us in each of the four Tests.'

Yet New Zealand won the series by three Tests to nil, with one draw. Great Britain had admittedly handicapped itself with some odd decisions – Welsh loose-forward Ray Cale's exclusion for being too physical is undoubtedly the unlikeliest reason why any player has ever been denied a trip to New Zealand. The All Blacks won on the back of grinding forward dominance and the calculated kicking of Otago outside-half Laurie Haig. Bleddyn Williams returned to Wales and reported, to a disbelieving public whose image of New Zealand rugby had been formed by the Kiwis and their predecessors of 1935 and 1924, that, 'every young boy wished to become an All Black forward and not a back'.

Rugby history might be seen in terms of a dialectic between defence and attack, with defences closing off the game as fast as attacking innovation or rule changes open it up. The 1950s were to be a time of defensive domination in Europe as well as New Zealand, South Africa and Australia. The Five Nations Championship generated an average of 13 to 15 points per match during the early 1950s, declining to single figures in 1959 when England's four matches produced a total of 20 points.

One element in this is scoring values. A try counted only for three points in 1953, the same as a drop goal (reduced from four as recently as 1948) or penalty, with two for a conversion. Another is the comparative scarcity of penalty goals. Those Five Nations clashes averaged about one penalty goal per game. Kicking was much tougher. Wales kicker Gwyn Rowlands remembers: 'It wasn't so bad on dry days, but on wet days, when the ball got heavier and you had to dig it out of muddy ground, it was very difficult.' Leather balls and boots made the toe-end style of kick – less accurate than the soccer-style instep-kicking that came in during the 1970s – all but mandatory. Sheer physical strength was a factor, with powerful forwards like Bill Tamplin and Ben Edwards almost as likely to kick as backs. Opportunities were limited: 'You would often only get one or two kickable chances per game,' recalls Scott.

There were, though, other reasons. Much more of the game was spent on set pieces – Skinner remembers that matches with 50 or more scrums were quite common. While South African techniques were tipping the balance towards the team with the put-in, the scrum was still much more of a contest for possession than it has become in more recent times, with strikes against the head still common. Nor were the scrum-half's difficulties ended by a successful strike – he was subject to harassment from his opposite number and loose-forwards, given much greater liberty than they are now, and would often have to battle merely to pick up and get his pass away. That pass might simply be transferring pressure to the man outside – the first five-eighth in New Zealand or outside-half in Britain. Clem Thomas was later to recall having 'a licence to kill outside-halfs'. As he explained: 'It was legally possible to arrive at the outside-half before the ball by taking a flyer as the ball came out of the scrum.'

Wingers, not hookers, threw into the lineout, where blocking was still permitted, allowing specialist jumpers like Tiny White and Wales's Roy John space to operate. The clean possession this supplied was, however, largely negated by the absence of limits on the length of the lineout, allowing back-rowers to mark the opposing midfield. The midfield gap between the two lines had yet to be instituted, so they could be within touching distance of each other.

As well as having minimal space to move in, the player of 1953 also had to contend with limitations on his handling. If the ball went to ground from a tackle, anyone wanting to pick it up had first to play it with his foot. With time and space limited, dribbling was still one of the game's basic skills. The ball had to be caught cleanly – any adjustment, even if did not go to ground, was likely to be penalised as a knock-on. Little wonder there were so many scrums.

Kicking to touch was still unlimited, and would be until games in the 1960s with more than 100 lineouts compelled a rethink. One consequence was that full-backs were expected to concentrate on defensive duties. The full-back who joined his three-quarters in attack, as both Scott and his 1953 All-Black deputy Jack Kelly were wont to do, was still regarded as a risk-taking rarity. The modern reader may wonder how anybody ever managed to score a try, or that the game was capable of attracting substantial audiences. Yet it did, and nowhere more so than in New Zealand.

CHAPTER 2

WHENCE THEY CAME:

(I) The All Blacks

The 1953 All Blacks came from a country close to the peak of its defining mid-century trends. New Zealand's population had doubled since 1905, passing two million in 1952. More than 90 per cent were European in origin, the vast majority British. Nearly 30,000 Britons emigrated to New Zealand in 1952–53, although this trend was slackening as Britain recovered economically from the war, so the government was encouraging Dutch immigrants 'of a good type'. The war had not only strengthened emotional connections. It had tightened economic links, the bulk purchasing agreement which lasted from 1939 to 1954 both guaranteeing prices for New Zealand agricultural produce and securing food supplies for Britain. In 1950, 66 per cent of New Zealand exports went to Britain – only 2 per cent to Australia and 10 per cent to the USA. Britain accounted for 61 per cent of New Zealand imports, up from around 50 per cent in the inter-war years and compared to 12 per cent for Australia and 7 per cent US.

The year 1953 accentuated New Zealand consciousness of those links. Three and a half months before the 30-man All Black party was announced, Edmund Hillary and Tenzing Norgay had become the first men to climb Mount Everest. Both Britain and New Zealand were happy to regard the achievement of an Auckland beekeeper and a Nepalese mountain guide as a British triumph. It also had a considerable Welsh dimension. Expedition leader John Hunt was in the Arms Park committee box on 19 December wearing a large Wales rosette, while his deputy, Charles Evans, was a Welsh-speaker who would become principal of the University College of North Wales, Bangor. Hillary was immediately knighted by the new monarch, Elizabeth II, whose visit to New Zealand at the end of the year would create genuine mass enthusiasm, – the 'Day of Joyous Tumult' hailed on her arrival in Auckland just before Christmas was reproduced all over the country. The monarch's birthday had become a public holiday only a year earlier.

The holiday was introduced by the National Party government of Sidney Holland, which ended Labour's 14-year rule in 1949. Like the British Conservatives who regained power from Labour in 1951, it left the bulk of its predecessor's reforming legacy in place. It had, though, adopted ferociously repressive measures to suppress the docks strike of 1951, one of the bitterest disputes in New Zealand history, invoking in justification the 'Red Menace' of the early Cold War years. National would stay in power until 1957, although Labour was finding a fresh generation – less than three weeks before the Wales match, the *Christchurch Press* reported that a 30-year-old engine driver named Norman Kirk was one of five newly-adopted Labour candidates. Twenty years later Kirk, as Prime Minister, would order the cancellation of the 1973 Springbok tour of New Zealand.

Economic circumstances were on National's side. While the Cardiff *Western Mail*'s description of 'Conservative prosperity' in New Zealand reflected naked political partisanship, it had some basis in reality. This was a time of extremely full employment, when the *New Zealand Herald* could advertise 825 jobs in a single issue, and report that only 12 of the 25 people appointed by an Auckland shop one Friday had turned up to work on the following Monday. Much of this prosperity was rooted in agriculture, still accounting for one-third of national income and accorded such importance that the *Herald*'s report of the All Blacks match against Cardiff was squeezed by coverage of a demonstration of new dairy processes aimed at producing better quality butter in the Waikato. The Korean War wool boom was excellent news for a country with 35 million sheep, while crop farming was becoming more sophisticated – on the morning of the Wales match, the *Herald* devoted considerable space to the thirty-eight firms, compared to five only four years earlier, providing aerial topdressing.

Prosperity was reflected in car ownership – with 285,000 on the roads, roughly one for every seven people, compared to one for every twenty-five in Britain. Most – roughly 82 per cent in 1955 – were British-built. Motorways had been introduced in 1951, while plans for the Auckland Harbour Bridge, which would open in 1959, were announced the week before the Wales match. Foreign travel was, however, still a rarity, although Canadian Pacific's announcement of plans to introduce jet aircraft on routes to Vancouver from 1954 was a clear glimpse of the future.

Whether New Zealand was also becoming more sophisticated is less clear. Warwick Roger, in his affectionate but incisive memoir of the 1956 Springbok tour, points to 'a rather flat mental and social landscape'. In that year, the 300,000 plus inhabitants of Auckland had a choice of 48 cinemas, showing exclusively imported films – only 5 homegrown features were produced between 1940 and 1972. New Zealanders are, against stereotype, great readers. The most impressive public building in many towns is the library. During the All Black tour, reviewers in the New Zealand press were to enthuse over first novels by Nadine Gordimer and Patrick O'Brian. Yet this coexisted with a censorship system so undiscriminating that the Lone Ranger was to be banned in 1956 because wearing a mask was an offence in New Zealand. Television had yet to arrive – a female BBC engineer arrived in Wellington to conduct tests the day before the Wales match – but radio was firmly established, its hours extended from 6 a.m. to 11.20 p.m every night in November 1953. Roger recalls that McCarthy's status as a national hero was rivalled by quizmaster Selwyn Toogood.

While higher education was still a minority pursuit, a 12,000-strong student body, most preparing for careers in teaching or agriculture at the still-federated University of New Zealand, compared proportionately very favourably to Britain. Plans for expansion were evident at Canterbury University College, Christchurch, where the rector H.R. Hulme – shortly to become famous in horrific circumstances when his teenage daughter and a friend killed his wife, one of the most notorious crimes in New Zealand history and inspiration of the film *Heavenly Creatures* – announced plans to move the city-centre campus to a suburban site at Riccarton.

This was still the New Zealand of 6 o'clock closing – upheld by referendum as recently as 1949. There was heated debate whether women should be allowed in bars – the Minister for Women and Children, Hilda Ross, wanted to ban them, while an Auckland publican argued that: 'New Zealanders don't know how to drink in the company of women. Women only make them want to drink faster and more. They're not content to linger over their beer and natter like the English or French.'

The 1950s saw, Jock Phillips has argued, 'the triumph of the New Zealand male stereotype', reflected in the strength of the Returned Servicemen's Association and a boom in the holy trinity of 'rugby, racing and beer'. Per capita beer consumption all but doubled between 1945 and 1958. A 1952 survey found interest in rugby at an all-time high: 'More players in the game than ever before, more public interest and record crowds for the Australian tourists. In fact, the attendance of 31,000 at Christchurch for the First Test was the greatest ever to watch an Australian side in action in New Zealand. Another record crowd, the highest ever for an inter-union match in New Zealand, attended the Auckland-Waikato Ranfurly Shield game at Auckland.'

In 1953, Arthur Swan was to write in his officially sanctioned history of New Zealand rugby, 'everything was given over' to the impending All Black tour. This perhaps slightly understates the importance and excitement of the Ranfurly Shield campaign, where Waikato, which had held the Shield since 1951 with a pattern of play in which loose-forward George Nola contrived a fair imitation of Hennie Muller, was defeated by an audaciously attacking Wellington team based round a brilliant young Victoria University back division.

Yet 'the biggest sporting elimination trials ever held in New Zealand' inevitably overhung the remainder of the season. Many were called – 195 players, representing every union playing provincial rugby, took part in 12 matches packed into 3 weeks in August and September 1953 – but only 30 could be chosen. It was, recalls loose-forward Bill Clark: 'a complete ordeal. You knew it was your one chance to go on a tour of Britain – there wouldn't be another tour until 1963. So many good players had missed out because of the war, or loss of form at the wrong time, or an injury. Only a few people had any firm indication that they were going.'

Wanganui first five-eighth Morrie O'Connell was hailed by the *New Zealand Rugby Almanack* as, 'the nearest approach to A.E. Cooke we have today', the best in his position and one of its five players of the year. After a Palmerston North trial which his team won 39–3, it had been said that, 'he can start packing his bags'. Nola was reckoned the most destructive tackler in New Zealand while A.W.C. McPherson of Canterbury was rated by the *Almanack* as one of the two best centres in the country. Not only were they not chosen, but none would ever be an All Black.

The announcement was made on 15 September 1953, following the final trial at Athletic Park, Wellington. The three selectors – two former All Blacks, Tom Morrison of Wellington and Merv Corner of Auckland, plus a former trialist, Arthur Marslin of Otago – confirmed their selections to the NZRU council in the committee rooms as journalists, including McLean and McCarthy, stood outside with their ears to the door. Then, led by their chairman Cuthbert Hogg, the council members marched along a corridor to the tea-room, which was packed with expectant players. Bob Stuart still remembers the silence as they walked in. Thirty names starting with two full-backs, John Kelly and Bob Scott, both of Auckland, were announced to the assembled company and a live radio audience. Bill Clark, who won his first All Black selection, says: 'You'd waited for weeks for this announcement. When it actually happened, you were in a daze.'

The final selection shows the brevity and transience of international careers in those days. Only seven had played in the previous season's Tests against the Wallabies, while eight had gone to Australia in 1951. Fifteen, half of the party, were new All Blacks. Scott, the only Kiwi, and Skinner, the most experienced Test player with 13 caps, were the only survivors of the 1949 South African tour.

In other ways, they faithfully reflected the society for which they now became ambassadors. Around a quarter of New Zealand males still earned their living from the land – the chosen thirty incorporated six farmers, an agricultural contractor, a milkman and head yardman, and an agricultural economist. There were three teachers, a less recognised but still consistent presence in All Black parties. Following your father's trade – be it farming, butchery, dentistry, mining or teaching – was still common. Names and descent were overwhelmingly British or Irish –

nothing as exotic as Svenson and Robilliard of the 1924 Invincibles – with three part-Maoris concealed behind common British surnames.

Some groups were notably more prominent than in New Zealand as a whole. There would be six former university students plus a trainee accountant in the team that played Wales. Roman Catholics were just under one in seven of the national population, proportionate to two in a rugby XV. Three from a single school, St Kevin's, Oamaru, would play against Wales. Skinner, one of the St Kevin's trio, remembers that there were nine Catholics in the party who toured South Africa in 1949. He recalls the coaching of Brothers Skeehan, an Australian, and Ryan, and says: 'Guys that took on that vocation were often keen on sport. We got a lot more coaching than we would have had at a state-run school, and without family responsibilities they had more time.' The school, with little more than 100 pupils, produced half a dozen All Blacks between 1935 and 1960.

Another St Kevin's alumnus led New Zealand against Wales. Tour captain Bob Stuart, a 33-year-old back-row forward from Canterbury, was regarded as a surprise choice. Speculation, and Stuart's own ambitions, had focused on his younger brother Kevin, a full-back who had missed out. There had been no obvious captain. Lock-forward Bob Duff, destined to be captain in 1956, had pulled out for business reasons. Skinner had led the All Blacks against Australia in 1952, but when sounded out declined: 'I didn't like making speeches. If it had been Australia it wouldn't have been too bad, but I knew that English rugby was a bit dinner-suity. That wasn't my style and I felt I'd make a better contribution as a team member.'

Stuart himself was not completely surprised: 'I had no evidence for it, but I had a feeling I was going to be selected.' He knew Marslin and Morrison. Corner had sought him out to discuss players after a provincial match. He was the captain of a leading province and had led New Zealand Universities in Australia in 1951. Canterbury selector Jack Rankin had told Winston McCarthy: 'So long as Bob Stuart can crawl on to a football field and I am a selector, he'll be the captain of my team.' He had led the winning team in the final trial.

Against this he had played only two Tests, as vice-captain in the shadow team against Australia in 1949. Memories of that year also cautioned him against over-confidence based on trials: 'I played in the final trial, was told it was the best game I had ever played and I wondered who the other 29 going to South Africa would be, but I wasn't chosen. It was a blow at the time, but a blessing in disguise.'

The choice was greeted with some scepticism. One paper said there was 'no doubt' that New Zealand would be led in Tests by Laurie Haig, the vice-captain. Yet Stuart was peculiarly well qualified. His 6 ft, 14 st. 7 lb frame and keen analytical mind had experienced many of the forces that had shaped his squad. A forward for the whole of a senior career started as a Massey University student chosen for Manawatu in 1941, he had been a full-back at school. Aside from Catholicism and St Kevin's, he was a university graduate employed in agriculture – as an economist with the Ministry of Agriculture and Fisheries – and had learnt much from war service.

Royal Navy service from 1941 was in retrospect a good preparation for captaining a touring rugby team: 'I was away for nearly five years, first on a destroyer in the Channel, then on corvettes for three years. Being on a corvette, living at close quarters with 80 or 90 people from different parts of Britain and Ireland, most of them older than me and many with greater experience, and being in charge of them taught me about living with other people and about handling men. You could also see rugby as a substitute for war. Both are about discipline and teamwork – you have to plan and be prepared. Everyone has a job to do, and you are all interdependent.'

War experience supplemented the analytical intelligence evident in his postwar resumption of interrupted studies – a Masters in economics followed his commerce degree, both from Canterbury University College. Then came the job with the Ministry: 'There was a lot of travel. I was responsible for the whole South Island, working on new methodologies developed in conjunction with the Cambridge School of Agriculture, and I was quite often away in the wilds for a fortnight at a time.'

He brought the focused seriousness of his work into his rugby. Lindsay Knight, historian of the All Black captaincy, described him as 'the most passionate theorist' of his time – an attribute shown in finding an answer to Otago after a ferocious beating in 1948. It took a rebellion before a 1950 Ranfurly Shield challenge, leading to Stuart being hauled up before the selectors to explain himself, to get his ideas accepted.

Following his advice 'not to get sucked into the ruck unless we're there first – in which case you get in, drive and keep going', Canterbury ended Otago's reign with an 8–0 victory. Stuart remembers: 'We lost the Shield in our next match, but that was the beginning of a great era for Canterbury rugby. We were strong in 1951, '52 and '53 when I was captain, and almost unbeatable in 1954, '55 and '56.'

In 1953, rugby union still numbered players like league, starting with the full-back at number one, the half-backs at six and seven and the forwards from eight up. So full-back Bob Scott wore number 1 against Wales. Scott, 32, conspicuous both for his bald head and extraordinary brilliance, had given up big rugby after the visit of the British Lions in 1950. He remembers: 'I was in business, though not very successfully. Then, round about Christmas 1952 Clarrie Gibbons, a leading member of the Wellington Rugby Union, came to see me and said Tom Morrison wanted me to make myself available for the tour. The selectors were worried they would be short of experience.'

Scott's experience went well beyond his 12 caps. He was a veteran of the Kiwis and, before that, four and a half years' war service: 'North Africa and Italy. I was a driver, no. 281904, and I didn't like authority. I obeyed the rules, but didn't always like them – it was a colonial thing. There was a story about a British brigadier complaining to Freyberg that New Zealanders never seemed to salute. Freyberg said, "If you wave to them, they'll wave back."'

The war was 'the turning point in my life in many ways'. He met his English wife Irene, who spent five war years in the London Fire Brigade, at the New Zealand Services Club. His rugby brilliance was not part of the attraction: 'When I sent a cable to say I'd become an All Black, they didn't know what it meant.' He played league until he was 19, reaching senior grade before joining up, then received 'my rugby education' in the high standard of games played among thousands of young men gathered together in the allied forces. His league past nearly cost him selection for the Kiwis as he waited impatiently for his reinstatement by the New Zealand Rugby Union to be confirmed: 'I had to wait in Austria with 50 or 60 other players who were having trials. I saw another part of the world, but the wait was frustrating and I nearly gave it away and came home.'

League had sharpened natural gifts as an attacking runner, still rare in a union full-back: 'In league you ran, knowing that if you got tackled you could still play the ball', and as a kicker: 'You couldn't kick directly to touch.' His 1953 teammate John Tanner believes it marked him as well: 'Bob never used to tackle low, possibly because he'd learnt in league, and he scarred me twice.'

McLean has written: 'It is unlikely that any All Black has known so difficult a childhood.' Scott had polio at five, spent three years in a Salvation Army hostel when his parents' marriage broke up and was to recall, when a teammate complained of tough meat during the 1953 tour, the time when he and his father – a railway worker who never fully recovered from wounds at Gallipoli and died in 1934 – had only rice to eat: 'We were always hard up and inadequately clothed,' he has written.

Rugby acclaim was no guarantee of prosperity. Scott had progressed from the early postwar days when he was earning £5 a week as a painter and paperhanger and paying £2 for the room he and Irene lived in – itself an improvement on his employment at 17 working a fleshing machine which took fat off carcasses – but his mercer's business was still struggling.

Poverty left him, he would write, for a long time 'with a complex that I was not quite as other people' and a distrust of anything that seemed good. He treated rugby with a mix of this wariness and supreme self-confidence. In spite of the invitation, he did not assume he was a certainty for the 1953 tour: 'I never felt sure, and was always thankful to be picked for any team. But at the same time I couldn't imagine anyone could play better than I could.'

Nor, it should be pointed out, could anybody else. Skinner, himself incontestably great, recalls: 'He was already a legend to the rest of us.' Hennie Muller called him: 'The greatest footballer I've played against in any position.' Bob Scott's perceptions of his rugby echo the sculptor who, asked how to sculpt an elephant, said it was a simple matter of taking a stone and removing everything that was not an elephant. Bob Scott could see the elephant: 'I had the ability to spot the weakest link in the opposition, so I did not run into danger. Someone once asked me what I was thinking under a high ball. All I was thinking was "I'm going to catch this ball" – all the rest was in my subconscious – if there was an opponent nearby, I knew where he was, how fast he could move and what I'd have to do to get away.'

Innate game sense and explosive speed over 10 to 20 yards from a standing start made him an attacking force at a time when full-backs, as Welsh counterpart Gerwyn Williams later bemoaned, were seen as purely defensive.

Off the field, McLean saw him as a 'responsible humourist', probably the best-read of the All Blacks, with a taste for biography and travel, who would 'talk willingly enough about anything and, if the subject were rugby, with a perception that was evidently the fruit of incessant reflection'. He was, McLean said, 'serious, conscientious, relaxed and yet with a flash of schoolboy fun'. On the field, relaxation and fun, for Scott at least, were swamped by an intense competitiveness unusual even in an All Black. He says: 'I wasn't a pleasant person on the rugby field, and I really couldn't take losing.' The game was not played for enjoyment, even though he brought great pleasure to thousands of spectators. 'There's no such thing as a game, only competition against yourself and an opponent. Satisfaction comes from your own and your team's performance, and from winning. I was once asked what my most enjoyable international match was, and I said there wasn't one. International rugby was too tense and too important,' he says.

He was wont to blame himself for defeats, a dangerous habit for a goal-kicker in an age when a match might offer only one or two shots at goal. More than 50 years on, he can offer a vigorous defence of his much-criticised goal-kicking on the 1949 tour of South Africa. Kicking was shared in Britain with number 2, the left-wing Ron Jarden, whose similarly receding hairline at 23 was no advertisement for the job. Jarden was also, according to the *Western Mail*'s man in New Zealand, the one absolute certainty to tour, 'the most brilliant wing three-quarter seen in New Zealand since the war . . . the glamour boy of New Zealand rugby'. Even so, he had his critics. Winston McCarthy, admittedly never knowingly understated, recalled that depending on who you were talking to he was 'either a champion or not worth a pinch of salt'. Jarden was mildly dismissive of his own abilities. A national junior 440 yards record-holder, he said: 'My only quality was speed and I soon discovered the safest place on the football field was over the goal line.'

He made his first impact in 1949 as a Victoria University student winning selection for New Zealand Universities and Wellington. Two years later, he and centre John Tanner went straight from the

Universities tour of Australia to join the senior All Black party. He scored 38 points with 6 tries and 10 conversions in a single match against Central West New South Wales, and totalled 88 points in 6 matches. His tries and goals, including all the points as the Shield was taken from Waikato, were vital to Wellington's Ranfurly Shield run.

Teammates had no doubt he was a champion. Allan Elsom, a frequent adversary for Canterbury and New Zealand's right-wing against Wales, remembers him as 'the complete rugby player, with terrific acceleration and a huge range of skills'. Tanner recalls his 'knack of picking up a bouncing ball and accelerating tremendously, so he went straight past opponents'. He had developed an intuitive understanding with flanker Bill Clark, a colleague in 230 games for Victoria, Wellington, New Zealand Universities and the All Blacks. Clark remembers: 'Ron never died with the ball. He played on the left, was left-footed and was good at cross-kicking into the middle. It did produce quite a few tries, although not as many as people used to think.'

Effectiveness was increased by powerful build – he was 5 ft 8 in. tall and 13 st. in 1953. Morrie MacKenzie said he had 'the most powerful thighs I've ever seen on a rugby player' and credited him with the rare combination of 'brains, quickness and speed'. The brains earned him a degree in history from Victoria and by 1953 were at the service of the Shell Oil Company, although he admitted to being a decidedly intermittent presence between April and September.

Inside him at centre, wearing number 3, was his 1951 Universities and All Blacks colleague, known to the New Zealand Rugby Museum website as 'the surprising John Tanner' for his habit of winning selection unexpectedly. This was no exception. Tanner was left out of the later trials and heard the news at his Auckland home. But like Bob Stuart, he was not as surprised as others: 'I had an idea I was in with a chance. Tom Morrison and Merv Corner always encouraged me, and Merv had hinted that I might still be OK.'

He suspects Auckland University's victory over Victoria a few weeks earlier – 'they had Ron, Brian Fitzpatrick and Jim Fitzgerald who all went to Britain, but we outplayed them' – may have been decisive. Ironically, selection was not the source of ecstatic delight one might expect. Tanner was decidedly laid-back about his rugby career: 'I was always pleased to be chosen, but I never thought ahead or worried about whether I was going to be picked. I played because I enjoyed the game, not because I was desperate to become an All Black.' He was not, however, wholly without All Black competitiveness: 'I found it difficult just to stop and shake hands at the end of a match after you'd been trying hard to win. It took me about ten minutes before I could wind down and relax.'

Tanner was yet another following the paternal trade – dentistry, in partnership with his father. From Auckland Grammar School he went to dental school at Otago University and within a year broke into the provincial squad. His first senior coach was Vic Cavanagh, who called him 'Junior'.

Rugby success took an academic toll: 'I was getting marks in the 70s, but when I got into the Otago team they dropped to the high 50s. We were training three times a week and playing at weekends while whole weeks could be write-offs – I went on a tour of the North Island that lasted two weeks.' There were also injuries. In 1948, he broke his arm, but was tempted back into action by Cavanagh's promise of a trial for the South Africa tour: 'I was running around with my arm in plaster after two weeks. After five it was X-rayed at the dental school, they said a callus had formed so I cut the plaster off and went out practising. I did play in the trial. Halfway through the game I made a tackle, and broke the arm again.'

He graduated in 1948 and returned to Auckland, where he was called up from the fringes of the provincial side for his All Black debut in the Fourth Test against the 1950 British Lions: 'I had no idea I was in contention and I hadn't played for three weeks before the previous Saturday. We trained Monday, Tuesday, Wednesday and Thursday, running hard all the time. By Friday my calf muscles were incredibly tight. I spent three hours on Friday night and again on Saturday morning soaking them in the bath as I could hardly walk. I wasn't not going to play, but my calves were like knots. In the first few minutes, Jack Matthews put the pace on, went at the new guy and ran through me. He didn't do it again – next time I got him, but I took about 20 minutes to loosen up.'

The following year he was vice-captain in Australia, earning a much-cherished place on the roll of All Black captains in the second game against Newcastle. He enjoyed rooming with Jarden, and genial rivalry with a new teammate, Victoria University second-five Brian Fitzpatrick, who remembers that they invariably seemed to end up pursuing the same girl. Acquaintance, and rivalry, were to be renewed in 1953.

A British team would have listed and numbered Tanner and Fitzpatrick consecutively as the two centres. In New Zealand's formation, number 4 was the right-winger Allan Elsom, 28, previously capped at centre and a veteran of navy service in the Pacific war. 'I was a submarine detector, that's why I'm deaf today,' he explains. Surviving that, he found peacetime rugby more perilous, breaking his neck in 1946: 'Tackling was one of my strong-points, but I hit the hip of the player I was tackling straight on. I can still remember the ambulance arriving at Lancaster Park and one of the medical officers saying, "He hasn't got much time left."'

Paralysed for a while, he recovered well enough to respond to an appeal from his club Albion in 1949: 'In my first match, I was quite frightened, but a Canterbury selector walked on to the ground just as I scored a runaway try – three weeks later I was in the Canterbury team against the [West] Coast.' A fast, powerful player – at 6 ft the tallest of the All Black backs – in 1951 he had 'a good run, scoring lots of tries' for Canterbury. He, five-eighth John Hotop and centre Tom Lynch received offers to play rugby league for Halifax. It was, he recalls, 'a substantial offer. I was in the real estate business and could have purchased three houses with it.' He turned it down, but Lynch went.

His choice was vindicated a year later by two All Black caps against Australia. He still remembers his excitement: 'I was rooming with Peter Eastgate. We were given our jerseys, went back to the room and couldn't get the jerseys on fast enough. He was saying, "How do I look, how do I look?"' Rugby fame had collateral benefits: 'A developer placed an entire new estate with me for sale. I made a year's pay in a week.'

Off-field, McLean found him a mix of 'rowdy clown' and 'a serious-minded man whose discussions on land agency, his business, were singularly well informed. A man of intense nervous energy, he was seldom still in tongue or body.' His invariable partner-in-crime was fellow-Canterbury wing Morrie Dixon, also a 1953 tourist. Stuart remembers their joining the 1951 Canterbury team: 'I'd never seen anything like them. He and Dixon were an amazing couple with their tongues permanently in their cheeks.'

Brian Fitzpatrick, number 5 as the second five-eighth, made his Test debut against Wales. While still only 22, his debut was overdue. At 20, he went on the 1951 tour of Australia as first-choice second-five, but was thwarted by injury. He remembers: 'It was my first time out of New Zealand. In those days it was a big thing to travel to Australia – by the time my children reached that age they had been three or four times. I did the lateral ligament in my knee in the first game and that was it. I played three more games at the end of the tour, but the Tests had gone.'

The injury that wrecked his 1952 season remains a vividly unpleasant memory half a century later: 'I went to fend a chap off. I accelerated, but he did too. There was a 'squelch' and I had a full dislocation of my elbow at right-angles with the palm facing upwards. I let out a shout that could be heard all over the park. I knew All Blacks aren't supposed to show pain, but when it hurts that much it doesn't matter what shirt you are wearing – you still shout in pain. And, of course, I still had my jersey on.'

Fitzpatrick was a powerful and aggressive player: 'I was supposed to be a bit of a hitman like Jack Matthews', but credited by Jarden 'with the uncanny gift of playing his wing-three-quarters into perfect position for the overlap'. While he came from Gisborne, in the north-east corner of the North Island, he was by 1953 firmly associated with Wellington, where in both Varsity and provincial teams he built a highly effective partnership of complementary talents with centre or second-five Jim Fitzgerald: 'The Fitzes. I was the hard player, while Jim supplied the subtlety – he was one of those players who could go one way, and then suddenly be going the other, like Christian Cullen.' He had again been injured in the tour trials, making his selection 'a bombshell' for one paper, but reckons Wellington's Ranfurly Shield run played its part: 'It does put you in the limelight. And we were a very good team, something different in the rugby of the time because we ran from everywhere.'

After leaving Victoria, he joined a bank, but by the 1953 tour he was a clerk with Shell Oil. He had spent the summer as a farm worker, hoping outdoor work would strengthen an already formidable physique. At 5 ft 10½ in. tall and 13 st. 8 lb he was jointly with number

6, Laurie Haig, first five-eighth and vice-captain, the heaviest All Black back.

Haig was the one immigrant All Black. He was born at Prestonpans, Scotland, in 1922 and moved at three to New Zealand with his miner father. He too followed his father's trade, making him in pleasingly counter-stereotypical fashion the only miner on either side against Wales. A scrum-half at school, he moved to first-five at 16 to accommodate younger brother Jimmy, who played twice for the All Blacks in 1946 before turning to rugby league and playing Tests for another decade. His first Otago appearance had been as far back as 1944. Teammate Kevin Skinner recalls him as a tough, tactically astute player who rarely missed a tackle and 'had a clever boot and would never give the ball to anyone in a worse position than himself'. He was a kicker rather than a runner, recalled by Scott as uncannily accurate with the grubber kick, whose talents ideally fitted the restrictive All Black game against the 1950 Lions.

Supplanted by Hotop against Australia in 1952, he had played himself back into the team in the trials, when McLean reckoned him second only to Scott in quality, while the *New Zealand Rugby Almanack* called him: 'A master tactician with the ability to direct the attack in any manner he pleases. He stood out head and shoulders above his fellows.' To McCarthy he was, 'the old maestro', but the radio commentator remembered one New Zealand expert warning him during the trials that Haig kept fit working at a coal face in the mines and he would not be getting that opportunity on tour. In addition, he said, Laurie was lackadaisical at training and had to be kept up to the collar all the time. He doubted that he would be any more enthusiastic on tour, saying that he would put on weight around the hips and thighs, and lose speed. He was dead right'.

Haig was partnered by scrum-half Keith Davis, number 7 and yet another Catholic, albeit not from St Kevin's. His faith is of lifelong significance: 'It gave me the disciplines that go with it, good teachers and a school I was proud to go to when we moved to Auckland.' Described by McLean, in an extremely rare slip, as the only Maori in the party, he was in fact one of three. Auckland prop forward H.L. 'Snow' White, had grown up speaking Maori in the Bay of Islands but looked completely unlike the stereotypical Maori. The other, more experienced scrum-half, Vince Bevan, was related to Davis: 'He was my third cousin, although that made no difference to the way we competed in the trials or for a Test place. Morrie O'Connell was a relative of Vince's. If he'd gone, there would have been three of us from the same stock.'

Davis's family history was an echo of New Zealand's. His great-grandfather, Roger Gray, a soldier from Enniskillen in Northern Ireland, had fought in the British Army in one of the great battles of the Maori Wars, Gate Pa. 'I had ancestors on both sides,' he recalls. His father had been a farmer, but the Davis family were among the earlier participants in an internal migration that was to be the defining Maori experience in the middle decades of the century. In 1945, when they moved from Whakatane to Auckland, only one in five Maoris lived in towns. Within 30 years, that figure would have increased to 75 per cent.

Within two years he was in the first XV at Sacred Heart School and playing for Auckland schools. In 1948, Sacred Heart were Auckland champions and in his final year, 1949, Davis captained the school. He still has the newspaper photograph of a visit paid to his school by members of that year's All Blacks: 'I was shaking hands with Morrie McHugh and Kevin Skinner. They were like gods to me and I said to myself, "I want to be like them."'

He went straight to a job at Dominion Breweries: 'I studied accountancy for a while, but rugby got the better of it,' he recalls. By 1951, he was playing for Auckland, coping with the buffeting experienced by the mid-century half-back: 'At the scrums you'd get the siderow men coming through with the ball. They didn't have to stay bound.' Even so the 5 ft 7 in. tall Davis was rapidly recognised as quick in thought and movement, always likely to make a dangerous break.

Though technically New Zealand's incumbent scrum-half after making his debut in the second Australia Test in 1952, he was far from confident of selection. His place may have been sealed by the trial at Palmerston North: 'I had a bit of a shoulder injury and didn't think that I'd last very long. So my game plan was to do something quickly so even if I had to go off the selectors would remember me. In the first few seconds, I made a break and scored under the posts. After that, I had an armchair ride while Vince Bevan, the opposing half-back, had a really hard time.'

It is at this point that New Zealand and British numbering really diverged. The Welsh numbered forwards league-fashion, giving the front row the lowest numbers, then working their way back though the second and back rows. New Zealand numbered from the back, and reflected their 3–4–1 scrummage formation. So the man at the back of the scrum was number 8, the flankers (still often called siderow men) were 9 and 12 with the locks packing between them at 10 and 11. The front row wore numbers 13 to 15.

Bill McCaw wore number 8. He was 26 and a schoolteacher, following his father, who was for many years principal of Surrey Park School, Invercargill. Being an All Black did confer a certain local celebrity in the rugby-enthused deep south, but he recalls that most of his pupils were too young to be impressed: 'I was infant mistress,' he says with quietly self-effacing humour. Older pupils were more aware, but might have begun to wonder if being an All Black was quite such an extraordinary achievement. 'It was a two-teacher school, and the head Tubby Hulme had been an All Black half-back.'

He had been at St Kevin's for his last two years of school following a slightly retarded earlier rugby education: 'I was at a small school, Edenvale, outside Invercargill. We only had house games because it was wartime and there wasn't the petrol.' The shortage of adult players and clubs during the war also pitched St Kevin's into senior rugby: 'It meant that I never played any grade rugby, but always at senior level – although it wasn't desperately strong in Oamaru.'

Training college at Dunedin was possibly more important: 'We had a lot of returned servicemen and excellent backs with players like Les Dees, who was New Zealand's full-back in 1949. We didn't have a very strong pack, but we played some very entertaining rugby and I had a most enjoyable couple of years there.'

Returning to teach in Invercargill and play for the Marist club brought a change of position: 'Until then I had played siderow, but the coach decided I would be better as the back-row man at number 8, doing the cover defence that was the position's main role. You'd play at the end of the lineout, with your first job to see the opposing half-back didn't break. You'd drive them out, then peel off behind in case anyone broke through. From the scrum you'd position yourself in relation to the opposing backs, so that if anyone broke, you'd be in a position to pick them off. It meant you did a great deal of running, often to little purpose, but were always there if there was a breakthrough.' McLean was to term him 'Johnny on the Spot'.

In 1949, he won selection for South Island – one consequence of the All Blacks touring South Africa during the domestic season was that a fresh cohort of players received representative opportunities – but was ruled out of trials for the Australia Tests by a broken hand. His All Black breakthrough came in 1951: 'I was picked for the tour of Australia. I played in all the Tests, which were closely contested, but the other games were fairly easy. I remember the feeling of euphoria that comes with being made an All Black, and also a lot of excitement locally. There were three of us in the touring team, which was a big thing for Southland.'

The journey was also memorable: 'We went to Australia in a flying boat, which took seven hours. It was so boring and we moved around a bit in the plane. The captain came on the public address and said, "Will you fellows stay in one place."'

He'd missed out in 1952 with an indented cheekbone, so Hugh McLaren of Waikato played the Tests against Australia: 'I had to push my own barrow and get re-established in 1953,' remembers McCaw. McLaren led the North Island team that beat the South 15–14, while McCaw was not chosen for the final trial, but he was confident this was a good omen: 'I'd had a reasonably good run and when I looked at the other people who were not required – players like Bob Scott, Laurie Haig and Kevin Skinner – I realised that I was in good company.'

Stuart wore 9, and an extra-large number 10 shirt was reserved for another of the men with nothing to prove long before the final trial. Richard White was 6 ft 2½ in. tall and listed as weighing 16 st., although seven weeks into the tour was probably nearer 16½ st. Bob Scott was to recall: 'Not one of his hundreds of ounces of weight was superfluous. His chest was 45 inches and his waist 35 and his trunk swelled out like Sandow's. The calves were the biggest I have ever seen on a man. They must have been 20 inches or more in circumference and, when they were flexed, the muscles and sinews stood out like iron bands.' The New Zealand taste for ironic understatement ensured that he was invariably known as 'Tiny'.

Of all the 1953 All Blacks following the family trade, none was quite so predestined: 'My parents were farmers. My father had started in a bank before the First World War, but afterwards followed his father into farming. My younger brothers were farmers, while my sister married a farmer.' His elder brother somehow contrived to become a teacher. Yet there was nothing predestined about an All Black career for an adolescent known in his native Gisborne for his size and lack of coordination: 'I think it eventually helped me, because I was determined to prove to myself and the world that I could achieve things.'

As a 14 year old in 1939 he had been told after a school rugby trial: 'Sorry, Richard. We can't pick you. You're just too big.' Hopes of studying agriculture at Massey University were thwarted by the war: 'It was more important to help my father. There were virtually no young men in the district so I did a lot of work for neighbours, mustering sheep for shearing and docking. But I injured my stomach helping clear flood damage and was effectively disabled for a couple of years.'

Gisborne High School Old Boys were unimpressed when offered his services in 1945: 'You could see them thinking, "Don't give that oversized, clubfooted so and so a game, he'll bugger the system up."' Disappointed, he remembered his father's words in 1939: 'Never mind, you'll show them one day' and turned up the following Saturday to find GHSOB one short: 'They found that the over-sized, clubfooted so and so wasn't such a bad player after all.'

Having missed the war, he volunteered to join J-Force occupying Japan: 'It was the thing to do something for your country.' It did something for him as well. His wife Elsie remembers: 'It changed the rest of our lives.' Not only did soldiering suit him: 'I had only one day in the ranks and ended up as a Regimental Sergeant Major, the last one in the battalion, picking up a lot of experience on the way', but his rugby also blossomed under the tuition of former Kiwi Pat Rhind: 'He encouraged me to develop the skills I had, which might not have happened at that time in New Zealand with the dominance of the Otago style.' While not wholly eschewing bars in his free time, his main leisure activity was getting and staying fit, running every morning and competing for his battalion in the 440 and 880 yards, and the mile.

Returning to New Zealand, his service earned him a place in the Returned Servicemen's ballot for a farm: 'I drew the second-to-last marble – a thousand acres, 99 per cent of it scrub. It needed a lot of hard work, but that was the place I farmed for nearly 30 years. Finance was made available at a special interest rate and it took me a few years to pay it off.'

The farm's location and topography helped develop distinctive training methods: 'I was 15 to 20 miles out of Gisborne, so I had to train by myself. I did it by running. You've got to have a hill to run up, you can't train just on the flat. I was out in the fresh air doing hard physical work all day and at the end of it I'd put on a pair of sandshoes and go out and run. It wasn't a chore, but a pleasure – once I got fit it became something to look forward to. Then once or twice a week I'd get in the truck and go into town for training. I played on Saturday and, if there was a representative game the following week, there was a run out on the Sunday.' He reckons he anticipated Arthur Lydiard's 100-miles-a-week formula, credited for the success of New Zealand runners in the 1950s and 1960s, by five years.

He returned from Japan too late to be considered for the 1949 tour of South Africa but rapidly attracted the attention of All Black selector Norm McKenzie, based just down the coast in Hawke's Bay: 'He reckoned I was the cheapest All Black he ever found – just the few shillings for the train fare. He picked me straight out of club rugby for an All Black trial. I was expecting a lecture before the game, but nobody said anything. When I asked Norm what to do, he said, "Just go on doing the things I saw when I came to Gisborne."' Since these included dominating the lineout – he could jump and clap his hands above a 10 ft 6 in. crossbar – and running amok in the loose, he was selected for the Australian Tests and held his place against the 1950 British Lions, where he fought a magnificent lineout battle with the slighter but equally upwardly mobile Roy John.

Even by the standards of the All Black tight-forwards of the time – two 1953 props would become presidents of the New Zealand Rugby Union – White had a mind of his own. He did his own body massages and had the makers add extra ankle supports to his boots: 'The ankle is the most vital part of the body in taking thumps and bumps, so I had a couple of inches added to protect it. I see modern players with no support on their ankles, and I don't wonder that they pull muscles.'

He was also prepared to argue tactics, advocating a much more mobile style than the dominant Otago method. As well as evolving a method of rolling his head and shoulders which enabled him to escape from scrummages, and sometimes get to the breakdown ahead of outpaced (and occasionally shouldered-aside) flankers, lineout mastery allowed him to catch two-handed and pass straight to the scrum-half or first-five. Otago orthodoxy demanded that such possession be brought straight down and driven. White argued that fast ball from the top of the lineout could outpace the fastest cover, and that this would be much more productive. His fervent conviction brought him close to mutiny against the Otago-dominated leadership of the 1951 tour of Australia. A lesser player might have been discarded. White, though, remained an All Black fixture.

Good second-row partnerships often operate on contrast. Nelson Dalzell, number 11, was also a sheep farmer and immensely strong, but otherwise very different. McLean described him as 'a quiet man, not given to thrusting his views forward'. In the lineout, Davis recalls: 'He never jumped. He'd stand there and get the ball as it came down.' Local legend in Culverden, North Canterbury, credited him with the ability to lift a 44-gallon drum from the ground onto a truck. That strength made him a formidable scrummager – Skinner, a connoisseur in such matters, recalls: 'Once he got his arm around you and went down, you knew you wouldn't move. He was completely unselfish and buried himself in the hard work.'

At 32, he was one of the oldest debutants in All Black history, yet the truly remarkable thing about Dalzell – 'Dad' to his teammates – was that he was there at all. He had been, recalled one friend, 'blown over the moon' by a Japanese shell while taking part in the infantry landing at Guadalcanal. Doctors wanted to amputate a leg, but he refused. Dalzell took two years, most of them in hospital, to recover and retained one of the more alarming scars seen in a rugby changing-room. 'He still had a big hole in his leg. He used to pack it with wadding, strap a shinpad over it and go out and play,' recalls Elsom, who was to become his brother-in-law.

Number 12 was another debutant, albeit eight years younger, the Wellington flanker Bill Clark. His father had played for Golden Bay-Motueka (a union subsequently amalgamated with Nelson) against the British Lions in the 1920s and his last two years of school had been at

Nelson College, the cradle of New Zealand rugby. For all these historical trappings he was in 1953 the epitome of rugby modernity. Jarden said he 'changed the character and nature of New Zealand forward play' by proving 'the value of intelligent loose-forward play'. Norm Mackenzie pointed to him as a consummate team player, brilliant in cover defence and with an uncanny gift for charging kicks down. Cliff Morgan, outside-half for both Cardiff and Wales in 1953, remembers: 'Rather than running straight, he came at you in an arc, so you never knew exactly where he would be.'

In spite of his lineage, Clark played only limited rugby before going to Victoria University – restricted at his first school in Mapua by its small size and wartime petrol shortages and, once he moved to Nelson College, by being thin and underweight. He played his schoolboy rugby at five-eighth and believes this helped his subsequent career in the pre-replacement era when a forward who could switch to the backs – and Clark's speed of thought and movement made him ideal – was a necessity for every team.

His time at Victoria was more productive in sporting than academic terms: 'I was supposed to be studying accountancy but the real answer is "mainly rugby" and the studies got pushed aside. I didn't graduate.' He remembers, though, a most enjoyable period of rugby: 'It was an era of no-risks rugby. University teams couldn't cope with clubs or provinces in weight and size up front, so they were very keen to move the ball. Our success influenced the style of the provincial team and we had a good Ranfurly Shield run in 1953. I've no doubt that influenced selection for the tour, as it put a spotlight on us.'

J.J. Stewart argues that, protestations to the contrary notwithstanding, 1950s flankers did little pushing in the scrums. Clark is one who does not protest: 'Our coach at Victoria worked on the theory that you could work the scrum with seven tight-forwards and one out and out loose-forward. Scrummaging was not ever one of my responsibilities.' While he was listed officially at 13 st. in 1953, he says: 'I don't think I reached 13 st. until I started doing weights before the 1956 series against the Springboks.' He worked as a clerk in MacKenzie's, a Wellington store, but like many university players stayed with the club even after leaving the institution.

The sight of Kevin Skinner, winning his 14th cap, in a number 13 shirt was enough to convince the most hard-headed opponent that there might be something in superstition. Skinner, 26, was in Scott's words, 'a great player with a great mental attitude'. Tiny White recalls: 'He was without doubt the best prop I ever met – a very strong player who could take all the pressure I could apply. It was because of his strength that I was able to develop the technique of rolling away from our scrum. He was also very astute, a good thinker and talker about the game.'

The third of the St Kevin's alumni, he had made his Otago debut in 1945 as a 17-year-old second-row forward: 'I was thrown into the front row when we went down to play Southland for the Shield in 1947. It was a choice of not being in the team or putting my hand up and saying that I had played prop at school. We won the Shield and I never played anywhere else after that, and the truth is that I wasn't really big enough to be a lock. I looked at people like Tiny White and Tiny Hill, and thought that the front row suited me fine.' He became one of the key figures in the Otago hegemony that followed, inspired by Cavanagh and Charlie Saxton, who had also coached him at the Pirates club: 'I was lucky to have a good grounding at school followed by people like Vic and Charlie. They had charisma and were the sort of people you would put your body on the line for.'

His raw power was supplemented by technical mastery and some delicacy of touch: 'Has Catley and Ron Hemi liked to strike for the ball on the opposition's head, which meant that you had to scrum a little differently to give them room to strike. You had to balance on your inside foot – the left in my case as tight-head – and follow the ball in from the half-back, bouncing on the leg. It was a bit of an art.' Nor was his role confined to scrummaging: 'Props had been expected just to scrum and block in the lineout, but after 1949 you learnt to be a bit more useful in other phases, taking the ball up, following up kicks and winning the odd lineout – the sort of thing modern players expect to do.'

Skinner, 16 st. 4 lb and 6 ft tall, had also, famously, been a good boxer: 'While I was at school, I went to a gym in Dunedin. A guy there got me doing a bit of sparring. I enjoyed it and within a couple of years I was in amateur boxing and won the New Zealand championship. That was as far as it was ever going. I wasn't going to go professional –

there were hardly any heavyweights around in New Zealand, so I would have to have gone to Australia for contests. It was never an alternative to rugby but a means of getting and keeping fit. The gym work for boxing helped quite a bit, but when I started chucking weights around for rugby the boxing trainer got crook at me because he said it would make me too muscle bound.' He finished after winning the championship in 1947 – Morrie McHugh, who beat him in 1946, would be a 1949 All Black colleague.

There were, though, hints of the boxer's introspection in his preparation for matches. McLean wrote that he 'brooded upon the important matches for perhaps 36 hours beforehand, turning very quiet, writing letters and keeping himself to himself'. Skinner appreciated the opportunity to concentrate not always available at home: 'At home you were working Saturday morning, so if you had a 1.30 game it was enough of a battle to get to the game, never mind prepare. I liked to be able to switch on a couple of days beforehand and prepare mentally for what lay ahead – and if possible I'd get away for half an hour before the game, lie on a bench and go to sleep. So I used to get crook at club players who'd talk about what they were backing at the races or what they were planning to do that night.'

A butcher by training – something that came as no surprise to opposing props – Skinner had gone into the family grocery business and joined up with his brother in running shops in Central Otago before buying him out.

If he had been a certainty, then hooker Ron Hemi, number 14, was the justification of those exhaustive trials – the man who had emerged from nowhere. Or, more precisely, from Waikato's reserves when the veteran Has Catley, 37, but playing well enough to be 'a problem for the selectors' was injured as they lost the Ranfurly Shield to Wellington on 1 August. The eight matches Hemi, 20, had played on the tour were more than half of his total first-class career.

Only three years on from a final year at Hamilton Boy's High School in which, Bob Howitt records, 'he captained the rugby team and the cricket team, took out swimming and athletic titles and was the college's head prefect' in addition to opening the batting for Auckland, Hemi was one of those players who arrives in top-class rugby fully formed. Snow White recalls: 'He had all the skills. He was a good hooker, he was fast and he was intelligent.' Skinner believes that even though one of his most important skills, dribbling, has become obsolete, 'modern rugby would have suited him down to the ground'. A trainee accountant, he was to take, and pass, the secretarial practice paper of his examinations, by special arrangement with the University of New Zealand, in Cardiff.

Alongside him at number 15 was another Waikato debutant, the 22-year-old prop forward Ian Clarke, beginning one of the longest All Black careers. Clarke was a farmer, one of five brothers who all played first-class rugby and whose remarkable fitness was based on improvised training facilities. Younger brother Don, a 1953 trialist who as a siege-gun kicking full-back would rival Colin Meads as the All Black icon of the later 1950s, recalled that: 'We built weightlifting gear with great chunks of firewood on the ends of heavy piping. Ian packed down against fence posts to build up his strength and shoulders.'

Snow White, a rival for a Test place, reckoned he was not yet the scrummager he would become, but he was well adapted for the more varied game described by Skinner, who says: 'He was very strong, very quick, anticipated play and could handle well.' Norm MacKenzie, calling on memories of half a century of rugby, reckoned him: 'a rugged, skilled footballer . . . one of the few props, indeed one of the few forwards I have seen who is able to pass on one foot and deliver it on the other'.

Teammate Peter Jones noted his good humour: 'You'd never see him looking tired or lazy and you'd never find him in a sour or gloomy mood.' It was perhaps for this reason that, as McLean wrote: 'The extremely favourable impression he made during the tour was by no means confined to men.'

The selected 15 had emerged from the 30-man touring party over a trip that was already 2 months and 13 matches old. The first All Black team to visit Britain in 18 years, they had already been to three of the four home countries in a trip that for many of them was their first experience of foreign travel other than trips to Australia. Preparations had begun from the moment of their selection for the tour on 15 September.

CHAPTER 3

HOW THEY GOT THERE

The month between selection and departure on 15 October had been, Clark remembers, 'crazy'. Players had to arrange leave from jobs, put businesses or farms in safe hands, get kitted out with their tour outfits, say goodbyes and also go to the American Embassy to obtain visas for the final leg of the tour by swearing that they were not, nor had ever been 'a Communist, Fascist, Nazi or Falangist'.

The craziness also incorporated another important match, Canterbury's Ranfurly Shield challenge against Wellington on 19 September. It was Stuart's 100th first-class match and a chance to answer critics of his selection: 'I felt we had to win it,' he remembers. They did, winning 24–3. It was, he recalls with some understatement 'quite a week'. Clark's memories are less fond: 'I always disliked playing on heavy ground. It was a wet spell in Wellington, the drainage was not very good at Athletic Park and the conditions were disgusting. I went in to tackle Ross Smith and lost all interest in where the ball had gone because I couldn't feel my shoulder. It went numb temporarily and I could see my tour going.' Fortunately, the shock was greater than the injury and he, although not Wellington, rapidly recovered. The result inaugurated Canterbury's three-year Shield run, but, in Morrie MacKenzie's view, put the New Zealand game back by almost as long by its triumph for 'the strong arm and the big boot'.

Players had a little over three weeks to prepare for five and a half months away. Personal situations varied. As a public servant, McCaw was given automatic leave on half-pay for representative rugby – if he had been married it would have been full pay. Dominion Breweries went on paying Davis's salary, while Tanner's father took on his share of work in their dentistry practice. Families or temporary managers filled in for farmers, while Skinner's partner ran his grocery business.

With characteristic generosity, the home unions 'after the fullest consideration of the matter' rejected the New Zealand suggestion that players receive a daily allowance of 10 shillings (50p), opting instead for 7s (35p). It was, remembers Scott, 'back to army pay'. The *Daily Herald*, British Labour's paper, was outraged, asking: 'How far does seven shillings go when you are living in expensive hotels and continually travelling. How can hospitality be returned on such an allowance?'

The answer for some was that clubs and friends raised collections. Brian Fitzpatrick recalls the Wellington aficionado Caesar Cohen, famed for owning a house called 'Rugby': 'He held a "Rugby Ball", got all the card sharps in and relieved them of £800 which he divided between three of us.' Keith Davis was thrown a farewell party by his club: 'I was handed an envelope with money in it and told it was a gift. It was nothing to do with playing rugby' – a sensible thought given the rules on amateurism – 'But for me to enjoy myself and make life more pleasurable.' For others it was tougher. Scott had no pay from his job and his club raised around £80 for him. He says: 'I was lucky that my wife was an exceptional housekeeper, but she was living on charity, really. If I think about it, I should probably never have gone.'

Both the Prime Minister and Leader of the Opposition spoke at the team's farewell dinner. The mere manner of its departure made history – the first All Black team ever to go on a major tour by air rather than sea. A half-year which Jarden was to compute as totalling 35,000 miles, 25,000 of them by air, started with the eight-and-a-half-hour-slog from Evans Airbase, Wellington, to Sydney by flying boat. Tiny White says: 'I remember looking out of the window and seeing a ship below us. I went away, had a cup of tea and a game of cards, then looked out again – and the ship was still there! It looked as if the ship was going faster than we were. The old Empire flying boats couldn't do much more than 120–150 knots.' Prop Peter Eastgate recalls 'wondering when the rubber band was going to break'.

The rest of the journey was done in rather more rapid four-engine Constellations, but still took the best part of a week, including an extended stop in Singapore. They arrived one short – Canterbury wing Morrie Dixon, ill at Singapore, was administered penicillin and succumbed to a virulent allergy. Delays at Singapore to load 1,800 kg of gold bullion forced an unplanned stop at Basra, while fog meant a stop in Zurich before crossing the Alps. Not that the players minded. McLean recorded: 'Two or three entered a combined beauty-salon-tobacconist's store. They stayed only a few minutes because we were about to leave – but I noticed each of the girls in the shop was wearing a silver fern, which seemed to suggest fast work.' In an era before international travel became commonplace, the trip was an experience in itself. Davis remembers 'seeing armed police for the first time in Djakarta, feeling the heat of the desert at Basra, and how beautiful Beirut looked from the air as we cruised above it'.

Traditional critics saw a sea voyage as time for a team to bond. McLean argued that, as with the 1949 All Blacks, it also risked their losing fitness and gaining weight. Clark recalls: 'All apprehension was gone by the time we reached Singapore. We'd all got to know each other, and proved that you don't need six weeks on a boat. I can't imagine what it was like for teams who had to do that.'

Arriving at Heathrow Airport on 21 October, some acceded to photographers' requests to wave as they came down the gangway, all performed a haka on the runway and a Rugby Football Union panjandrum underlined Scott's veteran status with the words: 'Of course I remember you, Scott. You played here after the first war, didn't you?' Manager Norman Millard promised, within a couple of hours of landing, that the team would try to play in an open, attacking style.

Millard, 63, had been on Wellington Rugby Union executive since 1916 and chairman since 1937. He would keep both roles until 1964. He was also a member of the New Zealand Rugby Union executive and a former president. As head teacher of Hutt Valley High School he had been famous for knowing every child's name by the end of its first month as a pupil – this saved time with the 1953 All Blacks, as Jarden and Jim Fitzgerald were alumni – but in spite of his invitation to 'call me Norman' some players, not to mention McLean and McCarthy, were not convinced that the schoolmasterly manner was ideal for the role.

Fitzpatrick, offering mimicry sufficiently vivid to suggest that he was one of the players who angered McLean by sending up the manager, recalls him 'speaking like a bishop'. Clark, who knew him from Wellington's away trips, remembers him calling the province's team together in a station café and saying, 'Hands up all of you who want a cup of tea.' Clark says: 'I respected him, but you had to wonder whether treating men who were well into their 30s and war veterans as though they were pupils at Hutt Valley High School was the right idea.'

His assistant was Arthur Marslin, a 52-year-old sheepbreeder from Alexandra in Otago, a former All Black trialist and a tour selector. Tiny White remembers him as: 'A man with a very astute rugby mind and a strong philosophy of the way the game should be played, according to the Otago style. To people he did not know, he seemed dour, but he was totally different beneath all that – someone who could pull your leg without blinking an eyelid, and totally loyal as a friend.'

The difficulty was that the assistant manager was expected to coach and, as Skinner recalls: 'He wasn't really a coach. There were good coaches in New Zealand at the time – we had Charlie Saxton and Vic Cavanagh at Otago, while Dick Everest did a good job at Waikato, but we didn't seem to get them for tours.' This was a strange weakness in All Black rugby. Britain might remain anti-coaching, but New Zealand players were, as Skinner points out, 'used to having club coaches – and some of them were pretty good'. Where the modern team goes on tour armed with the videos of their opponents' latest matches and a cohort of tactical analysts, only Stuart and Scott of the 1953 All Blacks had ever played in Britain (neither since 1946) and none had seen a British team since the 1950 Lions.

The All Blacks settled into training at Eastbourne College, where Scott amazed watching journalists by kicking goals barefooted from the halfway line. He was about to collect on a bet with one of them when he realised that accepting the money might make him, technically at least, a professional.

On the Saturday following their arrival, Stuart, Scott, Haig, Millard and Marslin went to Twickenham to see Harlequins play Swansea. They returned horrified, and not just because the Quins had beaten the only club side ever to have defeated the All Blacks. Stuart remembers: 'We were amazed at how much offside and killing the ball were tolerated. It meant that you could not get the ball fairly at the breakdown and that outside-halfs were battered to hell.' The conclusion, duly reported to their team, was, Clark recalls: 'Keep it tight and play the touchline.'

Forewarned as they were, there were further shocks when the tour began in the slightly unlikely surroundings of Hove greyhound stadium on Saturday, 31 October, against a South of England select widely assumed to be little more than cannon fodder. Watched by a 10,000-strong crowd, including 75 journalists, the All Blacks duly won 24–0 on an unpleasantly windy day. Critics were impressed by the pack, particularly McCaw, Tiny White and Clark, but unconvinced by the backs.

Nobody had expected to see Jarden, in the clear, overhauled and collared by centre Phil Davies. Nor were the All Blacks amused when Clark was refused a try from a charge-down. Clark remembers: 'The rules had only very recently been changed to allow you to get away with a charge-down,' but the referee seemed unaware of this.

Then there was Glyn Davies of London Welsh and Sussex, the South's captain. To E.W. Swanton of the *Daily Telegraph*, he had 'stolen the show' in the lineout, although the All Blacks felt his jumping unimpeded over a wedge of blockers was illegal. Keith Davis remembers: 'He was playing havoc with us. Something happened and he went down. Then he opened his eyes and said, "Wait till you bastards get to Wales."' McCaw, too, still vividly recalls 'this big redheaded guy and his voice booming out in the bottom of a ruck'. The refereeing was, McLean would write, 'the shape of things to come'. So too was Davies' invitation, or threat, but the All Blacks had not expected it quite so soon or so far from Wales.

Stuart also gave notice of his talent for deft, to-the-point after-dinner speeches, explaining that during the war he had 'many pleasant associations with Brighton and Hove. And I hope they are all married now.' Rugby players rarely love after-dinner oratory, but Stuart's efforts reinforced his team's regard for him. Fitzpatrick remembers: 'When Bob got up to speak, you could puff out your chest and say, "That's our captain."'

London left lasting memories. Elsom recalls: 'There was nowhere in New Zealand remotely as big, and we probably were a little overawed.' This was pre-Clean Air Act London, the four-day smog of 1952 a recent memory and Fitzpatrick remembers: 'I couldn't get over how dirty the buildings were. Even somewhere like St James's Palace was completely black.' Tiny White remembers the war damage: 'Parts of London were still flattened. Saint Paul's was there, of course, but a lot of buildings were rubble, lying where they had fallen. The hotel where we stayed in Eastbourne, the Cavendish, had one end totally blown away.'

Eight and a half years after the war, Britain still had rationing – restrictions on sugar ended three weeks before the All Blacks arrived, while the abolition of food rationing from the end of June 1954 was announced a fortnight after they landed. Tiny White remembers: 'We never went short of a decent meal.' Their plush hotel – the Park Lane – offered a different culture shock. Peter Jones recalled in his memoirs that New Zealand informality disconcerted hotel staff used to being treated as servants, while their non-tipping culture upset waiters until a collective end-of-stay payment was negotiated.

Some found British formality irksome. Snow White remembers: 'There were some people to whom meeting the All Blacks was just another part of their social calendar and a way of impressing people. They weren't really interested in us, and we weren't interested in them.'

Prominent New Zealanders were different. The team certainly were interested in the newly knighted Sir Edmund Hillary, in 1953 the one New Zealander likely to impress an entire All Black touring party more than they impressed him. He told them: 'Drop this Sir Edmund business. Just make it Ed Hillary.' General Freyberg, now Vice-Constable of Windsor Castle, gave them lunch at the castle, but remembered something both of rugby players and of the wartime proclivities of the New Zealand division. Snow White recalls: 'We had a great day with him. We enjoyed ourselves and felt relaxed. But he did say, "Don't forget, we're counting the silver. I know what you bloody Kiwis are like."'

Snow took away more London memories than most. One of three expectant fathers in the party, he learnt of the birth of his second child: 'We were training at the King's School ground and one of the journalists told me. I was rushed back to the hotel, rang home to see everything was fine and went back to training. The call cost about £4, a lot of money to me at that time.'

Perhaps the greatest novelty of all was television. McLean recorded that the cowboy series *Hopalong Cassidy* soon acquired a devoted following, while the televising of the Oxford v. Cambridge match in early December earned a surprised St Ives householder a roomful of New Zealand guests: 'We just knocked on the door of a house where we saw an aerial,' remembers McCaw. The home unions decided in early October that the Wales match would be televised 'as an experiment only', with clubs to be surveyed about the impact on attendances. J.B.G. Thomas wrote in the *Western Mail* that the broadcast would 'give players, particularly young players and their coaches, a chance to study the technical points of the game'.

Critics were, however, soon wondering how much there really was to learn from the All Blacks. An estimated 50,000 at Twickenham for the 11–0 victory over London Counties, the only team to beat the 1951 Springboks, was reckoned a record for a non-international in England. They won their matches, seeing off Cambridge (22–11) and Oxford (14–5) universities, London and Western (11–0) counties in the fortnight after their debut at Hove. The forwards won admiration – Vivian Jenkins, Wales's 1935 full-back, wrote of their 'immense vigour and drive' and warned 'make a mistake in the loose, leave the ball lying about unattended for a fraction of a second and you are courting disaster'. Scott was universally lauded. To Jenkins he was 'one of the greatest of all time, a supreme artist'; to Terry O'Connor, early in a long *Daily Mail* career, he was 'the glimmer in the Twickenham gloom'.

O'Connor also thought the London match an 'aimless display'. The quality of the backs, Scott apart, had been questioned since the trials and by the fifth match, against Western Counties, Larry Montague of the *Manchester Guardian* discerned a pattern: 'Slowness and less than strict accuracy in the pass from the scrum-half, the same unbelievable lack of speed off the mark and command of a flicked, crisp pass at five-eighth; the same monotonously tactically pointless and technically uncontrolled kicking ahead; and a seeming lack of a sense of anything but the most palpable of overlaps.' For all of the excellence of the forwards they were used 'almost entirely to drive in a wedge formation through every maul and every lineout and ruck they can transform into a maul'. The *Daily Express* renamed the fourth All Blacks 'the first dull greys'.

While unhappy at the virulence of some critics, the All Blacks knew they were not playing well. The difficulty was what to do about it. Stuart remembers: 'Arthur Marslin, Bob Scott, Kevin Skinner and myself discussed the tour endlessly and worried.' There was little disagreement with Stuart's belief that the Canterbury style was the only practical way under the rules, and in particular British refereeing interpretations, of the time. Marslin, Skinner and Stuart were aficionados of the South Island style while Scott, engagingly self-aware as ever, recalls that, 'I was always in favour of taking risks myself, but didn't trust other people to take them.'

Stuart denies McLean's report, in his book on the tour, that a decision was made to exclude tactics from team meetings. His recall is that, in a tour lasting over five months with around a hundred meetings it would have been 'folly to hammer tactics at even half the meetings. We tried to minimise boredom.' With a predominantly young team, he felt 'possibly the sort of warts-and-all sessions did not appeal as productive'. He points out that his own background with both University and Canterbury predisposed him to involving the whole team: 'But the coach and/or captain tended to predominate. Is the situation any different in this professional era?'

There was little or no dissent. Clark remembers: 'I can truly say that I didn't feel at the time that the junior members of the team were repressed or ignored. There were certainly players who were disappointed personally when they were not selected for the more important games, but it was generally kept at that level until hindsight came into the picture.' The difficulty was finding an alternative under conditions in Britain at the time: 'The referees did generally allow fringing around scrums, rucks and mauls, and I think the team generally accepted that to play too much of a free and easy style of rugby would have been suicidal, particularly against some of the stronger teams.'

There was tactical debate, on a strictly private, unofficial basis between Marslin and Tiny White, who remembers: 'We both enjoyed talking rugby and found that we liked each other's company. We used to talk about tactics and styles of play. I thought we needed quick ball from the top of the lineout and a more open style.' Those debates initiated a friendship that lasted until Marslin's death in 1977.

It was also clear how much the team relied on Stuart's leadership. McLean was to write that he 'personally revived great captaincy in New Zealand rugby', with his responsibilities going well beyond what happened on the pitch. Stuart remembers: 'I was effectively the coach as well. Arthur was an excellent selector but not a hands-on coach. There were also a lot of lunches, dinners and speeches.' Skinner recalls: 'Bob did a terrific job. He was a diplomat and knew how to handle people – he did a marvellous job considering he didn't have a coach and had to do most of that as well. Looking at that lot, you know why I didn't want the job!'

So the All Blacks crossed the Welsh border, via the A48, there as yet being no Severn Bridge or M4 – on 15 November, unbeaten and unbowed, but as yet unconvincing. They checked in to the Seabank Hotel, Porthcawl, which Fitzpatrick recalls would become a second home in four stays totalling four weeks over the next three months.

McCaw remembers: 'I had looked forward to it. I had heard so much about Wales and Welsh rugby – it was the epitome of rugby.' In London, Skinner recalls 'nobody really knew who we were'. This was more like New Zealand. Tiny White says: 'There was a deep sense of the love of rugby which was similar to home. Kids from school would follow you around. Sometimes, to get some peace, we'd turn our blazers inside out, but they'd still recognise us.' Tanner remembered Dunedin fervour from Otago's great days: 'But Dunedin only had 100,000 people. Here was an entire country who all wanted to talk about rugby and about their team.' Davis took to his hosts immediately, but had to disappoint them when asked if his name indicated Welsh ancestry: 'I had to tell them it was more Irish.' As in New Zealand, this enthusiasm has a down side. It was initially amusing to be told 'Wales are going to beat you' or some local variant concerning Llanelli, Swansea or Cardiff, but the All Blacks grew tired of the ritual. Before long, McLean recalled, many were answering 'get stuffed'.

Their first match, on Wednesday, 17 November at Llanelli, was a rousing rejoinder to perennially gloom-laden poet R.S. Thomas's question, 'Is there no passion in Wales?' Clark remembers: 'It was still a culture shock, even to a New Zealander. They were crazy about the game.' Tickets – 5/- for the grandstand, 3/- or 2/- to stand – had been sold out for weeks. A local half-holiday was declared, although the local police chief had opposed a two-hour opening hours' extension. Traffic queued three hours beforehand as an 18,500 crowd – more than half of Llanelli's total population at the 1951 census – shoehorned itself into Stradey Park. The *Manchester Guardian* writer felt there was a 'mystical quality' about the Llanelli fans, although McLean confessed himself less impressed by the singing once he went outside and realised the crowd was being conducted. The All Blacks, he recorded, were still 'exhilarated as they took the field, for this was the first time up against the representatives of an ancient and much-honoured enemy'.

Both representatives served their countries well. Tiny White remembers: 'A great contest, much more open than the games we had played up to that point.' Llanelli had held their own in the first half, equalising an early penalty when winger Tucker completed a 70-yard attack. New Zealand retook the lead when Tiny White scored from a Clark charge-down, then pulled away in the final 15 minutes to win 17–3 with Elsom, taking advantage of an injured marker, scoring three tries. He remembers: 'We got on top and started throwing the ball around. One or two of the pack reckoned we were killing them by whipping the ball out wide!'

It was, wrote McLean, the first time they had played 'as a well-integrated team'. Wilfred Wooller, yet another 1935 veteran watching from the press box, commented that while their tactics – 'working the ball down to their opponents' 25 by one means or another, and then every man in the team when near the ball goes flat out for the opposition line. Having applied the pressure they keep up relentlessly' – were not exciting, they would still be very hard to beat: 'The side to do it will have to have a good set of three-quarters behind a pack of forwards who can hold the All Blacks.'

Watching at Stradey were several players from Llanelli's next opponents, Cardiff. Outside-half Cliff Morgan remembers: 'Four or five of us went down in Rex Willis's car and stood behind the posts. Bleddyn Williams, our captain, said, "On Saturday, we'll throw a long lineout to engage their back row and make sure they can't knock hell out of you, Cliff." Then Rex said, "When I shrug my shoulders, that's the signal for the long ball." What we didn't appreciate was that Rex instinctively shrugged his shoulders, so everything went long.'

For the second time in four days the All Blacks faced a passionate crowd, 56,000 of them, compared to a revivalist meeting in one paper, and leavened only by the All Blacks' guests – 18 members of the touring New Zealand women's hockey team. Llanelli were enjoying their best season since the war. Cardiff had been the best team in Wales for most of that period and had been planning for the All Blacks visit. They had an almost all-international back division, a competitive pack and, as Gareth Griffiths remembers: 'Everybody played for the team rather than themselves – Bleddyn and Jack Matthews would not allow any other way.' New Zealand had to play without Stuart. A cut on his leg from the Western Counties match had turned septic.

This was arguably the greatest day in Cardiff's history, its exhilaration captured in a photograph, the more vivid for blurring, of Bleddyn Williams, face aglow with triumph, being carried shoulder-high from the pitch after their 8–3 victory. His plan was for Cardiff to score early, before New Zealand settled. All the points came in the first 15 minutes. Wing Gwyn Rowlands crossed-kick for flanker Sid Judd to score, converted and then, after Ron Jarden had kicked a penalty for New Zealand, scored himself: 'Alun Thomas put me away with 30 yards to go. I was half outside Ron Jarden, so he had to turn and that made all the difference – I went hell for leather.'

The remaining 65 minutes were in the words of one report: 'as fast, exciting, gruelling and determined a game of rugby union football as any normal man could wish to see'. 'Crisis followed crisis,' reported another, and Bleddyn Williams was to reckon it the most nerve-racking game of his life. Cliff Morgan recalls: 'I felt that every yard you ran you'd been pushed forward by the crowd and every time you kicked to touch the ball went 20 yards further, because the crowd was willing it to do so.' Prop Snow White suffered a shoulder injury that wrecked his chance of playing against Wales, but began a lifelong friendship with his opposite number, Stan Bowes.

While All Blacks scrum-half Vince Bevan famously told Morgan that he hoped never to have to play against him again, his team took, and still take, their defeat well. Stuart said, 'Cardiff play the kind of football enthusiasts wish to see.' McCaw still speaks for all when he says: 'We

were beaten by the better team on the day.' The critics had no doubt
New Zealand had missed Stuart, and that both tactics and execution by
their midfield backs were at fault – 'mere soundness and safety-first
tactics got them nowhere . . . the qualities of quickness and surprise
were, too, lacking,' reckoned the *Times*, while another reporter opined
that, 'Haig, as ever, was the completely solid and sound midfield player,
but not the swift, elusive first five-eighths for whom this New Zealand
team is still looking' and speculated that the 20-year-old Wellingtonian
Guy Bowers, who had played at Llanelli, might be the man.

It was probably a relief to leave Wales for three weeks. In the interim,
the All Blacks beat three Scottish regional selections with something to
spare – the early 1950s were Scottish rugby's historic low-point – then
squeezed out a 3–0 win over East Midlands at Leicester in a grindingly
tough contest, where the crowd's booing of Scott as he attempted a
penalty left 'an indelibly bad impression', and a 9–0 victory over South-
Western Counties at Camborne accompanied by a refereeing 'whistling
fantasia'.

Not, it might be thought, a bad run. There were gains – McLean's
belief that the mild-mannered Davis was transformed once roused to
angry aggression by an assault on McCaw at Galashiels is confirmed by
the player: 'I had been struggling a bit to start with. Then I saw Bill
being done over and I thought, "I can't let that happen, he's one of us."
It woke me up a little and things started to come right.' Scott continued
to inspire: 'The New Zealanders' secondary principles have not yet
become clear, except for Scott who is several principles in himself,'
wrote Denys Rowbotham in the *Manchester Guardian*.

Yet the problems identified in Wales persisted. Rowbotham also
wrote: 'When the New Zealanders are held in strength and adhesiveness
forward . . . it is as if they have no alternative tactics to dictate.' The first
half at Leicester was 'one of kick, hack, plunge and harry with scarcely
a first-class movement'. Haig's slow movement and distribution
continued to attract vigorous criticism. Worse yet, they were still
without Stuart, who, given a shot for his septic leg, turned out to share
Dixon's penicillin allergy: 'I was up in Scotland on a farm. One night
my chest started to itch and I came out in blisters everywhere. I was
taken back to London and they concluded that I had an allergic
reaction to the penicillin. While I was in bed it was reported that a

woman in Sydney had died from a penicillin reaction, which cheered me up no end. I was really ill,' says Stuart, who after two bouts of dengue fever during war service in Burma knew something of real illness.

He was still missing at Swansea on 12 December. Swansea were not having a great season, but neither had they been in 1935. More than 40,000 packed into the venerable St Helen's ground – to profound West Wales fury stripped seven weeks earlier of international matches from 1955 – ostensibly a 'temporary measure' pending modernisation. The *Western Mail* had reported plans to extend its capacity to 82,000 while McLean made, rather than wrote, news with a public plea for the ground's international status, saying: 'St Helen's means a good deal to New Zealanders because our roots in it are very deep.'

It was a ferocious, sometimes ugly, contest, which inspired fresh outbreaks of the barracking so deplored at Leicester. J.B.G. Thomas was outraged, writing, 'In Wales we enjoy a worldwide reputation of being good losers' – not the view of every visiting rugby team – and expressing his alarm that 'loud and persistent booing' would have been heard by radio listeners in New Zealand. 'It would be so wrong to allow barracking to make the headlines in New Zealand papers when the Queen and Her Consort are there as guests of the Dominion.'

Skinner, captain for the day and his front-row adversary 'Stoker' Williams both recall 'a fierce battle', and at the tour's end McLean wrote of the 'low packing of the Swansea scrum' as an exception to a fairly ordinary British norm. John Faull, a 19-year-old 6 ft 3 in., 15 st. centre destined to be a British Lions forward, son of the referee of 'Obolensky's match', kicked two monstrous long-range penalty goals. Williams remembers thinking: 'He'll never kick those.' They were cancelled out by two tries from Elsom, who was displaying a considerable taste for Welsh club opposition. Amid scenes of triumph reported as comparable to those at Cardiff, Swansea added a 6–6 draw to their 1935 victory.

New Zealand had dominated the lineout and won nearly two-thirds of the scrums, but, noted the *Manchester Guardian*, 'the complete ineptitude of the New Zealand back play again was painfully emphasised'. Haig had 'slowed down each movement', while his tactical kicking was 'ill-directed and presented no difficulties' – although other reports offered extenuation in the ferocious spoiling of Wales flanker

Clem Thomas. The All Blacks had spent 35 of 40 second-half minutes in Swansea's half without scoring a point. The *Daily Express* reckoned they had enough possession to have won three matches. The implications were clear, said a BBC commentator – Wales should beat New Zealand by ten points.

CHAPTER 4

WHENCE THEY CAME:

(II) Wales

The Welsh team who faced New Zealand the following week represented both a national game and a wider economy in a distinct upturn – synchronisation between the two applied for most of the twentieth century – following the misery of the inter-war years. The economy might not quite have been enjoying the 'Second Golden Era' for which David Parry-Jones argues in rugby terms – it is the nature of Golden Ages that they are discerned retrospectively – but, on and off the field, this was one of modern Wales's happier times.

Inter-war migration to Coventry, Slough and other points east meant that while New Zealand's population had doubled since 1905, Wales's had risen by less than 20 per cent, to just under 2.6 million, with a marginal decline since 1921. That population was, though, mostly in employment. While 25,682 jobless in June were 2,000 more than a year earlier – blamed on recession in tinplate and aluminium – they were by recent Welsh standards remarkably few. That minority, along with the poor and sick, also enjoyed much greater security thanks to reforms introduced under the postwar Labour government by Welsh ministers – national insurance by James Griffiths of Llanelli while national health was piloted by Aneurin Bevan of Ebbw Vale.

Both had been miners. Wales was still, as Dai Smith has written, 'dependent on coal extraction and steel production'. The 115,500 miners who fulfilled a long-cherished objective with another landmark Labour reform, the nationalisation of coal on 1 January 1947, may have been less than half of the 1913 number, but they were still more than one in seven of the Welsh labour force. Neath MP D.J. Williams, speaking as new pithead baths opened at Cwmgors in the Swansea Valley, prophesied that, with plans for the new Abernant pit, 'from the mining point of view, the security and future of the Swansea Valley was secured for the next 50 years'.

Steel too had revived. With the opening of the giant Abbey works at Margam in 1951, Kenneth Morgan has written: 'The Afan valley suddenly became a boom area of staggering proportions, with South Wales foremost among the steel-making regions of Britain once again.' New factories like the cold-reduction plants at Trostre, near Llanelli and Velindre, near Swansea; the industrial estate at Bridgend which provided 30,000 jobs; and the Usk power station opened two weeks before the All Blacks arrived in Britain underpinned an increase in output between 1948 and 1954 of 23 per cent, compared to 18 per cent for Britain as a whole.

Wales's political identity had been recognised, ironically enough, by the returning Conservatives in 1951 with the creation of a Minister for Welsh Affairs – the Scottish lawyer David Maxwell Fyfe, immediately rechristened 'Dai Bananas' in Wales. As the All Blacks arrived, politicians and local authorities were debating the designation of a national capital – the choice of Cardiff in 1955 was to coincide, wholly uncoincidentally in West Walian eyes, with the first year when there were no home internationals at Swansea.

Cultural identity was, as ever, highly contested. Though not the power it had been, organised religion retained considerable influence – the dry 'Welsh Sunday' was not to be challenged until 1961, while in 1950 Swansea had voted by only a small majority (Cardiff's result was more clearcut) to open its cinemas on Sunday. Among the diaspora, the Welsh Presbyterian congregation in Walthamstow, East London, announced plans to build a new chapel, since their current building could only seat 80 of their 120 members.

The 700,000 Welsh speakers found by the 1951 census were less than 30 per cent of the population. Goronwy Rees expressed concern at this continuing decline as he celebrated his appointment as principal of

University College, Aberystwyth, with a broadside at modern Welsh culture as 'a strange form of ancestor worship' characterised by 'rigid and unchanging habits of thought and belief'. It had been a bad year for poets – Idris Davies, author of *Gwalia Deserta*, died in April, followed in October by Dylan Thomas, his alcohol-hastened demise announced on the day that Llanelli's police opposed extended opening hours for the All Blacks match. A month earlier, Llanelli had lost its own great creative artist, the 1920s centre Albert Jenkins, who would have known how to use those extra two hours.

Wales's chosen 15 was, partly because of the opportunities offered by the annual Five Nations Championship, much more experienced than New Zealand's. Five had more caps than Skinner's thirteen. They had won all four matches in 1950 and 1952, although much more was made of the Triple Crowns these incorporated – the first since 1911 – than the Grand Slams, a concept yet to be recognised with the French, readmitted in 1947, still regarded as a marginal element. Wales had, though, fallen short against the 1951 Springboks, losing a match which surviving players remain convinced they should have won.

There were unprecedented crowds for most spectator sport. Cliff Morgan recalls: 'This wasn't because it was better than now, but because there was less to do. People did not have cars, computers or televisions. The best way to follow sport was to go and see it. If someone like [footballer] Stanley Matthews came to play in Cardiff, we'd queue to see him.' Welsh soccer was prosperous, with Cardiff City in the First Division – their record 57,800 crowd dates from April 1953 – and Swansea Town generating unparalleled talent, including the Allchurch and Charles brothers.

Cardiff, whose six-man contingent in the Wales team that played New Zealand was typical of the era, were not, in spite of beating the All Blacks, having a great season by their standards – they had lost to Swansea, Llanelli, Northampton and Combined Services. Yet 42,000 had attended the 15–6 victory over historic adversary Newport in early October. Welsh teams were, a survey of English clubs would show in the late 1950s, the outstanding attraction in the British game.

Of those originally selected, six – five Cardiffians plus Ken Jones of Newport – played for East Wales clubs. All six were backs, forming the entire three-quarter and half-back lines. All five from West Wales –

three from Neath, two from Swansea – were forwards. Llanelli were for once unrepresented, although full-back Gerwyn Williams had played for them.

Five of the Welsh XV were playing, and four more had played, in England. (One, a student, was playing both for his college and for Cardiff.) This is not invariably a source of strength in Welsh rugby – the choice of 16 English-based players out of 30 for the 1934 final trial had been evidence of the damage done by the inter-war diaspora. Strong external influences, like that of the English-born Nicholls, Winfield and Harding among the victors of 1905 or London Welsh's contribution in the 1970s, have often, though, been associated with prosperity.

Players tended to be the sons of, rather than workers in, coal and steel. Only one, with happy conformity to stereotype completing a front row alongside two employees of the Steel Company of Wales, had worked as a miner before joining the diaspora that has made the Rhondda one of Europe's great areas of depopulation. This team was typified not by pitmen, but by men who had grown up in the coalfields and later escaped via higher education and a job in teaching. Geoffrey Nicholson and John Morgan reported that Swansea frequently fielded nine students. Each September saw a specially chartered train leave Swansea High Street station for Birmingham, taking a considerable proportion of that city's teachers back to work from West Wales homes. Nine of the Wales team, including five backs and the whole back row, had been to college or university, way above the national average. War and the subsequent introduction of National Service meant almost all had served, or would do, in the armed forces.

While Wales was broadening its pursuit of talent – the Welsh Youth Rugby Union was founded in 1949 for youngsters who did not stay on into school sixth forms – six of the team against New Zealand had been educated in the private sector. Though in many ways 'a people's game', Welsh rugby has traditionally had middle- or upper-middle-class leadership and four of the public-school sextet would dominate the Wales captaincy for a decade.

Wales's captain was one of the four, the centre Bleddyn Williams. If Bob Stuart was a surprise choice, the only unexpected element in the 30-year old Williams' captaincy was it was so long coming. He had led Wales in the non-cap game against the Kiwis and was appointed captain again in 1950, only to be ruled out by one of the injuries that disrupted the middle of his career. An all-but automatic choice when fit, he played only once in the two Grand Slam seasons and not at all at Twickenham after 1948. Not until the start of the 1953 international season did he succeed John Gwilliam, and then only following an injury to Rees Stephens. New Zealand was his 20th cap, but injuries had cost him another 10.

He was the central figure in Cardiff's hugely successful and attractive postwar teams, scorer of a club record 185 tries and creator of many more. Built with, in the words of Gareth Williams: 'a torso like a tree-trunk and the muscular thighs of a Renaissance sculpture', he also had an intuitive rugby brain which made him equally effective in defence and was gifted with a natural rippling sidestep discovered while imitating one of his heroes as a child.

Those talents had taken him – one of eight sons of a coal-trimmer in Cardiff docks, all of whom played for the club – on a scholarship to Wilfred Wooller's old school, Rydal, as a 14 year old. He remembers: 'It was the finest thing that ever happened to me. I'd never been away in my life except for holidays in West Wales. I was homesick for the first couple of terms, but then I got into the first XV at the age of 14, which gave me a status that helped a lot.'

But for the war, he believes he might have played for Wales at 19 or 20. John Gwilliam, an almost exact contemporary, agrees: 'I've never seen anything like Bleddyn at 18 or 19. Later he had more experience, but not quite the zip he had then. He'd got it all – speed off the mark and perfect passing, kicking and sidestepping. He was quite alarming, really.'

Instead, he played social rugby in Arizona while training as an air force pilot: 'It was the first time I'd played under lights. All the pitches had lights, because it was too hot to play in the daytime.' He doubts he would have been commissioned without the public-school background, but this did not spare him a distinctly dangerous end to his war service: 'They were short of glider pilots after Arnhem and asked for volunteers. I didn't volunteer, but was told I was volunteering for it, and went through the Rhine operations.'

Discharged as a flight lieutenant in 1946 he would have liked to have gone to university but felt he owed it to his wife and young child to earn a living after more than four years away. In 1953, he was director of a coach company. Ostensibly an establishment figure, he was actually impatient of much conventional wisdom. While committed to amateurism, he was never anti-rugby league after encountering league players during the war: 'People like Gus Risman, W.T.H. Davies and Trevor Foster were great players and I learnt a lot from playing with them. They threw the ball about, because their game had rules that encouraged them to do so.' He had been a horrified spectator of the extraordinary incident in 1949 when a Wales teammate George Parsons was ejected from the train travelling to France when it was alleged he had committed the heinous crime of talking to a rugby league scout. He had also returned from the 1950 Lions tour of New Zealand convinced of the value of coaching: 'I came back and preached the gospel about coaching and how it should be started in Wales, but it fell on deaf ears for many years.'

Remembered by Cardiff and Wales colleague Gwyn Rowlands as 'a stabiliser', a figure of immense reassurance in a lightning-quick three-quarter line, Williams himself remembers his captaincy as a matter of 'going out, assessing the opposition and playing it by ear'. In this, he may under-estimate himself. At the very least the ear in question had perfect pitch. His centre-three-quarter partner against New Zealand, Gareth Griffiths, remembers him as an instinctive teacher: 'He talked to you as you went along through the game.'

This Wales team may in some ways have been counter-stereotypical, but it did live up to the national reputation for having a scarcity of names – in this period Trinity College, Carmarthen, was so overburdened with Davieses that one student had to be known as Hywel Lewis Walter Davies, there being two other Hywel Lewis Davieses in a roll of little more than 100. Wales wanted only an Evans (one would be forthcoming two matches later) for a complete set of the commonest Welsh surnames. Thus the full-back, wearing number 1, was another Williams – Gerwyn of London Welsh. He was 29, a miner's son who taught maths and physical education at Harrow Grammar School in Outer London. This Welsh archetype however concealed a complex progression.

He remembers: 'My father was a miner from Glyncorrwg who did not want his sons to follow him down the pit, so he moved to Port

Talbot in the late 1920s. He had played for Glyncorrwg, and encouraged me to play, but my mother hated all sports. He went down the pit at 14 and died at 55 of pneumoconiosis – we tried to get compensation but couldn't prove it had come from mining, which was the sort of thing that happened in the bad old days. But we were all very grateful he took us away from all that.'

He played rugby, at outside-half, and cricket for Wales schools at 14: 'Then when I was 16 both my parents died within three months of each other and I lost interest in sport of any kind. I was also diagnosed with "a tired heart". I had "presystolic beats", which means that it seems to miss a beat.' Having previously hoped to become a teacher, he left school: 'I had to go out and earn some money. One of my best friends at school was Richard Burton, then still called Richard Jenkins, a good rugby player and already a fine actor. He was terrific when we did Shaw's *Applecart*, although my mother thought I was much better than he was!'

Williams went into the steelworks as a clerk, while Jenkins worked in the Co-op: 'He used to give me clothing coupons during the war.' The war, and service in the navy, put rugby and teaching ambitions back on track: 'I was posted to a minesweeper in Scotland, but that was overruled by another order sending me to Portsmouth to do a course as a PE instructor. There I met Stan Bowes, the Cardiff prop and a real character, who made me play rugby whether I wanted to or not.'

Talent and enthusiasm rekindled, he played full-back for the navy and in 1947 fulfilled his ambition to go to Loughborough College, in his view the finest sports academy in Europe, on an ex-serviceman's grant which did not, however, cover the vacations: 'I had to labour on a building site to keep my family – we had two sons by then.'

He joined London Welsh: 'I used to travel down on Friday night, play Saturday and go back Sunday' and also played for English Universities when they beat Welsh Universities at the Arms Park, moving into contention for a Wales place, but never wholly convinced he would get it: 'You always felt at a disadvantage being outside Wales, as selectors were not likely to come and see you.' He played several trials, was reserve to Cardiff's Frank Trott for the whole 1949 season and felt his chance would come when Trott then retired: 'But they called up Lewis Jones. He was an immensely talented player but had never been a full-back in his life.'

The call finally came at the end of the 1950 season: 'I heard on the radio that I had been picked for the Triple Crown match against Ireland in Belfast. The one recollection I have is of afterwards when we were all in the changing-room, delighted to have won our first Triple Crown since 1911, and a BBC representative came in and asked if anyone could speak to the Welsh-language service – and nobody could. My parents spoke to me in Welsh, but I used to reply in English. I'd studied it at school and could read it, but couldn't speak a word.'

The slightly-built, redhaired Williams is recalled by Gwyn Rowlands as 'an immaculate, elegant footballer, never with any great sense of urgency as he always seemed to be in the right place – a complete contrast with John Llewellyn of Cardiff who never looked secure, but was also as safe as houses'. Williams remembers: 'Your role was completely defensive. The skills required of you were catching, kicking to touch and a skill which has now completely disappeared and used to frighten me – falling on the ball in the face of a dribbling rush by forwards. The only way to stop this was to fall on the ball correctly, with your back to the opposition so that if you were kicked it was in the back rather than the stomach.'

He was a thoughtful, analytical player who rejects suggestions that he had innate positional sense: 'Nobody has that. My play was improved by the fact that I had played at outside-half as a schoolboy. The outside-half is the catalyst for everything his team does in attack. If as a full-back you know what an outside-half has in his mind and what he is likely to do, you can move into the right position for the move you expect.'

After 1950, he had held his place for the next two seasons, winning a second Triple Crown and Grand Slam in 1952. He was equally proud of being, as a member of the London Counties team, the only Welshman to beat the 1951 Springboks.

Regular selection also introduced him to the legendary tight-fistedness of the Welsh Rugby Union: 'We were allowed nothing more than a third-class rail ticket. I was travelling down to Wales to play against England and I met the England team and Bill Ramsay, the Rugby Football Union treasurer whom I knew well from Middlesex and London. He invited me to come and sit with them and when the ticket collector came along he paid the difference, so I ended up travelling at

the expense of the English union – and we won the match!' He recalls
the case of a reserve scrum-half from West Wales as the epitome of
WRU attitudes: 'He asked for a hotel room on the Saturday night as he
wouldn't be able to get home after the dinner. Eric Evans, the secretary,
said that in that case he should miss the dinner. They were pretty mean
considering the capacity crowds they were getting.'

Williams played his entire big-match career in boots borrowed from
a Loughborough colleague: 'They were made by a company called Laws
of Wimbledon. On a schoolteacher's salary, I couldn't afford a pair of
my own.' His slight build ruled out goal-kicking, a job generally done
by the full-back at this time.

He spent two seasons with Llanelli while teaching in Aberystwyth,
but was confirmed in his 'out of sight, out of mind' theories when
dropped for Terry Davies as soon as he returned to London in 1953.
His recall against New Zealand was for his 12th cap, a tidy international
career by 1950s standards but merely a start compared to Ken Jones,
32, a fellow Loughborough alumnus playing on the right wing and
wearing 2.

Jones, the Newport fixture in otherwise Cardiff-dominated back
divisions – 'We always thought of Ken as one of us, however much Stan
Bowes used to joke about "those black and amber bastards,"' recalls
Gareth Griffiths – had 30 caps and was closing in on Dickie Owen's all-
time Wales record of 35. A sprinter who reached the semi-finals of the
100 yards at the 1948 Olympics and won a medal in the relay, Jones
'with his jet-black hair, his head slightly forward from his angular, bony
frame and his stamina and streamlined grace of movement . . . in flight
resembled nothing as much as a jaguar', according to Dai Smith and
Gareth Williams.

There was much more to him than pure pace. Scott, who 'had seen
too much of track runners who could not adjust themselves to jersey,
stockings and sprigged boots', found him 'the complete wing-three-
quarter' while Bleddyn Williams remembers him as 'a good footballer
with real tactical sense and an excellent defender – very little got past
him'. Jarden admired his 'ability to vary his running; with astute change
of pace and direction he would keep his opponents completely in the
dark' and reckoned him his most testing adversary, while for Cliff
Morgan he was 'with Gerald Davies, our best three-quarter of the last

50 years'. A teacher at Newport Boys High School, he had scored 15 tries for Wales, including 3 in the triumphant 1952 season, and 16 in as many matches for the 1950 Lions in New Zealand, including the long-range Fourth Test epic so vividly recalled by McLean.

The centre alongside him, Gareth Griffiths, wearing 3, was possibly even quicker. At least he had been while at school, breaking the Welsh Schools 100-yards record set by his Cardiff teammate Dr Jack Matthews, who was wont to tell him: 'But you had spikes, Gareth, I only had daps.' His normal position was right-wing, but that was nailed down for a decade by Ken Jones, while Gwyn Rowlands' form and goal-kicking won him the left. Griffiths was comfortable at centre and as scorer of three tries in the last two matches of 1953, his debut season, had to play.

Still only 22, he exemplified an extraordinary range of Welsh formative forces – the coalfields, the Welsh language, nonconformist religion, grammar schools, the forces and teaching. His was a deeply religious upbringing at Penygraig in the Rhondda Valley: 'Chapel dominated my own home and my grandparents. My grandmother ran the Zoar Chapel at Cwm Clydach, although as a woman she couldn't be a deacon. The visiting preacher, often a professor of religion, would stay with her and the parlour, one of only two downstairs rooms, was only ever used for him to have his lunch, then tea before the evening service. My father, influenced by my mother, became a deacon at Nazareth, the Calvinist chapel in Williamstown. We used to go to chapel three times on Sunday, quite often on a Monday and Thursday as well, all in Welsh.'

They were not, though, anti-sport. His father, who played tennis and cricket, was prepared to put studs into his best shoes when he went to Rhondda Grammar School in 1943: 'I didn't have football boots and you couldn't get them at the time.'

In spite of his athletic talents, he preferred rugby: 'I preferred being in a team game, and rugby can be quite easy if you are fast.'

At school, he learnt rugby from the Welsh master: 'It was normal for the Welsh or Welsh History master, rather than the PE master, to teach rugby,' using simple, effective methods: 'He put 20 to 30 of you on a field. As a 12 year old you had to watch and understudy the 15 year old in your position. I learnt from Hilary Howells, the headmaster's son.'

Sheer speed, he believes, earned him a schools cap at 14 and at every level afterwards: 'I was still a runner who was learning to be a rugby player when I got into the Wales team' – a progression he attributes as much as anything to luck. 'I never set myself targets, or thought that I would play for Wales.' Part of that luck may have been, in a echo of Tiny White, his physical surroundings: 'Rhondda mountainsides were pretty good places to train and the air was fresh even though the mines were still there.'

He believes his rugby benefited from his time in the air force: 'I was at RAF Upwood in East Anglia. Every Wednesday we had to test out a Lincoln bomber, the successor to the Lancaster. About 25 of us would fly over to RAF Marham, play rugby and come back. It was a lot cheaper and quicker than going by car. I played for the RAF against the army and navy – since I also ran for the RAF I had what was rather pompously called 'a double blue'. We also went to France to play provincial sides and to Germany where we lost to the British Army of the Rhine. They had the current England half-backs, but my grandmother knew why we'd really lost. She told me, "If you hadn't been playing on a Sunday, you wouldn't have lost!"'

A Cardiff debutant at 18, he was by 1953 training as a teacher at St Luke's College, Exeter, part of an immensely gifted team that would that year become the first British club to score 1000 points in a season. Hopes of playing four times against the All Blacks – Cardiff, Wales, Barbarians and South-Western Counties – were dashed when the Counties, 'as I can see at this distance was absolutely right' chose to exclude glamorous student transients in favour of county stalwarts, but he had played for Cardiff: 'Bleddyn asked me to come up for the four or five weekends before. It was a long way, and I had to get special permission from the principal to be away, but it was worth all the effort.'

Bleddyn Williams wore 4 while number 5, the Cardiff left-wing Gwyn Rowlands, might have found 19 December 1953 memorable – it was his 25th birthday – even if he had not been making his international debut. His selection concluded a progression more extraordinary even than Gerwyn Williams's. Rowlands was not merely eligible for England – a son of the diaspora born in Berkhamsted to Welsh-speaking parents who had left Penrhyncoch in the mid-1920s – but had very nearly played for them in 1949.

He remembers: 'We went on holiday to Wales, but it and rugby seemed a long way off. I played football until I was 13 or 14, and although I played and got into the first 15 as a day boy at Berkhamsted, we weren't very good – not for instance like Merchant Taylors, who beat us regularly.'

Between school and following his father's footsteps to London Hospital, he played a few games for a Harlequins midweek team, but it was medical school that would see his real breakthrough: 'The hospitals were very strong in those days, with the top four or five counting as first class. I started in the fourth 15 and worked my way up, but my big break was when Bill Chew, the first-team full-back who played for Eastern Counties, said he had been picked to play for them against Middlesex at Woodford, but he couldn't go and could I?'

He went up to Woodford, only a couple of miles from the hospital's ground at Walthamstow: 'It is a lovely ground, I played full-back, we beat Middlesex and I stayed in the team as a wing.' The story does not have a totally happy ending: 'We got to the County Championship final, but I couldn't kick a thing – nor could the other kicker, mind, and we lost 5–0', but the breakthrough into top-flight rugby had been made.

The Welsh knew of his eligibility – he was asked to play in a charity match for Welsh Academicals at Pontypridd: 'My centre was a Cambridge blue called Ken Spray who had a great day, so I was given every opportunity and ran in a few tries, all thanks to him. A Welsh selector named Enoch Rees was there. He spoke to me afterwards and said, "We'll earmark you for next year." I was young and rather innocent and this seemed very exciting.'

Came the following year's early Welsh trials, and nothing happened: 'Then I was called up for the England trials at Northampton and Cambridge. I didn't make the final trial because I spent both games like a spare part out on the wing, never getting a pass, and they brought the Oxford and Cambridge people in after the Varsity match. Then they published the teams for the final Welsh trial and I was playing for the Probables.'

The implications went beyond rugby politics. His mother, who had taken little interest in his rugby up to now, had sent him a telegram reading '*Cymru am Byth*' (Wales for ever) before his first English trial.

1905: BIRTH OF A SPECIAL RELATIONSHIP

The Originals: the All Black touring squad of 1905. (© Empics)

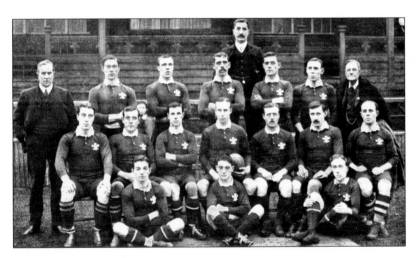

The Victors: the Wales team that beat New Zealand 3–0
on 16 December 1905. (© Empics)

THE VISITORS

'He personally revived great captaincy.' All Black captain Bob Stuart (left) confers with manager Norman Millard. (© Empics)

'Several principles in himself.' The incomparable Bob Scott practises kicking barefoot. (© Empics)

THE CONTEXT

How it was: Cardiff Arms Park in the early 1950s. (© Empics)

Always one step ahead: as the Combined Services scrum-half
passes, All Black back rower Bill Clark (21) is already on
his way to pressurise their midfield backs. (© Empics)

DRAMATIS PERSONAE, 19 DECEMBER 1953

Wales. *Standing (left to right)*: Dr Peter Cooper (referee), Clem Thomas, Sid Judd, Rees Stephens, Roy John, John Gwilliam, Courtenay Meredith. *Seated*: Stoker Williams, Gareth Griffiths, Bleddyn Williams (captain), Ken Jones, Dai Davies. *Front*: Gwyn Rowlands, Rex Willis, Cliff Morgan, Gerwyn Williams. (© *Western Mail*)

The All Blacks. *Standing (left to right)*: Dr Peter Cooper (referee), Brian Fitzpatrick, Allan Elsom, Bill Clark, Tiny White, Nelson Dalzell, Ron Hemi, James Fitzgerald (touch judge). *Seated*: Keith Davis, John Tanner, Bob Stuart (captain), Laurie Haig, Bob Scott. *Front*: Bill McCaw, Kevin Skinner, Ian Clarke, Ron Jarden (© *Western Mail*)

MATCH ACTION, 19 DECEMBER 1953

A giant called Tiny: All Black lock Tiny White passes to Bill McCaw (right) as Clem Thomas (15) tackles. Cliff Morgan (6) contemplates an interception, but Keith Davis (on ground) can only watch. (© Empics)

Long arm of the law: PC Dai Davies (middle) arrests the progress of Keith Davis (right) as Ron Jarden (left) intercedes. (© Empics)

THE NAVY'S HERE! STOKER WILLIAMS GETS TO GRIP WITH THE ALL BLACKS

On the charge: Stoker (with ball) faces the challenge of
Ron Hemi (right) as Courtenay Meredith (centre) looks on.
(© *Western Mail*)

At close quarters: Stoker (right) tangles for the ball with Allan Elsom.
(© Empics)

TRIES

Cardiff 1953: Ken Jones touches down for Wales's winning try. Stoker
Williams starts to exult while Ron Jarden (on ground)
and Brian Fitzpatrick are powerless to resist.
(Courtesy of the New Zealand Rugby Museum)

Wembley 1997, but a common image from all games since 1980.
Wales players gather under the posts to await the conversion attempt
following yet another All Black try. (© Empics)

FIFTY YEARS ON

The 1953 All Blacks at their 50th anniversary reunion. *Back row*: Colin Loader, Arthur Woods, Morrie Dixon, Doug Wilson, Stu Freebairn. *Middle*: Bob Scott, Bill McCaw, Brian Fitzpatrick, Kevin Skinner, Keith Davis. *Front*: Tiny White, Peter Eastgate, Snow White, Bob Stuart. (*Absent*: Allan Elsom, John Tanner, Bill Clark) (© Coxie/*Sunday News*)

History men: Kevin Skinner (left) and Bob Stuart reminisce at the All Black Centenary Dinner in 2003. (Marc Weakley)

'When I was chosen for the Welsh trial, she got very excited and insisted that I must play for Wales. I said, "I can't. I've just played two England trials and I can't just walk out. It would look as though I was grabbing for a cap." So I didn't play. My mother was very upset and took it very hard. My father had taken a rather more practical view, supporting what I did. She cast him out of the bedroom and never took him back. Her behaviour for ever thereafter became volatile and unpredictable. My father said to me later, "If you are ever offered a game again, for Christ's sake take it."'

He recalls: 'It was all very nasty, and not just in family terms. I learnt about the way the press would make things up or misquote you if they thought it would sell papers. I learnt a great deal and matured very quickly.' He ended the matter by writing to the Rugby Football Union explaining that, for personal reasons, he did not wish to be considered for England.

After qualifying, he was appointed to a job in Newport, and joined Cardiff: 'I started in the Rags [second team] and thoroughly enjoyed it' and when he joined the RAF received a helpful posting to St Athan near Bridgend. He played in all three Welsh trials in 1952–53 without winning a cap and both, either side of scoring one try and making the other in Cardiff's victory over the All Blacks, in 1953–54 as well as having a highly successful day with the boot when the selectors watched Cardiff play Gloucester. He remembers: 'There's no doubt that I peaked at the right time. Even so, I don't think they ever forgave me for what had happened in 1949 and I don't think they'd have picked me if they hadn't had to.' There were also suggestions that he was not quick enough: 'I think that was a little unkind. I wouldn't claim to have been the quickest – I was on the heavy side and didn't have blinding pace off the mark – and it didn't help playing alongside a sprinter like Gareth Griffiths. But I'd run in the hospitals sports against people like Arthur Wint.' He had, after all, been quick enough to hold off Jarden in the Cardiff match.

If Rowlands might have played for another country, it is impossible to conceive of his Cardiff colleague Cliff Morgan, outside-half and number 6, as anything other than Welsh. He was in Dai Smith and Gareth Williams's words: 'The identikit Welsh outside-half', inspirer among other things of the most vivid single passage in *Fields of Praise*, their remarkable centenary history of the Welsh Rugby Union, wherein he is described 'with the ball held at arm's length before him, his tongue out almost as far, his bow legs pumping like pistons, eyes rolling, nostrils flaring and a range of facial expressions seldom seen north of Milan' and as the epitome of 'the Welshness of a non-conformist home where Mam ruled and Sunday was for chapel'.

The son of a Rhondda miner – he claims not to have known a Conservative until he was 26, an age he would not reach until 1956 – he was the protégé of one of those remarkable teacher–mentors who proliferate in Welsh rugby history. Ned Gribble of Tonyrefail Grammar School was to him what T.P. Williams had been to Cliff Jones, that Bill Samuel would be to Gareth Edwards, and Geoff Davies to Robert Jones.

Like his All Black marker Bill Clark, he had seen academic studies (at Cardiff University) derailed by rugby commitments and was working for the Wire Rope Company in Cardiff, learning the business and travelling down every day by bus from Trebanog. 'Two shillings return,' remembers Griffiths, who came from slightly further up the valley and paid an extra fourpence. Celebrity, rapidly acquired following his first cap in 1951, had brought Morgan some small privileges: 'My house was about 30 yards from the bus-stop. If I was still having my cup of tea indoors, the driver would toot his horn and stop outside my house, and I'd run out and jump on.'

He was an exemplar of the intuitively inventive individualist school of Welsh back play: 'I played to show off really', a runner rather than a kicker and a challenge to the alertness of teammates as well as opponents. 'Cliff would always look to see if there was anything he could do. If there was, you knew he'd have a go – and he'd go like bloody lightning,' recalls Griffiths, who had known him since the early 1940s. He found more than just self-expression in the game: 'I learnt discipline, which is a delicate balance between freedom and accountability; I learnt to love the game and its nuances, to understand and discuss them; and a deep love of Welshness, which is like a beautiful wine you can never chill.'

Beautiful wine was not, however, on the menu in the evenings he most cherished after practice with Cardiff: 'You knew there would be a free pint of beer and a kipper, which you cooked in front of the electric fire in the dressing-room. You'd talk and there was a togetherness about it all. It was a club that had personality. You had Bleddyn, with his command of every situation; the youthful exuberance of Gareth and Gwyn; Sid Judd, who was a wild, extravagant, terrific forward; and the most remarkable chap of all, Stan Bowes, a gale of humanity whose great phrase was "we have wooden ships, steel ships and hardships" and who kept us all together until he died.'

Contact with opponents was just as important: 'You'd knock lumps out of each other, but afterwards you'd share ideas and ideals and there was a closeness, a respect for somebody else. To play rugby properly you've got to respect your opponents and each other.' He had grown up on the shared legends of Wales and New Zealand, and invited his opposite number Laurie Haig to lunch: 'He came to the Wire Rope Company. He was a hell of a nice fellow and I remember giving him a miner's lamp because he was a miner.' In the circumstances it was perhaps slightly ungrateful of Haig, running the line in the Barbarians v. All Blacks match at the end of the tour, to flag Morgan for a foot in touch, ruling out a spectacular try. Morgan knew he'd not been in touch, and recalls in his memoirs meeting Haig years after in Dunedin: 'I told him so. "Ah," he said, "but I had the flag." We left it at that.'

Typically, Morgan has provided the definitive picture of his scrum-half (Morgan called him his 'better half' for his unselfish play), Rex Willis, yet another Rhondda-born Cardiff man, wearing 7 and playing his 12th international: 'He was posh, drove fast cars, had long hair and looked an unlikely scrum-half. But he also had big shoulders, a strong frame and was prepared to defend you against all opposition. I never recall him giving me the ball when it wasn't a good ball for the outside-half to receive. He never passed it on just to get out of trouble himself.'

Willis was 29 and a company director, scion of a family who owned cinemas in Cardiff and the valleys, and named the Rex cinema in Aberdare after him. He needed the half ton of coal Winston McCarthy bestowed on him after winning the Porthcawl Rugby Club Christmas raffle less than anyone in British rugby – although McCarthy could hardly have been expected to ship it home.

He had an early brush with sporting greatness as a 12-year-old Llandaff Cathedral School boy – presenting a silver salver paid for by his parents to Welsh boxer Tommy Farr after his victory over ex-World heavyweight champion Max Baer in 1937. He had commanded a landing craft in the invasion of Europe. His rugby, though, was confined to the 'Rags' until Haydn Tanner retired in 1949. His subsequent ascent was Hemi-like, taking him into the Wales team after only a few first-team games and the Lions tour of New Zealand at the end of his first season. He had been a regular ever since. He rarely made breaks (but suffered a nasty one, playing most of the 1952 victory over Scotland with a broken jaw) and was never to score in 21 games for Wales, but was noted for the length and accuracy of his dive-pass. Bleddyn Williams remembers: 'He was very strong, an additional forward, who could stand up to and tackle opposing forwards. He wasn't as quick as some scrum-halfs but a good passer. Terry Holmes is a fair comparison.'

The prop forward W.O. Williams, 24, number 8 and winning his 11th cap, had also served in the navy – hence his nick-name of 'Stoker' – but there the similarities to Willis stopped. A crewcut and the bus into Swansea from his lifelong home in Gowerton, source of New Zealand's twin nemeses in 1935, were more his style. A range of identities – he also went by 'Billy' and 'W.O.' – decorated a strong body and personality formed by elementary schooling: 'I never went to secondary school. I had all my schooling at Gowerton Primary, and left when I was 14' and a working life that began immediately afterwards with an apprenticeship as a boilermarker – his father's trade – in a dry dock in Swansea. When his father died, he inherited his job at RTB Gowerton, where he was working in 1953: 'I'd go in on Saturday morning if I wasn't playing for Wales, or for Swansea somewhere like Leicester or London, and was back in on the Sunday morning.'

Like the otherwise dissimilar Rowlands, he had come to rugby late: 'I played soccer until I was about 17 – none of my family played rugby. Then not long after the war, I'd been playing soccer on the common in Gowerton and was walking home and someone from the rugby club came to me and said they were looking for a big bloke to go in the second row. I gave it a try, had three seasons with Gowerton, who were a good club in the West Wales Rugby Union, and then in 1949, Swansea lost a bloke named Les Pearce to rugby league and they came for me.'

It was as a second row that he played for Swansea: 'They called it a gentlemen's club, but it was a great club. We were on tour in Cornwall when my father died and they did everything possible to look after me and get me back as quickly as possible. My father was my greatest fan. If you believed him, I was always outstanding!', but his elevation to the national side as a prop came as the Welsh selectors looked for power in preparation for the visit of the 1951 Springboks. The day of his selection was memorable even by the standards of such occasions: 'I was playing for Swansea against Harlequins at St Helen's. Glamorgan Cricket Club ran a tote and I won it, about £100 which was a lot of money then. After the game, I went back to the bus station and everyone was saying, "Congratulations, W.O." and I wondered how they knew about the tote. I got on the bus, went back to Gowerton and went into the café run by my father-in-law. Everyone was there – my mother and my brother included – and they said, "You've been picked for Wales in the front row." I said, "Now I know you're lying, I've never played there in my life. There must be a mistake." Somebody wrote to the *Evening Post* saying he couldn't see how they could pick me as there were better props in Wales, and I had to agree with him because I never had played there.'

Armed with a crash course in propping from the recently retired Cliff Davies – 'I learned all about "boring in" and "dropping" and how to get under an opponent's neck,' he has told David Parry-Jones – he played against France in Paris: 'John Robins was the other prop and I asked him, "What do I do?" He said, "I'm the tight-head", so I ended up at loose-head!' The novice survived to play against South Africa and stay a regular through two years in the navy, where becoming a stoker was the price of being posted to Devonport – whose rugby team was stronger and played regularly in Wales – rather than Portsmouth. His selection, he acknowledges, was a stroke of near-genius: 'I've criticised the Welsh Rugby Union more than anybody, but you have to say that was a wonderful decision. If they hadn't wanted a big front row, I don't think I'd have had a cap – there were a lot of good second rows in Wales. I'd played against Rees Stephens and Roy John and knew I had no chance against them.'

Stoker Williams certainly merited the description of 'a hard boy', the favoured term of approbation of the man packing alongside him, number 9 and hooker, David Davies, 28. Similarly rich in identities –

Dai or D.M. to fans, Dave to his wife and 'PC Davies' to his superiors in the Somerset Police – he was another Rhondda native, like Griffiths from Penygraig, and the team's ex-miner: 'I went straight down the pit from school. There was nothing else to do in the village. I was a face worker, a tough life. They'd put a youngster in with an older chap.'

It was to escape the pit that he followed his brother Rhys and numerous inter-war Welshmen before him, to the Somerset Police in 1948: 'It was a good life, much better than the pit, although it was still physical work, on the beat around Taunton, sorting the drunks out.' The police offered a good standard of rugby and support for those playing at representative level: 'You'd have no problem with your shifts and I was paid when I was away with the British Lions in 1950.'

He had made his debut, and played every game, in that Grand Slam year – and would do so again in 1952. His talents were greatly appreciated by Gwilliam, captain in those years: 'He was very athletic, with very square shoulders and a tapering build. He knew all about what went on in the centre of the scrum and appeared quite fearless.' The cunning inherent in hooking was apparent to Stoker Williams on his debut in 1951: 'He was tapping me on the shoulder and I wondered why, then I realised. When we were giving away penalties, he wanted it to look as though he was not to blame!'

Gwyn Rowlands remembers 'a great humourist whom I'd got to know in the trials. He'd slap you on the back and tell jokes.' He had been a popular and successful Lions tourist. Bob Scott remembered his 'lovely tenor voice' while Bleddyn Williams was to write: 'We always had to persuade Dai Davies to sing his solos, but he did like being persuaded!' and on the field he replaced Lions captain Karl Mullen in two of the four Tests.

The front row was completed by Courtenay Meredith of Neath, 27, wearing 10 and winning his second cap. He was a slightly unlikely figure in the richly demotic world of the front row, possessor of a cut-glass accent which belied a Pontypridd birthplace and a rugby upbringing in the fiercely competitive West Wales Rugby Union with the Neath Valley club Crynant, the local power of the time: 'Nobody knew where he had got it from,' confirms former Wales coach Ron Waldron, a Neath teammate.

A graduate of Cardiff University, he worked as a production engineer for the Steel Company of Wales at the Abbey Works. He applied that expertise in stress, pressures and breaking points to formidable effect on the rugby field. Stoker Williams remembers: 'They told me that Skinner was a man-eater – and he was pretty good. But he didn't give me as much trouble as Courtenay. Nobody did.' To his delight, Meredith was similarly complimentary about him in a rare interview a couple of years ago. Waldron says: 'He had it all, and he knew how to use it. He was a terrific scrummager and, in the phrase of the time, a vigorous forward. He trained very hard and was pretty mobile, as well as being useful in the lineout. I was glad he was on my side – he could be murder in training.'

Neath teammates remember him saying of opponents 'this chap has got to go'. Former England cricket captain Tony Lewis, full-back for Neath under Meredith's captaincy in 1958, has recalled the going of George Hastings, one of that notoriously delicate and retiring race, the Gloucester and England loose-head. Hastings changed sides in the scrum: 'He had had enough of Courtenay. Our leader moved across the front row to follow him, grabbed the shirt of John Dodd, our loose-head, and swung him across to the tight side before turning to Hastings and announcing in cut-glass English, "Oh no, George, you can't get away from me as easily as that." Wham! The scrum engaged and another Meredith victim buckled and groaned.'

Meredith was the first of a Neath trio at the core of the Welsh scrum. Both locks – Rees Stephens, 32, wearing 11 and winning his 19th cap and Roy John, 28, number 12 and winning his 18th – also played their club rugby at The Gnoll. This was yet another second-row partnership based around compatibility, complementariness, and a personal friendship that earned the duo the joking label 'Mr and Mrs Stephens' from 1950 Lions captain Karl Mullen. Bob Scott recalled them hiring a tandem for a companionable exploration of Nelson. Scott also noted a belief about Stephens 'so strong among Welshmen, that he was lacking fire and gave up the ghost too soon', yet Bleddyn Williams reckoned him at his best in a tight battle and that 'John lacked Stephens' virility and vigorous intensity of purpose'.

John, a surveyor, was the line-up jumper whom McLean reckoned could 'do the Indian rope trick without the benefit of a rope'. Cliff

Morgan remembered that he 'seemed to stay in mid-air'. He could match Tiny White – who reckoned him an exceptional opponent – in both lineout and leaping at a cross-bar. He lacked the New Zealander's power but was possibly even more mobile. 'He was very tall and stringy, but pushed his weight in the scrum and could handle and run like a three-quarter,' remembers Gwilliam. John Morgan and Geoffrey Nicholson noted his 'astonishingly prescient covering in defence'. Scott thought he was really a number 8 'who had drifted to lock because nobody had thought of playing him anywhere else'.

Stephens had played at number 8 – like many versatile players his international career suffered through doubts about his best position and, although a Wales player since the visit of the Kiwis, was an intermittent presence in the early 1950s. At the same time, he was regarded as a likely captain and had led the Probables in the last two final trials. He was, remembers Gerwyn Williams, 'an excellent blocker, not as mobile as Roy around the ground but an important scrummager. He was a bit of a strong lad afterwards and enjoyed himself in the evenings!' He came from a wealthy family, whose extensive business holdings had included coalmines, and had attended Llandovery. His father Glyn had led Wales against the New Zealand Army in 1919 and was currently Vice-President of the Welsh Rugby Union. He was, remembers Cliff Morgan: 'a great lovable man, but a hard devil, like his father'. The newcomer Gwyn Rowlands remembers him as one of the players who went out of his way to make him feel welcome and at home.

Neither used his given first name. John had been christened Ernest Raymond, while Stephens' given name was John. Three other members of Wales's originally chosen 15 also used their second names, compared to a single New Zealander, Dalzell. When one considers the results of Wales teams that included Erith Gwynne Nicholls, Daniel Clive Thomas Rowlands, Thomas Mervyn Davies or Thomas Gerald Reames Davies, this may be one of the unlikelier indicators of Welsh success.

Listed in the programme at number 13, a designation that would prove another victory for superstition, was another of the five, the uncapped N. Glyn Davies, 26, he of the voice memorably issuing threats from the depths of the ruck at Brighton. A basketball international, he was known as 'Shorty' on the same principle that made Richard White 'Tiny': 'a tall, lanky beanpole with red hair,' remembers Griffiths.

Davies came from the East Wales valleys – by way of variation the grandson rather than the son of a miner. Born at Cefn Forest near Blackwood, as a small boy he met the Prince of Wales on the famous tour of the valleys that led the (briefly) future Edward VIII to proclaim that 'something must be done'. He attended Lewis School, Pengam – later to incubate such diverse talents as John Dawes, Neil Kinnock and Professor Phil Williams.

He had grown up in a rugby- and New Zealand-conscious home: 'I'd known rugby from the time my brother and I would play around with a pair of rolled-up socks on the bed, and my father was very proud that we had cousins in Mount Maunganui. He taught us to love and hate the All Blacks – that they were great people, but dreadful people on the rugby field.'

His initial sporting success was, though, in basketball and boxing – he was Welsh Universities light-heavyweight champion while studying French at Cardiff University. There were hints of rugby talent: 'I played occasionally for Blackwood and scored two tries when we took Cardiff Athletic's ground record' but, he recalls: 'I used to play rugby for exercise and never made the university team.'

Nor was taking a job at Lewes in Sussex the obvious route to rugby preferment. He remembers: 'I was teaching French and PE, and had become very fit. I joined Lewes for exercise. The rugby was rather gentle compared to Wales and I scored a lot of tries as a "roamer" in the pack and got into the Sussex county team.' His habit of running through the streets of Bexhill at night also created a stir: 'The police pulled me in and told me they'd had complaints because I was frightening the old ladies – I think it was a bit of a joke as they had quite a few rugby players in the police.'

Even playing at this modest level, Davies had a sense of predestination: 'I always had the notion that I would one day run on the field in a Wales jersey. I was clear that this was going to happen.' His break came courtesy of Dai Gent, England's Welsh-born scrum-half of 1905, *Sunday Times* writer and intrepid enough when well into his 70s to be the only British print journalist to follow the 1950 Lions. He also took International XVs on tour to Cornwall. Davies remembers: 'This old man introduced himself and said he'd like to take me with his team to Cornwall. I said, "But I'm not an international." He said, "No, but I think you could be." I went to Cornwall and scored a couple of tries. On the way back, Vivian Jenkins, or maybe Arthur Rees, asked me, "Who are you playing against next week?" I said, "I think we're playing Eastbourne" to which they said, "Oh no, you're not." They contacted Blackheath and the following Saturday I was playing for them against Leicester.'

His season with Blackheath, 1952–53, was memorable for playing against Newport twice: 'Newport! I'd been a small boy looking through the railings at Rodney Parade. We had a special game for the 100th meeting between the two clubs – I had a good game and the crowd liked me, and then I was chosen to play for the Barbarians. They were special days for me.' Advised, in one of those messages via intermediaries with which rugby authorities were wont to communicate with players, to move to London Welsh, he duly did so for the following season: 'Brigadier Glyn Hughes, a great man who ran the Barbarians for years told me, "Go with our blessing."'

Then came Southern Counties v. All Blacks and two Welsh trials: 'I'd idolised the All Blacks, and people like Sid Judd and Clem Thomas, and suddenly I was playing against them and found I could cope.' In the midst of this inexorable progress came a jolt: 'I started getting trouble with my back. I went to the doctor. He told me that I had a degenerative disc and said, "No more rugby for you." I said, "Don't be daft" and explained that I was hoping to play for Wales. So the doctor said, "OK, carry on, but you'll think of me and what I told you in 30 years time." He was right as well.'

Among the memories of his selection, heard by phone at his digs in Lewes, was the pride and delight of his family and in particular his father – as undemonstrative as most Welshmen of his generation – hugging him and saying how proud he felt. Similar feelings were abroad in New Zealand: 'My cousins there were thoroughly assimilated and they told me later how proud and excited they had been "even if I was playing for the wrong bloody team".'

Number 14 would nowadays be the number 8, the man packing at the back of the scrum. But then John Gwilliam, 30, a schoolmaster winning his 22nd cap, always was a little different. He had been captain on 12 appearances, winning 9 of them. He is still the only Welsh captain to have won twice at Twickenham, led through two Grand Slam seasons and would, if he had been available, have captained the 1950 Lions.

There was a sense of detachment about Gwilliam. In part, this was mere geography, a life lived outside Wales since he had gone up to Cambridge – for a student career interrupted for five years while he curled and contorted his 6 ft 3 in. frame into a standard issue British Army tank – in 1941. From Cambridge he went to teach history at Glenalmond, joining Edinburgh Wanderers: 'The club rugby was of a decent standard, and the border teams were very good. Schools rugby was strong as well.' He grew accustomed to training by himself, and to endless odysseys to get to games in Cardiff: 'I'd leave on Thursday and get there on Friday afternoon.' On one occasion this meant explaining to the schools inspector studying his history lesson that he wouldn't be around to answer questions until the following Tuesday. There were, in an age of food rationing, other benefits as well: 'On one occasion we played in Dublin. I got the ferry to Belfast and the train down to join the team. There were no boats back to Scotland until the Monday, so when the rest of the team went off on Sunday they left me in the hotel eating a steak.'

He had moved to Bromsgrove, creating speculation that he might rejoin Newport: 'I thought about it. But it was a two-and-a-half-hour journey each way, against an hour and a quarter to Gloucester.' So Kingsholm, always appreciative of tough, resourceful forwards was his home ground in 1953.

It was also, though, a matter of upbringing and personality. He played his earliest rugby as a primary schoolboy in Pontypridd: 'We were taught by Ronnie Boon, the old international player, who wore plus fours.' At 11 his family moved to Monmouth, and he went to the town's public school: 'It was a complete change. Rugby in Pontypridd was about excitement and *hwyl.* They took it very seriously at Monmouth.' He retains vivid memories of battles against Llandovery, including Rees Stephens, and West Monmouthshire, whose star was Ken Jones. Then came Cambridge and war service, including officer training at Sandhurst, where Matt Busby, between his two careers as a Scottish international footballer and the architect of Manchester United, was one of his instructors.

He was physically imposing, quietly spoken, religious and austere – the phrase 'Cromwellian' tends to recur in descriptions. Cliff Morgan says: 'You always felt you should call John "sir".' Gerwyn Williams remembers: 'We always got on well. Both being schoolmasters and playing outside Wales gave us something in common. In a way we were both outsiders.'

Gwilliam himself recalls 'I had developed the habit of talking through games' – disconcerting teammates such as Wales prop John Robins, convinced by one loquacious display that Gwilliam had formed a violent dislike of him.

His style and outsider status meant he was never likely to become a popular hero in the way that Bleddyn Williams was. He was the sort of player wont to be described as 'The thinking man's . . .' A thinking man is what he was, a student of rugby and other history who had read Gallaher and Stead and appreciated its lessons sufficiently to introduce a seven-man pack and an extra back when it seemed the best use of his school's playing talent: 'It caused a terrible fuss. Not British, you know,' he says with the disarming chuckle that is at odds with that Cromwellian image. Glyn Davies recalls him as, 'a terrific analyst of the lineout'.

There were advantages to being an outsider. Ray Lewis, for years a key member of the Wales set-up as physio and masseur, once told him that it insulated him from Wales's endemic backbiting and in-fighting. Gwilliam agreed as captain he had been, he recalls, 'coach, captain and Father Christmas all rolled into one'. But never a selector: 'They never talked to me. If anybody chose the team it was J.B.G. Thomas of the *Western Mail.* They all read him and he had a great deal of influence. And of course Cardiff had a lot of very good players at the time.'

Public school and Cambridge were also the educational background of number 15, Clem Thomas of Swansea, winning his seventh cap: 'Clem had one of the most affected public school accents I've ever heard, but it became a part of him. He grew into the persona, but we did pull his leg about it,' remembers Gareth Griffiths. That privileged upbringing did not remove any edges: 'He was never too fussy where or when he hit you if you were playing for Cardiff against Swansea. The accent might have made him sound different, but he was the hardest man in the team' recalls Cliff Morgan. He was to inherit the family butcher's business and his Cambridge teammate Peter Robbins, a man of similarly rumbustious character, alleged that he was the only man allowed to practise his trade on a rugby pitch.

He had been capped at 20 – even before he won his Cambridge blue, postponed for a year when his captain took exception to a misdirected punch laying out one of his own forwards and told him, 'We'll have none of that Welsh thuggery here, Thomas.' Gwilliam remembers: 'He was too young and he wasn't really strong enough for international rugby.'

By his recall in 1952, he was, Gwilliam recalls, an entirely different proposition: 'He was very strong and fit and by 1952 he was really a very good player. He had a remarkable match against Ireland. Jack Kyle was a brilliant player, but Clem simply swept him away – something that very rarely happened to him.' He had given Laurie Haig a similarly miserable time for Swansea against the All Blacks a week earlier.

It was those destructive talents that earned him most comment in the week before the Wales v. New Zealand match, as the press analysed the likely course of events at a length unusual for 1953 (although it looks astonishingly restrained 50 years later). Most critics felt that Wales would win, because of the power and experience of its backs, the brilliance of its back division and the evident creative limitations of the New Zealanders.

Rather less was made of Clem Thomas's attacking talents. In particular, nobody appears to have remembered that in Wales's last match, against France in Paris, he had created a try for Gareth Griffiths. With a cross-kick.

CHAPTER 5

THE MATCH

'Wales was the match that mattered. Of course we wanted to win against England, and the other Test matches. But Wales was the one,' remembers Keith Davis. His teammate Bill Clark agrees: 'It was the Wales game that was talked about on the radio and in the newspapers. We were aware of the history, and Billy Wallace, who had played in 1905, was still very much around and willing to talk about what had happened, and what to expect.'

Leading up to the international on 19 December, New Zealand had the rare luxury of a week without a Wednesday match. McLean remembered their training sessions at Porthcawl as the hardest of the tour with the still convalescent Stuart 'driving himself and the team with the insistence of a regimental sergeant-major'. He described one session, which started with Stuart leading the backs, Haig the forwards: 'Both groups worked purposefully for half an hour. Following this the team did about 20 minutes combined running, and at the end there was about half an hour of simulated game. Both the ground and the ball were exceedingly slippy, but there was no rest and when the practice ended with a run of about 1,200 yards, everyone was quite satisfied that he had earned his keep for the day.'

New Zealand announced its selection on the Wednesday. A few days earlier Stuart had not expected to play, but now he was named as an either/or with Des Oliver, an Otago medical student who was monitoring teammates' weights as research for his thesis. Davis and Bevan were also either/or, while, according to David Owen and Wilfred Wooller: 'Welsh critics were delighted that Haig was once again at outside-half and that the midfield players were selected more for defensive qualities than attacking.'

There was a scare on the Friday. Elsom remembers: 'I dislocated my shoulder at training. Doug Wilson and I were working a move, he accidentally ankle-tapped me and I landed on the point of my shoulder. It was one of the most painful injuries I ever had,' he recalls – not a light statement from a man who broke his neck, ankle, kneecap, fingers and 'my nose about ten times' during his playing career. Looking back he says: 'I probably should not have played.'

It was particularly tense for the five new caps. Clark recalls: 'It was useful that you had people in the team who were older, wiser and had been around. Kevin Skinner in particular was that sort of guy.' If promises that 'Wales will beat you' and predictions of the same in the press were intended to intimidate, they did not work. Tiny White was quoted as saying that he had never been so determined in his life.

Wales, whose team had been announced on the Thursday before the Swansea match, assembled on the afternoon of Friday, 18 – the earliest International Board regulations would allow a home team to congregate. Rees Stephens was under no illusions, telling McLean: 'It will be harder than hard. That is unless your boys have changed a lot. They haven't, have they?' Gwyn Rowlands, possibly not helped by his medical knowledge, had been suffering 'chronic hypochondria from the moment I was chosen – every time I went to the lavatory I was convinced I had appendicitis. Every little twinge and tingle was an omen of impending doom.' Glyn Davies, by contrast was 'walking on air. There were dozens of letters and cables. Cliff was there in an old grey polo-neck, others in tracksuits.'

Rowlands remembers a gentle workout: 'We ran up and down and threw the ball around.' The forwards scrummaged. Davies recalls: 'I was feeling really good. Then Bleddyn said, "Scrum down again." We went down, and it happened. There was a crunch and I thought, "Oh my God." A couple of the other forwards said, "Set off, get off, go home." They were pleased for me that I had been selected and knew that if I only played for ten minutes I would get my cap. But I knew I couldn't do that. It had started to stiffen up and I had to withdraw. I remember Ivor Jones, who was the touch judge the following day, saying to me, "Glyn, we won't forget what you've done." I think he was implying that they would make sure I got a cap one day.' Implicit promise or not, Davies was 'absolutely devastated. I was in a complete daze. I remember my mother crying and my father being very upset.' This was not the only Welsh worry. Clem Thomas had been in a motor accident in which a woman cyclist from Worcester had been killed. It was reported overnight that Thomas was unhurt, but 'naturally very upset'. Wales might lose two-thirds of its chosen back row.

While the All Blacks rested at their hotel, Wales dispersed. Morgan and Griffiths took the bus up the Rhondda Valley, Stoker Williams and the Neath trio rode the train west and Gwyn Rowlands went back to RAF St Athan. This, it was reported, was not 'stringent economy on the part of the Welsh Rugby Union but a belief that players prepare themselves better for a big match if they stay in their homes until the last minute'. The players themselves were less convinced. They reassembled in the morning, a familiar routine to Stoker Williams: 'I'd go down to Swansea station to catch the 11.05, which would pick up Roy, Rees and Courtenay en route. We'd go to the Royal Hotel. They'd introduce us to each other again in case we'd forgotten from yesterday and we'd have lunch.'

Brian Sparks of Neath, of whom Morgan would write: 'I never had a really good club game against him' was there as the official back-row reserve and would presumably have replaced Davies. Except that when Clem Thomas was in doubt, Sid Judd, Cardiff's first try-scorer against the All Blacks, had been called up as further emergency cover. When Thomas declared himself fit, it was Sparks, not Judd, who was left out. By Saturday morning, Sparks knew that he would not be playing.

How this came about is a mystery. The selectors, both Bleddyn Williams and John Gwilliam make clear, were not in the habit of discussing decisions with their captains. They were, though, in the habit of baffling switches of direction. It was only 18 months since they had summoned Dr Jack Matthews at short notice from Cardiff to Twickenham as replacement for the injured Bleddyn Williams, only to tell him on arrival that they were going to play Alun Thomas. David

Parry-Jones records that Matthews 'was (and still is) livid about his treatment'.

If Bleddyn Williams had been consulted, Judd would have been chosen in the first place: 'I was disappointed none of the Cardiff pack had been picked after the way they had played against the All Blacks, and Sid should certainly have been in. He was a hugely intelligent back row forward who led by example.' The influential J.B.G. Thomas had written much the same.

Judd, who inherited the number 13 shirt, was 25, a teacher who had played all four Five Nations matches in 1953. He was also the one person in Wales who made Clem Thomas look shy and retiring. He had been something of a legend at Trinity College, Carmarthen. My father Stan Richards, a fellow-student, remembers Judd getting the entire student body in to see veteran heavyweight Tommy Farr fight at Carmarthen Town Hall in 1950: 'We were crowded outside the gates with Sid at the front, armed with a hacksaw blade, sawing away at the chain on the gates. When the boxers came out, there was a great roar, Sid shoved at the gates and we all ended up in the hall.' College lore credits him with cracking the wall in his room, beating it with his fists when trying to silence the early morning prayers of fanatically observant Welsh Bible College students.

Gwyn Rowlands remembers: 'Sid was a hero, a great character, a very good footballer and an extraordinary womaniser – there were times when he had to be hauled out of bed to play. He and Stan Bowes were the life and soul of Cardiff, always funny, forever having a go at each other.' Cliff Morgan recalls: 'There was a presence about him. He was big, and you knew he'd be there at the crucial moments. He was a good ball player and there was a sense of indestructibility about him.' Gwilliam says: 'He was coming to his peak, while some of us were a little past ours. We needed a bit of go in the pack.'

It was a long morning for the debutants. Rowlands, recipient of a pile of telegrams congratulating him both on his birthday and his selection, says: 'Lunch seemed to drag on for a long time. Then we walked to the ground through the streets, packed with people in red hats. That was more exciting.' This was part of the day the more experienced Stoker Williams always enjoyed: 'You'd walk through the crowd and you'd hear people saying, "Look, there's Roy John, there's Rees Stephens, there's

W.O. Williams." It made you feel six feet tall and they should do that with players nowadays.' McLean recorded that the 'streets outside Cardiff Arms Park were swarming with people for an hour or so before kick-off'. Not all were happy. The *Western Mail* recorded that touts, who had been getting double face value for 15/-stand tickets earlier in the week, were finding no takers as the fans who might previously have been their market opted instead to watch the game on television.

For New Zealand, Stuart had been passed fit on the Friday and Davis, reckoned a better bet than the more experienced Bevan in dry conditions, was the final choice at scrum-half. The All Blacks came by coach from Porthcawl. Elsom remembers: 'We could hear the singing from miles away. The atmosphere was fantastic, and I think it inspired us.' Stuart recalls 'packed streets and all the tension. You didn't have to say anything to convince our players that this was important.' Clark remembers 'prematch tension, which was somewhat extended by the bus trip from Porthcawl, was mainly centred around one's own desire not to let people down – the people in your own team and the people in New Zealand – relations, friends, even the selectors'.

Both changing-rooms were quiet. Clark recalls: 'The atmosphere in an All Black changing-room before a Test match was never anything but quiet. It was, and still is, a serious business playing rugby!' Davis says: 'We had a job to do. We didn't make a noise or smile, but were concentrated on the game.' In the Wales changing-room Gwyn Rowlands read the programme for information about his opposite number, Allan Elsom: 'It said he also played centre, so he was obviously a good footballer.' The sole Welsh debutant, he says: 'I was in with a team of old-stagers who'd seen it all before, so I doubt they had half the butterflies and tension I was feeling.' Neither captain was of the histrionic school. Rowlands says: 'There was nothing tactical in Bleddyn's talk, just a reminder that we had been chosen as the best 15 for our country and it was up to us to go out and show that we were.' Stuart says: 'There was no point in hectoring people like Kevin Skinner or Tiny White. They knew what was ahead, and what they had to do.'

Outside, it was noisy. Architecturally, the Arms Park was not that impressive – McLean's early impressions were that it was 'prosaic' and 'overpraised and deprived of true rugby atmosphere by the lighting stands for the greyhound racing track outside the rugby field proper'.

Bleddyn Williams also thought the lighting stands 'ridiculous'. The ground was in much the shape it would be, improvements on the south side for the Commonwealth Games in 1958 the only exception, until its transformation into the national stadium in the late 1960s and early 1970s. The pitch was enclosed by the oval of the greyhound track, flanked to the north by a double-decker stand – seats upstairs, terracing below – not long fully restored after being bombed in 1941, to the south by a single-decker and on all sides by standing areas – banks at both ends and enclosures down the side. Of the 57,000 crowd, nearly 50,000 were standing. At the city end loomed the redbrick Glamorgan County Club, an uncompromisingly functional electronic greyhound totaliser scoreboard and a white-painted wooden rugby scoreboard bearing the names of Wales and New Zealand – no '*Cymru*' or '*Seland Newydd*' in those days. The flags of the two countries fluttered at the river end, while the Arms Park cricket ground occupied the space behind the North Stand used nowadays by the Cardiff club ground.

It was, though, incontestably atmospheric. Gwyn Rowlands remembers: 'When the ground was full the atmosphere was over-powering – to play before a full house was an enduring experience.' The journalist John Morgan, a spectator that day, wrote: 'The crowd look, as an Englishman once told me, like a soccer crowd. Not here the tweedy, bescarved, sunburned hearties, the pretty, healthy girls – they are Stand-people, not Field-people. Here are the blue-suited or brown-suited men, off the peg, who know what it's all about, this game, and didn't learn it at a public school.' McLean found it initially subdued, but by the time the radio broadcast to New Zealand began at 2.15, 15 minutes before kick-off in order to allow the singing to be heard there, the crowd was in full voice with a series of hymns.

There was a substantial audience in the early hours 12,000 miles and 12 time zones away. Don Cameron, then a young journalist at the *New Zealand Herald*, was single and living with his parents in Aorangi Street, Parnell, still in 1953 a working-class suburb: 'I'd been out, had a fair amount of beer with the lads, came home, went to bed and set the alarm for 2.30. I'd struggle out of bed and go and listen to the old valve radio – the reception was pretty average – in our front room. We lived on the side of the hill and I remember looking up the valley and watching the lights come on in every fifth or sixth house.' David Scott, in 1953 a small child in Blenheim, but 50 years on a London-based accountant and former political activist, speaks for his age cohort of rugby-minded New Zealanders when he says: 'My first non-backyard memory of rugby is hearing the singing at Cardiff Arms on the radio.'

In South Africa, cricket fans watching North-East Transvaal playing New Zealand at Benoni were puzzled by the continual stream of players heading for the broadcasting box in the main stand: 'It took a little time to discover that the New Zealanders had their ears glued to the radio which was relaying the All Blacks match,' explained McLean's cricketing counterpart Dick Brittenden.

McCarthy, recalled by Cameron as, 'explosive, but not very analytical', was with Welsh co-commentator G.V. Wynne-Jones in the greyhound racing judges' box on top of the South Stand – an ad-hoc studio reached through a trap-door by a ladder which had to be pulled up 45 minutes before kick-off. They did little more initially than act as comperes, telling their audience the names of the hymns being sung. The unlucky Glyn Davies had taken his seat in the committee box: 'Everybody was very sympathetic, but I was still in a cold daze. I sat with Sir John Hunt, just back from Everest for goodness sake, and the New Zealand High Commissioner Sir Frederick Doidge, who was telling me: "You come to New Zealand, young man, that's the country for you."' Not long before radio transmission began, the crowd roared at the news that Judd was playing.

The teams ran out, side by side, as the crowd was bringing forth its rendition of '*Diadem*'. Clark remembers: 'We had heard so much about the singing that we were determined not to be scared by it.' During what seemed 'an interminable wait' he noted that 'while they had a conductor, each side of the ground was singing to its own time and one stand seemed to be about 30 seconds ahead of the other!'

McLean retained slightly more elevated memories of '*Hen Wlad Fy Nhadau*', recalling in 1969: 'It is 16 years ago and yet I see him now as plainly as if it were yesterday; tall, strong, with a green cloth cap on his head and a green woollen scarf tied as a kerchief around his neck. He is standing just in front of the old wood stand of Cardiff Arms Park and his head is tilted a little as he sings, in a rich bass, "Dear Land of My Fathers" . . . more than 50,000 spectators are giving themselves over to their anthem. Not all of them are dressed like my man, my miner down for the day from one of the valleys, and not all of them can sing as well as he. But each and every one of them is possessed by a fervour. None sings for the sake of singing. All sing for the sake of Wales.'

Skinner had been surprised by the singing of Welsh crowds: 'I was used to crowds cheering not singing. When we ran out for the Cardiff game, I was behind Peter Jones, who was playing in one of his first big games, and I was concerned that he might feel intimidated. He said to me, "Don't worry, Kevin, they can sing in Awanui as well!"' What he hadn't appreciated, he remembers, was 'how much the crowd and their singing could inspire players'.

Not only Welsh players. Jarden would write that: 'The effect of the Welsh singing was merely to incite us to greater determination.' Davis says: 'It was like going into a lion's den. Just the 15 of us, isolated against all of them. It built up anxiety but also made us feel that we had to win, to go out and do it for New Zealand. I had never heard anything like it, but it inspired us in the same way as the haka, making us want to get on with the game.'

Next came 'God Save The Queen', still New Zealand's national anthem, and finally the haka, led not by Davis, who recalls: 'I was always a bit shy about it' but by Jim Fitzgerald whose tour had gone somewhat awry. Vivian Jenkins had classed him with Scott and Jarden among the players likely to leave a lasting impression, but he was not to play any of the Tests. He instead had become the regular touch judge (teams still supplied their own) and haka leader. Theirs was not quite as intimidating a version as the 1924 Invincibles, who had added to the effect by starting on their knees and rising, nor were Wales asked, as London Counties had been, to kneel in order to give spectators a better view. Gerwyn Williams remembers, 'looking straight at all those bloody great thighs'. But just as the New Zealanders took strength from the singing, Williams, like many opposing players before and since, found the haka inspiring rather than intimidating.

A roar of appreciation from the crowd, there was a pause to allow the St Albans band to take its leave and Wales, winning the toss, chose to play towards the city end in the first half, giving New Zealand the kick-off. The referee, Peter Cooper, a white-clad 38-year-old doctor from London refereeing his fifth international – he had already refereed the All Blacks at Bristol, impressing them with his 'inclination to severe interpretation of the laws' and, as one of the Rugby Football Union's medical officers, had treated some of them in London – blew for the kick-off.

Scott lined the ball up, but another All Black ran across and kicked to the left. Exactly who it was is unclear. McCarthy, whose vanity about his ability to identify players occasioned McLean much not wholly innocent pleasure, reckoned it was Clarke. McLean reported that it was Fitzpatrick which, even allowing for Clarke's unusual footballing skills – he would end his career in big rugby a decade later with a drop-goal on this very ground – seems more logical. Gareth Griffiths caught the ball cleanly and kicked it into touch, which was where it was to be for most of the opening exchanges.

The commentators had reckoned the conditions perfect for good rugby. Rain had been forecast, in line with conditions for much of the previous week. Clark remembers that it was chilly, but McCarthy told his listeners that, 'the sun is shining beautifully and there's a bit of breeze, but nothing that will worry anybody'. Tension and wariness however outweighed all. Wynne-Jones said after nearly ten minutes: 'We've seen no great football yet, but what do you expect in a Test match of this importance?' What they had seen was 29 stoppages including 17 lineouts, with Jones and Jarden, from the south touchline, doing most of the throwing-in. Rowlands' first touch, after nearly six minutes, was to throw-in at a lineout.

Not everyone on the crowded terraces was enjoying a clear view. John Morgan wrote: 'Before the game began, the crowd swayed behind me and I fought against the swell. I missed the kick-off. My first clear and honest memory . . . is of a lineout in the shadow of a grandstand, the only shadow on the sunlit ground.'

Wales had the early territorial advantage, but the first real threat came from the All Blacks. Davis, after six minutes, broke clear in the middle of the field, but McLean wrote, 'Where he might have kicked over Gerwyn Williams's head and so started a headlong rush, he answered a call to his left.' Quick, accurate passing might still have put Jarden into a scoring position, but the movement petered out before reaching the wing.

The first score came after 15 minutes. New Zealand won a scrum midway between their own 25 and halfway, but Willis, a noted harasser of opposing scrum-halfs, collared Davis. Judd hacked towards the right-hand touchline, where the ever-alert Jones kept the ball in play, kicked on, went in hot pursuit deep into the New Zealand 25 and grasped Scott by the leg when he picked up. Scott, true to form, remembers what happened next: 'They said I dropped the ball, but I didn't. I had the ball and was caught, but was still free to pass it. Brian Fitzpatrick had come across to cover and either he overran, or I dwelt on it for slightly too long. I tried to get the ball to him, it went loose and there was a mêlée on the goal-line.'

Gwilliam and Judd were there first – McCarthy said 'there always is Judd there'. Fitzpatrick dived back desperately, but the Cardiff flanker, as he had done a month earlier, seized the ball and crossed ten yards to the right of the New Zealand posts. Rowlands, kneeling to place the ball upright then retreating six paces before striking with his toe-end, converted.

Wales 5, New Zealand 0.

Rowlands had a fresh opportunity within another couple of minutes as the All Blacks were caught offside. It was a long-shot in every sense – between the New Zealand ten-yard line and halfway, five yards in from the right-hand touchline. An initial roar from the crowd indicated that he had struck well and accurately, but the kick fell short and was caught beneath the posts by Scott.

The try fitted the emerging pattern: 'a grim struggle, mostly a forward one' in McCarthy's words. When in play, the ball was on the ground as much as in the hand, kicked, dribbled and fly-hacked more than it was passed. Midfield backs did much more tackling than running – radio summariser Wilfred Wooller was to note the excellence of Tanner and Fitzpatrick's defence – while wingers were employed almost exclusively to put-in at lineouts, which at least kept them busy since there were to be 75 in all. They were, though, intermittently conclusive, often leading on to a scrum after the ball failed to emerge from an ensuing ruck or, if it did, somebody knocked on.

Scrums were frequently not settled first time – of more than 50 in the match, a good 20 needed more than one put-in – and had a marked propensity to lead on to a kick or scramble for touch and another lineout. Modern ears listening to the match recording are struck by the bittiness of the play, with endless stoppages and little handling. When

Wales met New Zealand 50 years later in the 2003 World Cup there were only 10 scrums and 27 lineouts, while the average for all 48 games in the tournament was 21 scrums and 33 lineouts. Yet one also notices the much greater urgency of re-starts, with scrum or lineout forming and receiving the put-in much more rapidly than 50 years later.

New Zealand were determined to close down the dangerous Welsh backs – in particular Morgan. Accounts and memories differ as to the effectiveness of Clark's marking, flying from the open side of scrums and running from the midfield at lineouts. Swanton of the *Daily Telegraph* felt Clark 'put a complete stopper on the outside-half', while McLean, noting the difference in physique – 'Clark is very tall and lean and Morgan tiny and solid' – reckoned, 'Clark could not quite get the mastery of Morgan'. Clark, amiably self-deprecating, says: 'I'm not sure I ever did catch him.' Morgan for his part remembers an exceptionally quick and difficult opponent.

What was not in doubt was that New Zealand were getting on top. Rees Stephens, leading the Welsh pack, said afterwards that the New Zealand eight were the best he had faced in an international, better even than the formidably powerful 1951 Springboks, while Skinner recalls his surprise that the All Blacks were able to dominate so completely. Dai Gent, in the *Sunday Times*, reckoned Stuart's presence transformed his team. 'He really led them and inspired everybody.' Wales were eclipsed in the scrum, no great surprise to O.L. Owen of *The Times*, who recalled that Wales had lost to those same 1951 Springboks through 'contempt for the set scrummage', while McCarthy reckoned the All Blacks were 'packing better than I have seen them all tour'.

In the lineout, Tiny White 'literally stood out head and shoulders' according to Ron Griffiths of the (Swansea) *Evening Post*, while the All Blacks ingeniously restricted the agile John's poaching by throwing in low. White, 'the strongest man I ever played against' in Gwilliam's extensive experience, was similarly prominent when the All Blacks drove forward, as Ron Griffiths wrote, 'clustered around the ball like a swarm of bees so close together that it was often difficult to tell them apart'. Outside them, Davis 'small, but exceedingly nippy and resourceful' was fighting off Willis's vigorous attentions to send out his long pass, while the Welsh scrum-half in his turn was being hampered by his pack's slow heeling and pressure from McCaw. Welsh resistance was heavily reliant on Gerwyn Williams – by general assent playing his best ever game for Wales – catching and clearing coolly and accurately.

New Zealand began to exert real pressure in the second quarter. Bob Scott attempted a giant drop-goal from a penalty awarded near halfway after 20 minutes. While it fell short, Griffiths sliced his touch kick and the All Blacks had the put-in well inside the Welsh 25. From the ensuing pressure, Wales were penalised at a scrum near their own line – McCarthy's shout of 'It's against you Rex' an echo of one of his many earlier incarnations, as an auctioneer. To create a kickable angle, Jarden took the ball back outside the 25-yard line. From five yards inside the right-hand touchline, into the sun against which referee Cooper had to shade his eyes and amid the silence of a crowd whose manners were not those of 2004 (outside Limerick at least), Jarden kicked high and accurate, permitting McCarthy the use of his catch-phrase: 'Listen . . . It's a goal.'

Wales 5, New Zealand 3.

Rowlands and Jarden both missed long-range opportunities in the next ten minutes. Rowlands remembers: 'The ball was different then and few players could kick for goal from afar with any certainty of success. Both kicks I missed were a fair way out. They would have been bonuses if they had gone over.' McCarthy said of Jarden's attempt that, 'it went outside the right-hand post but had everything else right'. Then, five minutes before the break, Scott, in his own words: 'Went down the sideline and hoisted an up and under. It wasn't brilliantly executed.' Griffiths was the unlucky man at the bottom of the flightpath. He recalls: 'I probably should have caught the ball. On the other hand, I had to come back for it and usually the full-back would come on to the ball, but I don't think it was as straightforward as that. Anyway, neither of us caught it.' Scott, Gerwyn Williams and Stoker Williams were in the vicinity as it bounced, but Clark, as so often, reacted first and quickest, diving to clutch the bouncing ball and touch down.

Memories fade, and not only because of the passage of time. Griffiths points out: 'It is all a bit of a blur. It is all adrenalin and excitement, and in a game of such speed and tension you live every second. The memory doesn't record anything you can recall easily except some tries and kicks. The rest is travelling 100 miles per hour all afternoon.'

Clark does not remember any great detail: 'It is likely that the lack of instant and interminable replays has a bearing on it,' he says, as well as suggesting that subsequent events during the match have clouded the memory. Feelings, however, are more readily recalled: 'I can remember feeling, immediately after the event, a feeling of great pride in the achievement coupled, of course, with the standard practice for the era of displaying extreme modesty and bashfulness. I know I had every right to be modest and bashful – I didn't beat anyone with ball in the hand – all I had to do was fall on the thing after somebody dropped it!'

Griffiths says: 'I was mad at myself and it probably shook me up for a while.'

Jarden, with Scott acting as ball-holder, landed the conversion.

Wales 5, New Zealand 8.

A brief Welsh flurry before half-time saw Gerwyn Williams breaking down the middle, but the first half, which had incorporated 85 stoppages including 43 lineouts, ended with the city end scoreboard still showing New Zealand three points up. The teams stayed out on the field – Clark recalls: 'In those enlightened days we were not allowed to leave the field. I still don't know for certain why! I think it may have had something to do with the International Rugby Board's dislike of coaches and coaching.' Scott remembers: 'I always stood with my own thoughts just waiting for the battle to begin again.' Neither can remember what Bob Stuart or anyone else said. Nor can Stuart. He says: 'There was a rest time of three minutes, so anything I said would be succinct. I would not have made any changes but encouraged a maintenance, and even more dominance, in the second half. Why take a watch to pieces if it is in good order?' G.V. Wynne-Jones told his radio audience of the way Stuart had spoken quietly and earnestly to his team at the break. Wilfred Wooller too would later note his low-key style: 'Seldom have I seen a leader obtain such excellent results with so little verbal effort. A quiet gesture with the hand was often sufficient to direct a line of attack or defence.' On the Welsh side, Rowlands remembers Bleddyn Williams offering 'just a few words exhorting the forwards to greater effort and more than a suggestion that the game was still there to be won'. Meanwhile, on the other side of the world at 3.15 a.m. on Sunday morning, thousands of New Zealanders were twiddling the knobs of their radios as the transmission changed wavelength.

Wooller, summarising for the radio, had no doubt 'this New Zealand team is playing a great deal better than Wales'. While it still had not shown much thrust behind the scrum, its forwards were dominating, particularly in the scrums and the loose, while Wales had never settled: 'The All Blacks are giving it everything they've got, while Wales seem to be holding back.'

Morgan kicked off the second half for Wales towards the river end, and his re-start was caught by the giant Skinner who called for and was awarded a mark. This might seem an odd action for a prop-forward, but he would do it again later in the half – and four of the five marks given during the second half were to be taken by prop-forwards, 'making themselves a bit more useful' with a vengeance. Skinner's kick, from just outside his own 25 to halfway between the Welsh 25- and 10-yard lines, immediately put Wales back on the defensive. Wynne-Jones remarked that the crowd were 'very quiet now – sad or disappointed and perhaps a little afraid'.

They had good reason for fear. Relieved only briefly when Rowlands kicked a penalty deep into New Zealand territory and Morgan and Bleddyn Williams combined to take play into the 25, Wales were pinned back, their scrum untidy and covering increasingly desperate. Ten minutes into the half, halting an attack in which Davis and Haig combined to send Tanner surging into the Welsh 25, Gareth Griffiths was injured. He remembers: 'I had the two centres coming at me with the ball. I don't know where Cliff was, but Bleddyn had to take the outside-half. I had to use what I used to call the 'basketball defence' where you pawed one of them to make him pass, but hoped to God you'd still be fast enough to get the other one. The problem was that when that happened you didn't hit him, he hit you – on this occasion I think it was Tanner. I couldn't move my right shoulder or pick up the ball. When I told Bleddyn I couldn't move my shoulder, he said "let's have a look" and then, "You'd better go off."'

Reduced to 14 men against opponents who were three points up and threatening to add more at any moment, Bleddyn Williams took Clem Thomas out of the pack to play on the left-wing, and moved Gwyn Rowlands into the centre. Wynne-Jones hopefully pointed out that the victory of 1935 had been achieved by 14 men after hooker Don Tarr (a naval man remembered by the commentator as Jack Tarr) had been seriously injured.

Now, though, began the Welsh Calvary. Wilfred Wooller may have opined, in his post-match radio summary, that Griffiths' absence made no difference given that New Zealand were already dominating, but that was not how it seemed at the time. As Stoker Williams says: 'It is bad enough playing against New Zealand with 15 men, but with 14 . . .' Pressure became a siege, with Wales pinned back inside their 25. The crowd, McLean wrote, was 'sad and melancholy' as the All Blacks pressed. Radio listeners in New Zealand had clearer reception as the swirling roar against which commentators had to compete was quietened.

Keith Davis remembers: 'We were so close, and we did everything we could to score. The defence took an enormous amount of punishment.' Stuart went close from a set move in which he moved forward from the back of the lineout, took the ball and crashed between the men at the front. He says: 'I hit the line with a pile of bodies on top of me. I have no doubt the referee was uncertain and in my opinion made the right decision. If there is any doubt in these positions, the referee must rule in favour of the team on defence.' There were also signs of greater fluency – Owen noted sardonically 'once the ball even reached Jarden'. McLean thought Fitzpatrick had scored, noting meaningfully that he touched down only ten yards from the spot immortalised by Deans, in the 17th minute of the half. Fitzpatrick recalls: 'It was a pre-planned move on our put-in. I ran blind on the left of the field and the idea was that you had to be level with the scrum when you got the ball, so you were in full cry before their half-back could move. It needed a clean hook and a quick pass, and it all went perfectly. I got extremely close and I'd have been in glory for ever more if I had made it, but I'm pretty sure I didn't score. I'd remember it if I had!'

Fitzpatrick was downed almost at the Welsh line by a combination of Gerwyn and Bleddyn Williams. Gerwyn, for whom it is one of the few details of the match still clearly recalled, says: 'I remember him coming towards the corner flag and I knew I had to take him low. I was only 10½ st., and we were very close to the line, so a man of his strength and power would still probably have scored if Bleddyn hadn't taken him high at the same time. I didn't see Bleddyn, but I sensed he was there.' Instead of a try, Fitzpatrick was penalised for a double movement.

Scott felt that Fitzpatrick should have scored – and nearly did so himself moments later with a drop-goal attempt Wynne-Jones described as 'just shaving the posts' after the Welsh penalty clearance missed touch. Rowlands, the penalty-taker, still remembers the groans of the crowd. He was in the one shaky spell of an otherwise highly composed debut. Shortly afterwards, Ian Clarke took a mark and hoisted his kick towards the Welsh line. Rowlands vividly remembers trying to take the catch under pressure from 'a giant New Zealander wearing a scrum-cap. Ninety-nine times out of a hundred I'd have taken it without any worry. I can still hear his breathing as he came towards me, and the ball went straight through my arms!'

Two minutes later, Wales were back to fifteen men. One subsequent account tells of Griffiths standing up in the dressing-room, insisting 'I'm going back on' and running down the tunnel to rejoin his teammates. The quote and the spirit of the anecdote may be accurate, but the location is fictitious. Griffiths, remarkably matter-of-fact about the whole business, says: 'I never left the touchline.' He remembers the WRU official surgeon Nathan Rocyn-Jones greeting him as he left the field: 'He said go and lie on the blanket. I did as I was told and in a few seconds he put it back in. It was aching, but it certainly wasn't excruciating. You have to remember that all the muscles and the bits around them were warm. At 22, I still had a young body and Rocyn-Jones was an expert orthopaedic surgeon, so it was simple for him to put it right back. I've never had any trouble with it since.'

Gwyn Rowlands confirms: 'You can put a dislocated shoulder back, but you need to do it within ten minutes or the muscles go into spasm and it becomes impossible – then you need an anaesthetic. But if you do it immediately it will go back.' He remembers performing a similar on-field operation for an army player who put his shoulder out. There clearly was some debate before Griffiths returned. Ray Lewis, the Wales physio, told the *Daily Herald*: 'He wanted to get back straight away – but at least he stayed while we struggled the dislocation back into place. Strapped up though he was, there was always the danger that any further tackle would send it out again and cause a lot of trouble, but he just would not listen.'

Wilfred Wooller's postmatch suggestion that, given the All Black forwards and a similar situation, the Welsh backs might have scored 20 to 30 points was over-excited – Wales would score 20 points only once in 73 matches between 1951 and 1967 – but there is no doubt this was the decisive period of the match. If they had made the most of their advantage, Bleddyn Williams readily admitted, 'Wales would never have recovered.'

But they did not score. The rules of the day, much more defender-friendly than now, certainly played their part. When the outnumbered Welsh pack was driven back over its own line, Willis was pulled down in trying to clear and Wynne-Jones reported: 'I can't tell you what is happening now, there are lots of bodies on the Welsh line.' The subsequent put-in, and two more as the All Blacks shoved them backwards, went to the Welsh.

At the same time as owning up to his own support for such tactics, Bob Scott blames 'that old New Zealand failing – safety first, keep it in the forwards and don't take too many risks. It has lost New Zealand a lot of Test matches over the years.' Elsom recalls: 'The ball never got beyond the five-eighths.' Bleddyn Williams remembers: 'Haig was still a good player, but not as quick or effective as he had been in 1950.' McCarthy, for all his admiration of Haig, noted that there were opportunities to move the ball, but 'Laurie was flat-footed and it'd go back into touch'. McLean blamed a straightforward lack of subtlety.

Yet New Zealand's failings were not the only reason Wales survived. Stuart and Davis both remember a remarkable defensive effort. Cliff Morgan is chiefly, and justly, remembered as an attacker, but on his return to New Zealand Jarden would tell how he 'kept up the morale of Wales by his superb clearing play during the long period when we were leading by eight to five and attacking all the time . . . on getting possession it would go straight back to Morgan who would run and kick beautifully'.

They had also worked out a way of turning Scott's incursions into the line, a significant All Black weapon, against them. Bleddyn Williams remembers: 'They didn't really extend us because, although they had two very good wings, they used Bob Scott to come into the line a lot. We realised this and shut up the middle of the field.' Cliff Morgan recalls that the tactics used successfully by Cardiff were applied again by the all-Cardiff midfield: 'There'd be a shout of 'Bob's in!' and the nearest man to him would go for the tackle.' Bleddyn Williams recalls: 'Bob was a truly great player, but as far as I was concerned they should have moved the ball wide to extend our defence. We would have given out in the end.'

Griffiths returned to what Clark recalls as a 'huge welcome', lifting crowd and teammates alike. Bleddyn Williams says: 'It made one hell of a difference. We'd been under this enormous pressure and suddenly there we were with numbers even again.' It was, correspondingly, a blow to the All Blacks. Clark says: 'It was frustrating for us. We knew we should have scored, and we had not.'

Matter-of-fact Griffiths may be, but Rowlands has no doubt 'what he did was exceptionally brave'. It doubtless aided the team's psychological momentum, as well as reassuring Griffiths himself, that he made two half-breaks in his first few minutes after returning, moving play back towards midfield and lifting the All Black stranglehold. The crowd, too, returned to the action. Tanner remembers: 'We were used to noisy crowds in New Zealand, but this was something different. The crowds in Wales were so engaged by the game. They wanted to be involved themselves. And the noise at Cardiff was so great that you could hardly hear to think, never mind communicate with your teammates.'

Even so, Wales still trailed by three points and had not threatened the New Zealand line since their try more than three-quarters of an hour earlier. Now came the next shift in balance as Bleddyn Williams – offside according to McLean, who reckoned this the one true stroke of luck in the whole match – kicked from midfield to within ten yards of the New Zealand line: 'We seemed to have a new lease of life. The pressure was relieved and from that moment the pack took over,' he remembers. From the subsequent lineout, Judd kicked ahead and chased, but as he dived was beaten to the touchdown by Davis.

Half an hour of New Zealand dominance had been fruitless, but Wales scored within five minutes. Jones charged up the right and kicked – 'a terrifically high one' according to McCarthy – to the centre. The ball bounced over Clem Thomas's head, but was gathered by Meredith 'who just flashed from nowhere' and charged for the line 'but Scott and Tiny White hit him hard at once' and brought him down a few yards short.

New Zealand won the subsequent scrum, but went down as they

drove forward. Referee Cooper blew for a penalty against Clark for playing the ball on the floor. Fifty years later the decision still rankles with the New Zealanders. Every one of the survivors remembers it as a harsh decision that may have cost them the match. Clark recalls: 'I was on the floor. I didn't know where the ball was and I had one leg trapped under Tiny White and was trying to push myself out.' Sixteen years later, watching Taranaki play the 1969 Wales tourists at New Plymouth, McLean found Clark 'gleaming with delight' at Clem Thomas's proclamation that it should not have been a penalty. Bleddyn Williams thinks the decision 'very harsh'. So, by all accounts, did many at Cardiff that day, although one report of the crowd 'silent in sympathy' with the penalised player hardly accords with the bellow of delight on the radio recording.

The kick was dead in front, well inside the New Zealand 25. Simple enough, but Rowlands recalls with feeling E.W. Swanton's comment 'if indeed any kick could be described as easy given the circumstances'.

Rowlands still remembers a feeling of time stopping: 'Bleddyn picked the ball up and walked slowly and deliberately towards me. It was just as though he was going plod, plod, plod in a dream. His few paces seemed to take an eternity. It was all in slow motion. Not a word was said. The stadium was still and hushed. I placed the ball and tried not to think of failure. I wondered briefly what my father, who was seated in the stand would be thinking. I tried to compose myself and just take my time. I looked at the back of the ball and did not move my eyes one inch.'

Dreamlike or not, the kick went over. Rowlands recalls: 'For a moment there was a stony silence, then the whole stadium erupted in a huge crescendo and I lifted my eyes from the ground to see hats, seemingly hundreds of hats of all denominations, flying in the air.'

Wales 8, New Zealand 8.

There were still eight minutes on the clock, but nobody would have objected to a draw. By now, though, the crowd was, McLean reported, 'utterly possessed', a continuous roar rising to deafening pitch whenever Wales threatened. The watching John Morgan recalled: 'Where I am becomes a jostling, mauling, howling place. I am kicked behind the knee. People are throwing other people's hats in the air. The crowd sways and fights bitterly against the sway. The Welsh team have gone wild, perhaps

because we have gone wild. The noise must impel them like a great gale.'
Three minutes later Wales drove forward again, Morgan kicked,
Rowlands scragged Elsom and Clem Thomas, following up, found
himself on the touchline with the ball in his hands . . .

Thomas did have alternatives to the kick he sent flying across the
pitch. McCaw remembers: 'You could almost see him thinking, "What
do I do now?"' He could not pass to Bleddyn Williams, who recalls: 'By
this time I was injured as well. I'd torn the ligament at the top of my
left leg, probably just after half-time, so Clem knew there was little
point in giving me the ball.' Cliff Morgan, though, was closing in fast:
'I was calling for the ball, "Clem! Clem!" I don't know if he heard or
saw me, but if he'd given me the ball I'd have been tackled and nothing
would have happened.'

So across went the kick, and in McLean's words: 'The whole world
was reduced to two flying figures, Ron Jarden and Ken Jones, a
bouncing ball and a vast Wagnerian chorus of sound.' Elsom, from his
vantage point on the right-hand touchline, recalls: 'It bounced high. If
it had been low. Ron would have had it.'

Bob Stuart says: 'Ron, who was usually very quick off the mark, held
back a bit while Ken Jones gambled and went all out for it.' Snow
White, watching from the stand, says: 'It was out of this world. Ron
didn't have a chance. Nobody would have.'

Scott was over on the right close to Clem Thomas. He is not amused
that McCarthy's commentary identified him rather than Jarden as Ken
Jones's rival for the vital ball, fixing him in this role for a New Zealand
public who, Don Cameron recalls, 'regarded everything McCarthy said
as gospel'. Scott says: 'You really can't judge exactly what a ball like that
will do, but Ken Jones was an excellent footballer and assessed it very
well and very quickly. Once he knew it was high, and bouncing back
towards him, he accelerated.'

Jarden himself recalled the moment some years later: 'From my
covering position in front of the goalposts I could see the ball going
over my head, and realised at the same instant that Ken Jones was flying
up on the attack.' If the ball had bounced his way, he reckoned: 'I doubt
if even Ken could have turned and given me 15 yards start in the length
of the field' – a view universally held by his teammates, although
Rowlands thinks Jones might have caught him.

That, though, is a matter of speculation. What really happened was described by Jarden: 'It landed on its point and bounced straight into Ken's outstretched hands. The swerve inside was the simplest of movements, and in a flash he was over the goal-line.' It was, as McLean was to christen it, 'The Bounce of the Century'.

McCarthy, drowned out by the Arms Park version of 'Gotterdammerung', told listeners of 'the jubilation and the crestfallen looking New Zealanders as they go back'. Clem Thomas was to recall 'there must have been hundreds of lost hats'. Rowlands kicked the conversion.

Wales 13, New Zealand 8.

Was it a fluke? That tends to be the view of the front row union, rugby's born sceptics. The All Black Peter Eastgate, watching with the other reserves in the stand, describes it as 'the biggest fluke in the world'. Stoker Williams told David Parry-Jones that 'with three bloody great All Black forwards bearing down on him, all Clem wanted to do was unload at all costs'.

Only Clem Thomas knew the truth, and, as one of nature's raconteurs, his story varied over time. He was quoted as saying that 'he just hoofed it across' but also that he had spotted Ken Jones in space. In 1994, he recalled that, 'There was a sea of black jerseys coming toward me. I was desperate to get rid of the ball. I thought of lobbing it to Bleddyn, but suddenly spotted plenty of unguarded space on the far side.' Cliff Morgan, close to the action, discounts the famous story that touch-judge Ivor Jones shouted to Thomas to kick while other teammates argue that the strongest evidence against this is the unlikelihood of Clem ever doing something simply because he was told to. Elsom, still closer, thinks there may be something in the Ivor Jones story.

There was, of course, also the largely forgotten matter of that cross-kick against Paris in 1952 – remembered, it would seem, only by the reporter from the *Daily Mail.* Clem may well have had 'the luck of the devil' as Vivian Jenkins put it. He was taking a risk that might have backfired and undone the recovery of the previous few minutes. But he was not launching completely into the unknown. And, as Gerald Davies, epitome of Welsh rugby at its imaginative best, has pointed out: 'Rugby is a game of calculated risks.'

The game, of course, was not over, even if McCarthy had said: 'No doubt about it, a winning try.' While there were four minutes on the clock, seven and a half would be played, thanks in part to Gareth Griffiths' injury. It was New Zealand's turn to press desperately, while Wales defended their lead. Cliff Morgan recalled in his memoirs: 'We defended, we fell, we tackled, we caught the ball, we scooped it away to touch.'

It was done, on occasion, in a manner that might have a modern referee reaching for yellow cards. Thus McCarthy, in conversational mode, addressed Roy John: 'Hey, you're offside, Roy', then in an aside to his listeners added: 'He doesn't mind being offside. He knows three points are not enough for New Zealand' – a refrain repeated a couple of minutes later as several Welsh forwards offended. Scott, similarly pursuing five rather than three, chose to hoist an up and under rather than go for goal, and kicked the ball dead. That he did so again shortly afterwards from open play shows that trying to rescue a match that should really already be won can induce error in the greatest players.

By the very end, McCarthy said: 'Wales are now an entirely different team. New Zealand seem fagged out. They've tried everything.' Wales broke the pressure again and Dai Davies was close to scoring. New Zealand won the 53rd scrum of the afternoon, Davis passed, Haig grubber-kicked and Morgan, on halfway, kicked to touch as Haig threw him to the ground and Dr Cooper blew the final whistle.

'Just how you summarise that – I don't know' were the disarmingly frank words of Wilfred Wooller as he did his best to do justice both to New Zealand's long superiority and Wales's remarkable late comeback. Ken Jones, had he been listening, might, given his role in the build-up to both earlier Welsh scores, have been surprised to learn that his try was 'the only thing he did all match', although not as surprised as disappointed and bleary-eyed New Zealand listeners who discovered, courtesy of the BBC Overseas Service's announcer, that they had sat up until around 4 a.m. to listen to 'Cardiff against Wales'.

Don Cameron, journalistic detachment perhaps outweighing New Zealand patriotism, remembers: 'I was not that disappointed. We knew that the Welsh were always worthy and dangerous opponents.' His compatriots 12,000 miles away felt differently. Keith Davis says: 'We felt that we had let the rest of New Zealand down. We were carrying a big load, we knew that thousands of New Zealanders would have been listening on the radio.' Fitzpatrick remembers: 'You could only feel for Bill Clark. Nobody blamed him, but we knew how he must be feeling.'

Clark himself says: 'We were bitterly disappointed, but we were inclined to blame the referee.' Radio and newspaper reports spoke of Scott scuffling for the match ball with Roy John – the Neath man winning the battle but handing the ball to his adversary. Scott has no recall of this: 'I did not and of course do not have that ball' or of Clem Thomas – according to Thomas himself – taking revenge for a confrontation the previous week at Swansea by telling him to 'stick that in your pipe and smoke it'. He does remember: 'I was shockingly disappointed. When Freyberg came in to our changing-room, I broke down. I felt we should have won and I took it pretty badly, and I didn't care who knew. It wasn't quite as bad as South Africa in 1949 because there we lost four Tests in a row, but this was out of the blue – like an accident that could have been avoided.'

One might expect his disappointment to have been mirrored by Welsh ecstasy. Yet Bleddyn Williams, so clearly and memorably exultant after Cardiff's win, was reported to have 'glumly exclaimed that Wales had no moral right to their victory'. He explains: 'I was disappointed because I felt we didn't really play until the last 15 minutes. The Cardiff game had been full of euphoria. I had hoped we would play as that, and we did not. We won the Cardiff game, but they lost the Wales match rather than our winning it.'

That has become the accepted version, with New Zealanders ready to accept Cardiff's superiority while feeling they should have beaten Wales. Not all Welshmen, though, felt disappointment. Gwilliam, who of course had not had the Cardiff experience, remembers feeling 'genuine joy – it meant so much to beat New Zealand'. Nor does he feel that Wales were particularly lucky: 'We scored two tries to one in spite of the fact that they had so much possession and we had to play for a while with only 14 men' – thinking in line with the *Daily Telegraph* headline that 'Intuitive Skill Won The Day for Wales'.

McCaw says: 'We can't complain. If you lose, you're always inclined to look at the referee, but we were chiefly disappointed in ourselves, that we'd failed to push home the advantages we had. For 25 minutes, we had done everything but score, but we lacked that ability to push home those opportunities.' Tiny White is in accord with Bob Scott's 'safety-first' explanation: 'We'd played a more open style against Llanelli, while we were more flat-footed in the Test match. That's not a criticism, it was just the style that we were playing. But if we'd played against Wales the way we did against Llanelli, I've little doubt that we would have won.'

Stuart remembers: 'I felt it would have been fair if it had finished 8–8. The try was a freak, but we lost, that was it, and we had to be gracious' – which he was in an after-dinner speech that is remembered, even by his standards, as particularly graceful and generous. It was not a long evening. Cliff Morgan remembers: 'The dinner started at six and was over by eight.' All dictated, the players felt, by the close-fisted determination of the WRU not to be paying hotel bills, but to have their players back in their own homes.

It is, however, possible that the blame attaches to their predecessors of 1935 who, Wooller remembered, had left a giant gorgonzola cheese stuck to the Queen's Hotel dining room wall 'like a school clock', swept glasses from a bar counter on to the floor to be 'jumped on in the manner of treading the grapes' and dropped a series of large earthenware pots down the stairwell 'with the noise of a bomb'.

The New Zealanders returned to their hotel, where Elsom's disappointment was compounded by a freak accident: 'We were signing autographs. We had finished and were going. I walked straight into a cigarette somebody was holding and it went into my eye. It was very painful and they were afraid I was going to lose the sight – it was right in the centre of the eye. But I was lucky with the specialist who came to see me. I can't remember his name, but he had done the first cornea graft.'

Elsom possibly was not comforted by the coincidence that Winston Churchill, ambushed by an exploding box of matches at Trinity House, also suffered burns in a freak accident that day. The unorthodox methods of Welsh medicine did however cheer him considerably: 'The doctors used to come and get me and take me out for a drink. On one occasion, we'd had a drink or two and one of them said, "I've got to get up to do an operation at 8 a.m. tomorrow – so this had better be the last."'

Nor was he the only victim of 19 December 1953. Elsewhere in the St David's Hospital was Mansel Davies, a bus driver who had realised that his bus, taking fans back to Maesteg, had caught fire. Crawling under the bus with an extinguisher to put out the fire, he had been overcome by fumes. Happily, Cardiff Fire Brigade finished the job off and Davies was released from St David's. No such luck though for G. Hawker of Risca, detained overnight with suspected internal injuries after a crush in the crowd, or Edward Parker of Monmouth, 59, who had died while a passenger in a friend's car, returning home after the match.

Gwyn Rowlands was back in his RAF hut at St Athan while the West Walian quartet had gone home, as usual on the last train of the day, the 11.05 to Swansea. Next day, Stoker Williams, bearing with him the pride and satisfaction of a job well done – 'You don't need people to tell you you've had a good game. You know yourself: and I know I had a good game that day' – was back on his normal Sunday morning shift at the RTB works, Gowerton.

CHAPTER 6

WHAT HAPPENED NEXT

New Zealand's tour still had three months and four more internationals to run. Clark remembers: 'The Wales match was so important to us that it did put something of a dampener on things.' McLean's report in the following Monday's papers was suitably complimentary to Wales: 'Never before have I seen an international team so decisively turn defeat into victory', but inevitably his main purpose was to find reasons for New Zealand's defeat. He was later to summarise the All Black team: 'Eight wonderful forwards, a truly great full-back and six other players whose contribution to the game was spasmodic rather than total.'

This seems unfair to Davis, acknowledged by British critics and McLean alike to have had an excellent game. British writers homed in on first five-eighth Haig. Larry Montague of the *Manchester Guardian* was typical, if more incisively graphic than most, in describing him as: 'The cold hand on the warm spirit of attack. Haig is a true footballer – experienced, cool, shrewd and solid in defence, but he has the fatal handicap for a stand-off half or five-eighth of being terribly slow for first-class football and by the time the ball had left him, so much precious time had been consumed that the movements were certain to be strangled.'

Haig's performance in the next match, a 22–3 victory over Abertillery and Ebbw Vale which had J.B.G. Thomas proclaiming: 'At long-last the Fourth All Blacks have revealed some of the qualities which have made the name New Zealand a household word in rugby football,' did not quieten the critics. Thomas still used his match report to bemoan the failure to make greater use of young Bowers – 'the answer to the obvious midfield weaknesses of the All Blacks'.

The chorus for Bowers took on a new dimension following the All Blacks' next match, against Combined Services at Twickenham on Boxing Day. For the All Blacks it had been overshadowed by the news from home of the Tangiwai rail crash. New Zealand's worst loss of life since the Napier earthquake 22 years earlier, it claimed 151 lives when a Wellington–Auckland express train crashed through a bridge. On Christmas Eve, the *New Zealand Herald* had broken long-formed habit by taking the advertisements from its front page in order to print pictures of the visiting Queen's first day in Auckland. Two days later, that front page was being used for news.

New Zealand post-Tangiwai sporting memories tend to focus on the heroics of cricketer Bert Sutcliffe, returning to the crease with a bandaged head in the Test match against South Africa to hit seven sixes in an innings of eighty not out, and still more of Bob Blair, who batted in spite of hearing of his fiancée's death at Tangiwai. It was also, though, a memorable day for the All Blacks, started by both teams and the 20,000 crowd standing for a minute's silence.

This was not some easy run-out to allow the All Blacks rest over Christmas. Combined Services were extremely strong in the 1950s, with National Service giving them the best young players in the country for two years, and the career forces considerably larger than they are now. They had beaten Cardiff. Six of their team were internationals. A month later their captain prop Bob Stirling would lead England against the All Blacks, and lock Peter Yarranton would become their seventh international. An eighth, lock-forward Rhys Williams, would become the best of the lot, remembered for his performances with the 1959 Lions as one of the best British forwards to visit New Zealand. They could still leave out Rowlands, Llanelli's Carwyn James – a navy coder who was learning Russian, and would return to haunt later All Blacks – and were debarred from choosing a black Cardiffian Lance-Corporal called Billy Boston, because he had signed professional forms with Wigan two months earlier.

New Zealand combined the Wellington midfield – Bowers, Fitzgerald, Fitzpatrick – with Scott at full-back and the lively Davis at scrum-half. They won by 40 points to 8, a massacre by 1953 standards, scoring nine tries. Fitzpatrick, a Wellington teammate who played second five in this match, recalls Bowers with immense warmth: 'He was a natural, with a lot of flair and when he put on the gas he really went.' This, in McLean's view, was 'his day of days' when, as Montague wrote, 'he abandoned kicking as a means to progress and relied on the old-fashioned but now largely neglected virtues of straight running and well-timed passing'. The one player, ironically, who did not benefit was Jarden. After the shock of receiving a pass from the first scrum – 'If he had dropped it in sheer astonishment, I should have been the last to criticise,' wrote McLean – he was injured and replaced on the wing by the pacy flanker Peter Jones, who took to his new role with enormous gusto, scoring a try. McLean thought it 'the most important match of the tour, but nobody appreciated it as such'.

What it did do was inflame New Zealand's incipient outside-half controversy. As ever with such polemic – Arwellians v. Jenkinsites in late 1990s Wales, Barnes v. Andrew for England a few years earlier or Fox v. Botica in late 1980s New Zealand – an argument ostensibly about individuals was as much about style and philosophy. McLean felt that the Combined Services match had shown New Zealand a better way of playing – and also that their true crime in selection was neglecting the attacking talents of Fitzgerald, deemed defensively suspect and marginalised early in the tour. It was Bowers v. Haig, though, that became the focus and proxy for argument about the way New Zealand played. A debate which McLean, writing six years later, would recall as 'in extent and passion . . . almost the fiercest in New Zealand rugby history'.

Haig had been an unanimous choice for the Wales game. Bob Stuart recalls: 'Guy Bowers was a lovely player, but he was young and had really been picked with the 1956–57 era in mind. If there had not been so much offside play, it might have been a different matter, but we didn't want him getting knocked about. He could never have stood up to it.' Asked about Haig's qualities at the end of the tour, he would compare him to an airline pilot: 'You'd hate to be up there without him.'

Scott felt similarly: 'I would always go for a sound, experienced player rather than a young, brilliant one – mind you, that could have been a fault on my part! So I always felt happier with Laurie. Nothing against Guy, but I preferred the tried and tested.' Skinner was not on the selection committee, but says: 'Guy simply wasn't experienced enough. We didn't really have an alternative to Laurie.'

Clark feels that Fitzgerald got a poor deal: 'I can understand the thinking, but I always took the view that you could tolerate letting the odd one through if you were scoring more tries at the other end.' He wonders what the purpose was of picking Bowers for the tour at all if the team was going to play a ten-man game to which he was patently unsuited.

McLean was to write that the selection committee 'for a long time voted for safety first and it never quite shrugged off its affection for this'. He felt this was the wrong choice. This was not the comfortable or easy viewpoint – McLean was, with McCarthy, an official member of the tour party. Given the sense of isolation of any touring team – '30 of us and everybody else was the enemy' in prop Peter Eastgate's words – criticism can easily be interpreted as disloyalty. McLean recalls that 'this did make things a little uncomfortable for a while' – but the men of 1953 were merely the first All Black team to be reminded that he was a journalist, not a cheerleader.

Bowers was preferred to Haig against Ireland on 9 January. Ireland's back row spoiled ferociously and, the All Blacks felt, illegally. McLean wrote of their Lions flanker Jim McCarthy that: 'There never was a more delightful young footballer as a man than McCarthy, and I doubt that many have so deliberately infringed the laws as he.' Yet Bowers justified his selection with a fine break, aided by Hemi, to create a try for Bob Stuart in a 14–3 win. Haig, though, returned against England and Scotland – aided by a penicillin injection, to which he proved happily non-allergic, administered by the versatile Dr Peter Cooper before he played against England. New Zealand won 5–0 in the Twickenham snow, with a try from the mighty Dalzell 'bustling forward as violently as an enraged bull' after Clark had once more gathered a loose ball. Hemi took eight strikes against the head, McLean reckoned New Zealand controlled 70 per cent of possession, and England were pinned into their own half for the entire second half. Montague felt that 'had the pitch been a thousand yards long, they and Scott and Haig would still have ensured that the game was played in the last 30 yards at England's end'.

Scotland, who had lost 12 games in a row, including the famous 0–44 'We were lucky to get nil' debacle against the 1951 Springboks, were expected to be the least of their problems. Instead, a pack led by veteran flanker Douglas Elliot and including a lock, Ewen Fergusson, destined to be Her Majesty's Ambassador in Pretoria and Paris, was possibly the best New Zealand met all tour. They were grateful to escape with a 3–0 win, courtesy of a Scott penalty.

There were also two more visits to Wales, and as McLean wrote: 'Although Wales has many attractive features, these tend to lose some of their fascination at their third or fourth time of asking.' The first visit was in late January, arriving back from Ireland. Irish rugby was tough at this time. Ulster (as in 1935) had managed a draw, while Bob Stuart and Kevin Skinner still remember vividly the desperate struggle the All Blacks had to subdue Munster 6–3. Ireland was, though, with a single exception, mercifully free of suggestions that Ireland or anybody else would beat them and 'Scott, who seems to have been the only one who heard the remark, was told it in undeniably funny circumstances'. By contrast 'at almost the first stop on the rail journey from Fishguard to Newport . . . a Welsh head poked itself in the carriage window and an unmistakeably Welsh voice cried, "Newport will beat you!"'

Newport did not, handicapping themselves hopelessly by playing their outstanding outside-half Roy Burnett when patently unfit, although scrum-half Onllwyn Brace neutralised the All Black loose-forwards with such aplomb that they wondered why he had not been considered for Wales: 'He adapted himself to the conditions by standing seven or eight yards behind the lineouts to wait for passes thrown directly to him by his forwards.' Tiny White, watching for once on a tour in which he played 30 out of 36 matches, doubtless noted this for his running polemic with Arthur Marslin – a debate which the assistant manager, to White's lasting pleasure, would ultimately concede. New Zealand won 11–6.

Nor had they lost three days earlier to Pontypool/Cross Keys, a contest headlined 'Roughest Match of the Tour' in which Elsom, playing for the first time since his mishap with the cigarette, added two more tries to his considerable Welsh haul in a 19–6 win. That title only survived for a week before a ferocious clash with Neath-Aberavon. Peter Eastgate, a Canterbury prop who spent his formative years on the West Coast and thus surely knows whereof he speaks, reckons this the roughest game of his entire career. Courtenay Meredith scored for the combined team, but the All Blacks won 11–5.

Wales, though 'racked by envy and jealousy' according to McLean – neither the first nor the last visitor to be astonished by the capacity for feuding that led Aneurin Bevan to allege that 'the politics of Westminster are in their infancy compared to those of Welsh rugby' – was mostly free of the occasional mishaps that occurred in England. Some were humorous – Fitzpatrick still smiles when reminded of the time he discovered that the driver he was trying, prompted by a mischievous teammate, to tip a shilling was Lord Swinton, a Cabinet minister. Some less so. Elsom remains staggered by the occasion after the England Test when he, Jones and other players went looking for a drink and were told: 'You boys wait outside and let the ladies and gentlemen have their fill – then you can come in.' A hard time had by all at The Gnoll, snootiness at Twickenham. Some things have not changed that much in half a century.

Rugby tours are not invariably happy, as the 1993 and 2001 British Lions, a shockingly large number of Welsh parties, the 1956 Springboks, the 1928 All Blacks and others far too numerous to mention would attest. Homesickness, factionalism, boredom, frustration and simple dislike of teammates or management can all play their part. What is striking about this team, asserted not only by its surviving members but by McLean, ideally placed to observe had it been otherwise, is how happy and united they were as a group, with respect and affection for Stuart the factor invariably cited. These may have been more deferential times, but Stuart and senior players like Scott, Skinner and Tiny White commanded respect through their skill as players, personalities and – for Stuart and Scott at least – war records.

If anyone was unhappy, it was Jarden. Separation is invariably a problem on tours and Jarden was only recently married. He was noted early by McLean as the most assiduous letter-writer in the party – his close friend Clark suspects he may have been the least: 'I think I only managed to write to my parents once' – although Tiny White was probably the best served for communication via his brother, an enthusiastic radio ham, who linked him up with his family in Gisborne on Christmas Day and other important occasions. Jarden had a frustrating tour as a player – *Playfair Rugby Annual* described him as 'so ill-served that he became a kind of Ken Jones, but without, however, the latter's cheery indifference to neglect'. Nor did some teammates help. For most, Elsom and Dixon were a source of (mainly) innocent merriment. Elsom's propensity for addressing teammates as 'Chutney' caught on through the party, while Clark remembers that 'he had an extraordinary ability for knowing how far to go without being offensive or causing real trouble'. But he, Stuart and others believed that Elsom and Dixon's mickey-taking of their fellow wing, an old adversary from Ranfurly Shield matches, while not malicious in intent, contributed to Jarden's unhappiness. McLean recalls: 'They were a couple of scoundrels really. They'd see Ron sitting and reading a letter from his wife, and they'd wind him up.'

Modern teams do little but train for and play rugby. This team, and those of their era, had other diversions and were encouraged in them. Stuart remembers saying to his teammates after the post-match dinner on Saturday nights: 'Right, I don't want to see you lot until Monday – get away and do something different.' Permission might also be granted for occasional midweek breaks. Certainly nobody could have begrudged White, amid his marathon playing stint, his couple of days off after the England Test: 'I'd bumped into a friend of my father's who was chief test pilot for Hawker Siddeley and he invited me to go and spend a couple of days with him at the airfield. They were testing jet engines in the tail of a Lancaster bomber, so I ended up flying over a good bit of the south of England in the number-two pilot seat of a Lancaster. A couple of times I even held the pole and flew it.'

White, along with the other farmers, was frequently invited to visit British farms and retains fond memories of a trip in the Borders to see the stock owned by Campbell Templeton: 'He had black cattle and I've still got quite a few pictures of them. I was reminded of the Waikato – green, rolling countryside and beautiful stock.' Bob Stuart still recalls Ian Clarke's amazement at visiting a small Irish farm with around a dozen workers: 'Ian and two brothers worked a hundred acres – it was a completely different type of farming.' Stuart's own agricultural expertise made such an impression, McLean wrote, that 'his career in this looked likely to become as international as his rugby'. On one occasion he was surprised by his teammates, to their great delight, kneeling and examining minutely the quality of the grass in the grounds of Windsor Castle.

Young men abroad have, of course, more traditional means of entertainment. Jimmy Duncan, the coach of the 1905 All Blacks, who died while his successors of 1953 were enjoying their stay in Singapore, had fondly recalled 'the numbers of young ladies and old widows who were desirous of taking me into partnership as a sleeping partner only'.

McLean remembered them as models of restraint and propriety compared to some teams he was to accompany, but the 1953 All Blacks still had their share of adventures. He recalled that, 'Ian Clarke could catch women with a flick of his wrist.' Tanner remembers: 'There were girls who followed us around, especially in Wales. I remember on one occasion going back on the bus to Porthcawl, four or five of us had girls with us. I said to mine, "How will you get home?" She said, "Don't worry about that." The following morning I was too embarrassed to go down to breakfast with her, I thought it wouldn't look too good, but when I got there the other guys had their girls with them!' Fitzpatrick recalled that the staff at the Seabank were accommodated in a separate annex behind the hotel: 'By the end of the tour there were more players sleeping there than in the main hotel.'

It was to the Seabank that they returned for the fourth and last time to prepare for their final match in Britain, against the Barbarians at Cardiff – the first All Black turn at a fixture gradually entrenching itself as the invariable tour finale. The brilliance shown against Combined Services had flared intermittently since – notably in extraordinary conditions against North-Eastern Counties at Bradford. McLean recalled: 'They had to use a harrow to tone down the icicles, which were sticking up like swords. The All Blacks played brilliantly and I remember the reporter from the *Daily Herald* saying to me, "First class, old boy, absolutely first class."' He himself wrote of his 'regret that many of the tough matches of the tour, including the international against Wales came so early'.

That thought was underlined by the Barbarians match, the All Blacks' third at Cardiff. They won 19–6 in the manner with which this fixture was to become associated. Scott had offered to stand down to allow Jack Kelly, a popular and adventurous reserve, a big game, but the offer was refused. He dropped a goal and White appeared somewhere a lock forward had no right to be to score the final try. Scott, called for by the crowd, and Stuart were chaired off, hands were linked, 'Now Is The Hour' and 'Auld Lang Syne' were sung. Fitzpatrick, on his return to New Zealand, recalled this match as the highlight of the whole tour. Scott remembers it as one of the highlights of a great career. It was, thought McLean, 'the finest display that I have seen by an All Black team', while J.B.G. Thomas wrote: 'How much more successful and enjoyable the tour would have been if they had played in such a manner from the start.'

Had they returned to New Zealand at this point, McLean thought, they would have received a warm welcome. Damage done to their reputation by the defeats against Wales and Cardiff had been repaired by the three subsequent international victories and the finale, 'technically and emotionally the game of the tour', against the Barbarians. Only by the standards of the 1888 Maori team could they have been accused of giving short measure after more than four months away and twenty-eight matches. Instead they went to France.

New Zealand had not played France since 1925, when they won by thirty points to six. France had still to win their first Five Nations Championship. Nor did they seem to be too excited about their guests: 'Nobody seemed to know that we were coming and we couldn't get a practice ground or a practice ball. There was something of a sense of anticlimax about it all, we were all rather unsettled and only Kelly could speak any French,' remembers Stuart.

That was even before they stepped on to the field to play South-West France at Bordeaux. White played, even by his standards, a remarkable game. He was, though, no more remarkable than the referee, M. Taddei of Brive, who did nothing to undermine Kevin Skinner's preference for neutral referees and is remembered by the prop forward for one particularly innovative ruling: 'He gave a penalty against Vince Bevan. Vince asked him what for and he said, "You put the ball in crooked" and Vince said, "I haven't even got the ball in my hand yet."'

Then came the international, at the Stade Colombes. McCaw remembers: 'We expected French rugby to be open, with the ball being thrown around, but it was the complete opposite. They just stood up and negated everything we did. The forwards dominated, but the backs could not penetrate.' It was, McLean would write, 'Wales over again'. He estimated that New Zealand had 70 per cent possession and 'the French seemed only too willing to allow New Zealand to win 70 per cent of the ball', confident that they were unlikely to do anything constructive with it.

Skinner cites this match, and the failure to turn pressure into points, as evidence that Bowers was not the answer to New Zealand's problems: 'We had the ball all day and we didn't do anything.' Jarden admitted to being bemused by the French ability to mix backs and forwards: 'Wherever I looked there was a swarm of swarthy, muscular figures, all of whom looked exactly the same and all of whom appeared to be capable of running like backs.' The only score was a try from Jean Prat of Lourdes, an already legendary figure winning his 32nd cap.

There was no disgrace in this defeat, at the end of a tough tour against what proved to be the first seriously powerful French team. France was about to share its first Five Nations title with England and Wales, would tie with Wales in 1955, and in 1958 would achieve two things as yet beyond New Zealand – winning a series in South Africa and a Test match at Cardiff. The first championship followed in 1959, and France was to be as far ahead of the rest of Europe over the remaining 40 years of the century as it had been behind in its early years. The New Zealand public were not, naturally enough, to know this. Part of the burden of 1905 and 1924 was that All Black teams were expected to win all the time. The odd lapse in Wales was perhaps to be expected, but losing to France, Lindsay Knight was to write, was 'remembered as a tragedy'.

This was the end of the serious rugby, yet there were still half a dozen matches to come – one was at Ipswich against South-Eastern Counties, technically an unofficial match to replace one snowed off earlier in the tour, in which Stuart played at prop, Dalzell at number 8 – from where he scored two tries – and a late rally was needed to secure a 21–13 victory. Then came the final leg in North America, the reason for those US visa applications six months ago, with three matches in British Columbia and two in California. Clark recalls: 'The rugby there was not so strong, but there were plenty of attractions off the field and the sheer novelty of being in those countries made it more than worthwhile.' All five matches were won in reasonable comfort, although McLean described a dire display in beating University of California 14–6 at Berkeley as 'the most excruciating experience of the tour'.

They landed at Auckland Airport on 21 March 1954. It was more than five months since they had left. They had gone round the world, travelling more than 35,000 miles in all, and played five Test matches, winning a permanent place not only in All Black history but also in that of the countries they had played in and against. Their experience was remarkable then, unrepeatable now. Brian Fitzpatrick says: 'We were a bunch of young guys who were seeing life – and in our case very much for the first time.'

CHAPTER 7

WHERE THEY WENT:

(I) New Zealand

After nearly half a year travelling in a tight-knit group, the return home was disorientating. Peter Eastgate recalls: 'We had a farewell do in Auckland, then all went to the airport and went home. Next day none of them were there – and you missed all of them.' Davis recalls: 'I found it very difficult to get back to normal life and settle down after such a long time away.' For some there were significant adjustments to be made at home – two of the team were introduced to children who had been born while they were away, while Bob Stuart's fourth child was born shortly after his return.

There was also a sense of anticlimax about the rugby scene. McLean noted that while Britain and France always had the Five Nations to look forward to, New Zealand would have only the Ranfurly Shield to provide excitement in 1954. The next major tour, to South Africa, was seven years away in 1960.

Stuart, Haig, Scott and Dalzell retired from big rugby, while Eastgate, to his disbelief – 'I told the doctor not to be such a bloody fool' – was later in 1954 diagnosed with tuberculosis. Happily, it takes more than that to finish off a prop from the West Coast, and Eastgate, who turned 77 in July 2004, lives in Christchurch and remains as forthright in his opinions as in the days when Arthur Marslin asked him at a team meeting, 'Are you feeling all right? We haven't had a complaint from you yet.'

Eight of the fifteen who played Wales had an All Black future when they returned to Auckland in March 1954. The bulk were forwards, with the 1953 party forming the core of the team who would subdue the Springboks in 1956. Among the reserves, flanker Peter Jones would also make an immense impact both on rugby and folk-memory that year – with an extraordinary long-range try in the decisive fourth Test and a postmatch confession, broadcast live to a rapt but still somewhat strait-laced nation, that he was 'absolutely buggered'. The forward coach of that team was to be none other than Bob Stuart.

Seven did not play for New Zealand again, the retirees plus McCaw and the midfield duo of Tanner and Fitzpatrick. None of the midfield backs who went on the 1953 tour ever played for New Zealand again. Bowers and the wing Stuart Freebairn, both supposedly being groomed for the future, turned out not to have one at international level. Of the backs against Wales, only Jarden was to play against the Springboks three years later.

One element in this was a tendency for players to retire in their late 20s. In some cases, family needs were the reason. McCaw recalls: 'I felt my wife and family suffered because of my involvement in rugby.' Many players retired when they got married, while others who carried on are highly conscious of the pressure that their rugby careers, and in particular absences, placed on their wives. Snow White says: 'Looking back now, I think that I was thoroughly selfish in those days.'

Work pressure also played its part. Fitzpatrick says: 'People were asked, "When are you going to get a full-time job?" Or, if they had a job, their employers were saying, "When are we going to get full use of you?"' Jarden acknowledged when he retired at the end of the 1956 Springbok series that it was time he repaid Shell Oil for the time off given him over the previous few years.

Even so, two of the team made the trip to South Africa in 1960 and one, in 1963, would become the first All Black ever to make a return trip to Britain. Two of the team would see younger brothers become All Blacks, one would father one and one player would marry another's sister, producing a daughter who married an All Black. One player would become president of the New Zealand Rugby Union, as would the rival he beat out for the game against Wales. Another would chair the International Rugby Board. Of the 15 who played against Wales, 10 are alive more than 50 years later. Sixteen of the thirty-strong touring team survive, with the oddity noted by Snow White, that 'it seems to be the young guys who have gone first'. The simple fact of being an All Black, the label is conferred for life, is a source of immense pride. The potential pitfalls of early sporting fame are exemplified in F. Scott Fitzgerald's former college footballer Tom Buchanan: 'One of those men who reach such an acute limited excellence at 21 that everything afterward savours of anticlimax', but the archetype seems to have few followers among the 1953 All Blacks.

Among their fellow travellers it was Norman Millard's fate to be commemorated as a grandstand. His 48 years of service to Wellington rugby led to his name being attached to the extraordinary Athletic Park landmark, the vertiginous steepness and vulnerability to local climatic idiosyncracy of which led columnist Tom Scott to nominate it as the perfect venue for the World Hang-Gliding Championships. Few grandstands anywhere have been likelier to draw the inquiry, 'What the **** is that?' from first-time visitors, or proved quite such a white elephant. Clark recalls: 'They found that they'd need about three internationals a year to make it pay.' Millard chaired the Wellington Rugby Union until he left the executive in 1964, and died aged 88 in July 1978.

Arthur Marslin had died the year before, aged 76, in his birthplace, Alexandra. He stayed an All Black selector until 1956, retiring after the triumph over the Springboks. A quiet, rather lonely figure on tour, he progressively became, his friend Tiny White recalls, the life and soul of the team's reunions as time passed.

Few lives were affected quite so much as that of the journalist Terry McLean. He would not have been appointed as the sole officially accredited reporter had he not already commanded serious professional respect, but as a colleague was to tell him on his return: 'You're out of the ruck now, McLean.' He consolidated the reputation earned by his dispatches from Britain – which he reckons totalled 170,000 words, or an average of 1,000 words per day, Sundays included, for five and a half months – by rapidly turning them into a book, *Bob Stuart's All Blacks*. He had a crisis of confidence early in the writing: 'I got stuck and thought, "This is too much, I can't do it." I stopped for three days, then came back and finished it. It was the beginning of my career.'

As press packs grew over the next quarter-century, he was to be the one invariable component in the group following the All Blacks, 'a white pointer shark among the minnows of New Zealand rugby writing'. His literate style was not invariably to players' taste – as in 1953 he was never a cheerleader and some felt the literary flourishes got in the way of the rugby: 'Four paragraphs of Omar Khayyam and then the match report' – but Tiny White considers him 'of all journalists, the one who best understood and explained international rugby'.

His 28 books made him probably the most widely read of all rugby writers, but not by himself. He gave up reading the published versions of his own copy after the 1953 tour, realising on the advice of his editor that this was the only way to avoid unproductive rage at the depredations of 'dumb sub-editors'. A secondary identity as 'T.P. McLean' emerged when he became the *New Zealand Herald*'s first by-lined sportswriter under an editor who disliked forenames.

McLean was knighted in 1996, the second sportswriter following the almost diametrically different Neville Cardus, a lyrical stylist who pleaded 'guilty to fiction if it told a deeper truth' and cheerfully admitted to having only one scoop in a lifetime of cricket writing. McLean recognised the irony that he may be best remembered for a story he did not get – being curtly and threateningly instructed by disgraced All Black prop Keith Murdoch that if he valued his personal safety he should get back onto the light aircraft from which he had just alighted in a small Western Australia settlement. Yet in a trade not always strong on journalistic edge – Chris Hewett of *The Independent* once memorably suggested that if British rugby writers had been reporting Watergate, Nixon would still be president – McLean was the man who had the skills and persistence to trace Murdoch, and the intestinal fortitude needed for what was almost certain to be an unpleasant confrontation. He died a few days before his 91st birthday in July 2004. His final years were spent in a retirement home in Auckland, where he was largely confined to a wheelchair by frail knee joints but opened windows and doors with the aid of a stick manipulated with the dexterity of the good golfer he once was. He went on writing and contributed a new chapter to an expanded edition of one of those 28 books, *I, George Nepia*, in 2002.

Winston McCarthy continued to provide the soundtrack for New

Zealand's most vivid memories until the British Lions tour of 1959 and wrote seven books, including *Round The World With The All Blacks 1953–54,* in the same conversational, descriptive style that characterised his commentaries. Cliff Morgan, whose credentials to judge are unmatched, rates him, 'The greatest of all rugby commentators, because he liked radio and he loved rugby. He talked to you, he had a wonderful voice, knew the game and could always find the phrase that would illuminate and charm.' He died in 1984.

Bob Stuart turned 84 in September 2004. Following retirement from rugby, he continued working for the Agriculture Ministry and fulfilled McLean's prediction that this too might become an international role: 'I was still working mostly in the field in South Island in 1959 when almost out of the blue I was appointed a member of the New Zealand delegation to the Food and Agriculture Organisation [FAO] in Rome. I went on a number of trade missions dealing with dairy products, meat and wool. This was a time of huge change in trade, with subsidised European goods like cheap butter coming into the market – it still goes on. Markets have been more volatile ever since.' He moved to Wellington in 1961 and served as executive director of the Agricultural Production Council.

Nor was the FAO the limit of his international services. For many years a member of the New Zealand Rugby Union executive, he served from 1977 as delegate on the International Rugby Board, a period which included the hosting of the first World Cup in 1987. He admits to having been sceptical about the idea: 'I couldn't see the British unions moving on the idea and while most New Zealand opinion was strongly in favour I had some sympathy with the British point of view. I felt that once you had a World Cup it would erode the status of all other international rugby and in particular the British Lions, and I wasn't at all convinced it would be good for rugby.'

He chaired the IRB in the late 1980s and was heavily involved in the reorganisation, based on a ten-year strategic plan, that provided its modern shape: 'We knew we had to take on the lot – management structures, regional organisation, laws, coaching, junior and women's rugby were just some of the aspects we considered. So it became a long process with faxes flying back and forth across the world.' He still sits on the IRB's laws committee and the NZRU judicial committee, which means that anyone getting into trouble in a Test, Super 12 or National Provincial Championship match has a reasonably good chance of meeting him. He received the IRB's award for services to the game at the banquet held in Sydney to mark the end of the 2003 World Cup.

Had work not got in the way, it is likely he would have coached the All Blacks. Co-opted in 1956 to organise the forwards against the Springboks, he coached his club Varsity in 1957 and the following year was nominated for South Island selector: 'I explained that, with all the travelling I was doing, I couldn't really do the job properly – for the moment I'd concentrate on club rugby and doing my job properly. Neil McPhail did the job, and went to Britain in 1963–64 as assistant manager – effectively coach.' Rome, then demanding jobs in Wellington, ended any further progress as a coach/selector. He had, though, the satisfaction of seeing younger brother Kevin, whom he feels was unlucky not to be chosen in 1953, attain his long hoped-for All Black cap against Australia in 1955. A nephew, Cameron McIntyre, was a regular member of the Canterbury Crusaders Super 12 squad in 2004, starting the final at five-eighth ahead of All Black Andrew Mehrtens, and is regarded as a likely future All Black.

His memories of the tour remain fond, but with a tinge of frustration. While every account of the match testifies to the impact his leadership had on the All Blacks, he wonders to this day whether he should really have played: 'I was fit, but not match fit, which is a different matter. It would have been different if I'd been able to play even one match before playing against Wales.' There are, though, no second thoughts about the tactics he used – he feels there was no option given British toleration of offside play and the resources at his disposal. He recalls telling British rugby officials: 'This isn't a problem for us – we're only here for a few months. But if you go on refereeing this way, your outside-halfs are going to be destroyed – they're taking a dreadful battering.' He still holds to the opinion he expressed on returning to New Zealand that his team's real deficiency was the lack of anyone to give the backs the leadership Bleddyn Williams supplied to the Welsh.

The man they needed was in Britain in 1953, but as unavailable as if he had been climbing Everest. Tom Lynch, the Canterbury centre who signed for Halifax Rugby League when Elsom rejected their offer in

1951 was, Stuart still believes, the All Blacks' missing link: 'He could play second five, centre or wing, tackled like a demon and could kick. He would have been our midfield anchor.'

He maintains contact with his former teammates, making sure they are kept up with news of each other. 'After all these years he's still our captain,' says Tiny White.

Bob Scott, a few months younger than his captain, turned 83 in February 2004 and lives in Whangamata on the Coromandel Peninsula. He remains fit, sharp-witted and with an affable tolerance of visitors who lack his uncanny spatial awareness when manoeuvring to escape his driveway. He is still frequently recognised: 'It helps that I was bald when I was playing. No matter where I go, I'll walk into shops and people will say, "It is Bob Scott, isn't it?" New Zealand is a small place where rugby still matters a great deal. I enjoy it when people know you. You're part of the public and you belong to them.'

While the French game was the last of his 17 caps, it need not have been: 'They asked me to make myself available again in 1956, but I couldn't do it. I was 35 and it would have been too much. I was still playing OK for Petone and I had the skills, but I wasn't playing at the same intensity. Age catches up with you.'

He also had a developing business to care for. Assisted by friends and admirers, who loaned him the capital, he bought a men's clothing store in Petone, just outside Wellington, not long after the 1953 tour: 'I don't think I was an outstanding businessman, although I had plenty of commonsense and I could always rely on the experience of Bruce Robb, who sold me the business but stayed on with me for 15 years.' A later partner was Andy Leslie, All Black captain in the mid-1970s. The business brought him financial security for the first time in his life. Retiring in 1978, he moved first to Tairua in the Coromandel and then, in 1988, to Whangamata.

He did some coaching and administration at Petone, but says, 'I was never any good as a coach. I can tell you the skills and give you advice that would make you more consistent, but not much more than that.' Part of the difficulty was that uncanny ball sense, which made coaching the vast majority of the population who do not possess it both difficult and frustrating. 'You can't coach what I had,' he says – not a boast, but an objective statement of fact.

He turned first to golf, which he rapidly played off scratch, and then at around 60 to bowls, a sport some might regard as an old man's relaxation. Not Scott. Rugby writer Bob Howitt, a fellow bowls player, confirms, 'Bob plays with all the intensity he used to bring to his rugby.' Scott also argues, with the conviction he brings to everything, that bowls is the most demanding game he has played: 'The demands of precision and accuracy are incredible and you're competing not just against each other, but the elements. People can talk about the pressure of putts in golf, but there you can hit earlier shots well and so give yourself some control. Unsurprisingly, he plays well: 'I could look at a putt in golf and read the break of it, so I could concentrate on the weight. Similarly in bowls, I can see the line I need. The weight and timing may need a little work, but I can guarantee that I won't be very far away.'

Part of the price of his skills and temperament is a sense of disappointment about his rugby career: 'I was always slightly disappointed with my own limitations,' he says, a feeling that places him in a minority roughly estimated at one. But what seems perversely self-critical to the normal human is, he insists, a vital element in driving performance: 'I'm sure you'd find with Tiger Woods that however well he plays and how many tournaments he wins, there'll always be that little bit of disappointment, that sense of something that is not quite there.'

Looking back on 1953 he says: 'We had good players, but I'm not sure we were a good team' – a tactical failure for which, as a member of the selection committee, he regards himself partly responsible.

Ron Jarden was the first of the New Zealanders to die, of a heart attack at home in Lower Hutt in Wellington in February 1977, when he was 47. The news dominated the front page of that day's *Evening Post*. Jarden also rates an entry in the *Dictionary of New Zealand Biography*, reflecting not only the seriousness with which his country takes sport but also his distinction in other fields.

The unhappiness of his 1953 tour was a minor setback in the career of, in Morrie MacKenzie's words, 'the best New Zealand wing between 1920 and 1960'. In 1955, he scored 30 tries, still a New Zealand record, including one in each of the three internationals against Australia. He followed up with scores in two of the four 1956 Tests against South Africa; although an extraordinary solo effort, contentiously ruled out by the touch judge, in New Zealand Universities' victory over the tourists is probably remembered even more fondly than either.

He retired, having scored 42 points including 7 tries in 16 internationals, after the Springbok series, citing moral debts to his employers. In addition, he told told Bob Howitt, 'I'd ascertained how good I could be and knew I could get no better'. That mental clarity was to serve him well in a business career that soon took him from Shell to form stockbrokers R.A. Jarden and Company, and onto several company boards.

It might still also have been put to the benefit of rugby. As a player, he had been such a hero in Wellington that, McLean once found, it was ill-advised to express the slightest scepticism about his talents. But when Jarden ran for the provincial rugby union excutive, he was rejected. Clark has little doubt this was a serious error by the clubs: 'Ron had an excellent business brain and might, for instance, have saved them from the mistake they made with the Millard Stand.'

Instead Jarden's energies were directed into the Music Federation of New Zealand, the National Art Gallery and National Museum – of which he was a trustee – and the Broadcasting Council of New Zealand, of which he was appointed chair after playing a prominent role in the National Party's 'Sportsmen for Muldoon' campaign at the 1975 General Election. Initially criticised as a government placeman, he was subsequently praised by opposition leader Wallace Rowling for his part in the restructuring that created two separate television channels and a radio organisation. He took up sailing in 1974 and within a year was representing New Zealand in the Admiral's Cup.

Jarden's teammate for both Universities and All Blacks, John Tanner, turned 77 in January 2004. He lives in the Auckland suburb of Remuera, perched on a bluff overlooking Orakei Basin and propels his car up what must be the steepest driveway in New Zealand. He still works Tuesday and Thursday mornings as a dentist, regularly runs six kilometres, plays golf – he was the best golfer in the 1953 party and played a round at Portmarnock with McLean, British Amateur champion Joe Carr and Ryder Cup player Harry Bradshaw – and is married for the third time.

Wales was to be the last of his five Tests for New Zealand. He was disappointed, feeling to some extent blamed for the defeat, but laidback as always, says: 'Not playing in the big games gave you more scope for enjoying yourself' – an opportunity not wasted on him. He continued to play for Auckland until 1957, completing a full decade in provincial rugby, but his most memorable post-1953 exploit was his try in the 1956 Universities defeat of the Springboks, an angled 70-yard solo run. He played for an Auckland dentists' team against visiting Japanese dentists in the late 1960s, by which time his game was hockey, which he played between the ages of 40 and 52. He then took up, and still practises, windsurfing.

Looking back on 1953, he adds substance to Stuart's theory about the backs: 'We needed somebody to organise the backs. There was nobody talking and getting everybody sorted out', and says that Fitzpatrick's individualism and unpredictability made him difficult to play with.

Fitzpatrick, who turned 73 in March 2004, also lives in Remuera and was at one time one of Tanner's patients. Like many New Zealanders he has a print of a magnificent composite All Black team picture, including hundreds of players from almost a century of rugby, put together a couple of years ago. He wonders how many have noticed the feature that makes it special for him – himself as a 20-year-old seated in front of son Sean, shown as a 30-something towards the end of a career that brought him an All Black record 92 caps.

His own All Black career ended with the 1953 tour, at the age of 22, leaving him with three caps and the wistful thought: 'I played in 22 matches for the All Blacks, and not once in New Zealand.' He moved to Auckland shortly after the tour and began a career in freight forwarding. He says: 'It does no harm if people know your name.'

His subsequent career was restricted by knee problems: 'The ligaments were perished and they couldn't do the things they can do today with injuries like that. I had a high pain threshold, but my legs got bandier and bandier.' He had replacement surgery in his late 60s.

While he broke only intermittently into the Auckland team, he too was to have a last hurrah for the Universities against the Springboks. Later he joined College Rifles, a second-grade club, and followed a pattern familiar to old players: 'They were just round the corner and said, "Come and have a run with us." I went over the wall a few times and next they asked me if I'd like a game. Before I knew it I was captain and my wife was on the committee.'

He took a relaxed attitude to Sean's rugby: 'He and his brother were out playing in the back garden when they were hardly bigger than the ball. I let them get on with it, although occasionally I might say, "No, don't do it that way", and perhaps that helped – it means bad habits are killed at the beginning.' One biography of Sean recounts how his father advised him to stuff newspaper into his shinpads to make his legs look more powerful. While enormously proud of his son's success, he does not claim credit for it: 'I suppose it is in the genes and a natural eye for the ball, but his achievements are his own.'

He retains warm memories of, and great affection for, his 1953 colleagues and has been an enthusiastic participant in their reunions: 'One thing we have done is to ensure that everybody pays the same each time, so if for instance there is a reunion in Auckland, all of us living here make a contribution to the costs, so that people who come from other parts of the country don't have to pay more. If it is in Wellington or Christchurch, the people from nearer there contribute to our costs.'

He remains disappointed, though, that two of his three Test matches were defeats and feels that the conservative tactics were a mistake: 'I think we had more talent than we showed,' he says.

Allan Elsom turned 79 in July 2004 and lives in the Christchurch suburb of Avondale. Friendships with Eastgate and partner-in-crime Dixon, who died in July 2004, have endured. His real estate business prospered and at one stage he owned 26 properties in Christchurch. Now retired, he retains some property interests and had been out chasing up overdue rents on the morning when he was interviewed.

His tour declined after the Wales match. While he recovered from the eye injury within a few days, the dislocated shoulder plagued him for much longer and his two tries against Pontypool-Cross Keys, giving him a total of seven in four matches against Welsh clubs, were the only sign of his old form. It was Dixon who played the remaining Tests and went on to a vital role in the 1956 series against South Africa. Elsom, though, did play all three Tests against the 1955 Australians, taking his total of caps to six, and had an All Black trial as late as 1957, when he was pushing 32.

He was also a regular member of Canterbury's Ranfurly Shield team, who retained the trophy for three years after gaining it in the match immediately after the 1953 All Blacks were chosen. He played until 1958, when he was 33. 'By then they were shouting, "For Christ's sake give it to Granddad" and printing my initials, which are A.E.G., as A.G.E. in the match programme.'

It was Elsom who at Jarden's funeral said to a forward teammate: 'All very well for you, but I think the big guy upstairs is starting from the edges.' Diagnosed as having a terminal illness in his early 60s, he showed the stubborn resilience that carried him through the war, his broken neck and that long list of injuries.

Laurie Haig, the vice-captain of the 1953 All Blacks died in Dunedin in July 1992, three months short of his 70th birthday. He had retired at the end of the tour, after winning his ninth and last cap against his native Scotland. Three years later he left mining, moving to Dunedin when an accountant brother found him a job as salesman and driver for Newjoy Ice Cream, a local company. Newjoy was subsequently taken over by Tip Top, which in turn became part of the General Foods Corporation. Haig prospered amid these changes and for ten years before his retirement was sales manager for General Foods.

Interviewed in the mid-1970s he said that it had been a solid team, but 'didn't have the players of brilliance' that would have been needed to go through the tour unbeaten. The constant menace of back-row play, practised on a scale the All Blacks had never seen before, was the reason why New Zealand never found a stable midfield combination, making changes at five-eighth after every game but one: 'We were trying to find the players to fit the bill and we never succeeded completely,' he recalled.

Keith Davis, who did play all five Tests on the tour, turned 74 in May 2004 and lives in the Auckland suburb of Torbay. The unsettled feeling he recalls after finishing the tour was to last a long time – no member of the team went through more different jobs during his working life: 'I was at Dominion Breweries, left and bought a service station at Penrose, which I eventually sold. After that, I went into the liquor trade as a publican at Waverley near Wanganui, and that's where I brought up my family – five daughters – before returning to Auckland in the 1980s. I was put on the scrapheap and getting on in age, and I went out selling on commission. It was lucrative, but I spent a lot of time driving and living in hotels, so eventually I gave that up and went and worked in real estate – my last job was with Barfoot and Thomson.'

All of his jobs involved dealing with people and he found that his rugby fame was useful: 'When I went into shops selling on commission, some people did recognise me and it did open doors.'

His international career illustrated the inconsistency of selection during the 1950s. One of the successes of the All Blacks, he then had to wait 18 months for the next international match, and played only the second of the three games against the 1955 Australians. He missed out in 1956 and was furious when not taken to Australia in 1957: 'I had what I thought was my best-ever game in a trial at Wellington. We won 40–3 and I kept on putting people in for tries. But I missed out completely.' A year later, with no great expectations, he played all three matches against Australia and then retired from international rugby: 'I was still only 27, but I got married and thought it was time to give it a miss.'

He did, though, maintain a lifelong relationship with Marist clubs in Auckland: 'I went on the club committee and helped the club establish its own headquarters, acquire land and then help develop it.' His jerseys went to the Auckland club, and he remains a regular supporter and fundraiser for North Harbour Marist.

He played for New Zealand Maori until 1959 and was a selector for several years: 'I had to give it away because of work, but I regard that part of my heritage with great pride.' He is strongly in favour of an inclusive attitude: 'It isn't your colour that matters, but what you are. If you've got the heritage you should play.'

Like a number of the 1953 team he has taken up bowls and takes part in the annual rugby players and writers tournament at Mount Maunganui.

He remembers the 1953 tour as 'a time when you made a lot of close friendships. You were travelling and living in hotels, but playing and training together and you got close to each other.' In particular a friendship with Brian Fitzpatrick has extended to both families.

Bill McCaw, who turned 77 in August 2004, lives in Christchurch, his home since the 1970s, in the suburb of Ilam. He spends a certain amount of his time explaining that he is not related to the current All Black flanker Richard McCaw: 'I'd be pleased if he were related. He's an excellent player,' he says.

He played no more international rugby after the tour. While a friend pointed out at a welcome-home party that 'Bill played in all the losses and draws', this was more a matter of ill-luck than any loss of selectorial favour. In the non-Test year of 1954 he captained South Island and played for New Zealand against The Rest. He was chosen as South Island captain again in 1955 – which suggests that the selectors saw him as a potential All Black leader: 'But I got a deep cut across my eye, had to withdraw and didn't make the Tests.'

He retired at the end of the 1955 season: 'They may have had me in mind as a possible captain, I don't know. But I think I might have lost my edge by then. I was getting married at the end of the year and I'd sort of made my mind up to myself that that would be it.' His honeymoon was close to Arthur Marslin's home at Alexandra. He dropped in to see the former assistant manager, still a selector, and was greeted by the words: 'I suppose you've come here to ask why we dropped you.'

He started coaching in 1956 and also became a member of the Southland Rugby Union executive, but eventually gave up due to family and work commitments: 'I felt that in some ways rugby is too demanding on people's lives and I felt my wife and family suffered from my involvement with it. Your family should have the first call on your time.' He and his wife Bernice, known as Bunny, who died in the summer of 2002, had four children. His teaching career led to a move away from the Southland to Christchurch to teach first at Kaiapoi, then at St Mary's School where he was principal for some time before his retirement in 1987.

He has no doubt that he would have enjoyed modern rugby: 'I was quick around the paddock and would have loved to play 8 or 7 in the modern game – although I look at modern players and realise both how unfit we were by their standards and that we never reached the level of ball skills they have.' He remains immensely proud of being an All Black: 'I felt, and still feel so proud, so important and so honoured. I hope that this isn't something that gets lost over time. When you put on an All Black jersey, you were putting on part of New Zealand, representing not only the present but also the past and the great legends of New Zealand rugby.'

That pride extends to the touring team he played in: 'You hear very little said about it, perhaps because we are considered unsuccessful for losing to Wales. But I do sometimes wonder why our team is slighted and not given the coverage that other teams have enjoyed.'

He does, though, admit to one strong feeling of disappointment about his time as an All Black: 'When I first became an All Black in 1951, I expected I would learn so much, but the policy of the time was not to provide teams with recognised coaches, so you only learnt from the other players. In 1953, we had some really good players and would love to have had more direction. It was asking an immense amount of Bob, who had so much else to do, also to do the coaching. If they had chosen their assistant managers on the ability to run a Test team rather than as a reward for services to the game, we would have learnt a great deal more and had better results.'

Tiny White still lives in Gisborne and turned 79 in June 2004. He played every Test until 1956, retiring as the most capped All Black after 23 consecutive Tests. He scored New Zealand's clinching final try in the third Test – yet another occasion when observers and opponents alike were left wondering how he'd got into the position to score – but is most remembered for the incident close to the end of the fourth at Auckland where, as Warwick Roger recalled: 'It looked as if we were seeing the making of a paraplegic right before our eyes' when White, after a scream of agony heard clearly above the crowd noise, was left lying on the pitch after a savage brawl and missed the final five minutes of his Test career. For more than 40 years, the perpetrator of the boot in the spine was the subject of speculation. Springbok prop Jaap Bekker's confession, not very long before he died, did not wholly impress the recipient: 'He was due to come to New Zealand and apologise personally, but he died a couple of weeks beforehand. Perhaps he knew and felt the need to clear his conscience, but it took him an awfully long time,' says White.

Warwick Roger's fears were closer to the truth than he knew. White explains: 'During the third Test at Christchurch, I started feeling a tingling down my left side. I went to see Bill Park, a surgeon. He examined me and said, "Hell's bells, you've got a dislocated neck" – the neck injury I'd had as a teenager had been aggravated. Bill put me in a steel brace. Tom Morrison rang Bill and asked if I could play. He said, "I don't know. If he wants to play, I won't stop him and if you select him, I won't discourage him." I took the brace off and felt good, and the Springboks had no idea. It was a very well-kept secret, but it was still at the back of my mind.'

He played a few games in 1957, but had no second thoughts about retirement: 'I'd had eight years of international rugby and I had three young kids and a farm. It had been costly in time and I felt I'd done my bit. Going to Australia in 1957 after the intensity of the Springbok series would have been an anticlimax, and I realised after the games I did play that I had to be 100 per cent committed or I didn't enjoy it. I was also subsconsciously aware of the neck injury.'

He coached Poverty Bay briefly in the late 1950s and helped set up Junior Advisory Boards for youth rugby in the district, but, as he says, 'Though rugby was important, it was never the be all and end all.' He farmed until 1976 when a tractor 'did what the Springboks couldn't do. I rolled the tractor down a hill and the frame saved my life. I gave up farming reluctantly, but the specialist said, "You'll kill yourself." I came into the city and spent 15 years doing life underwriting.'

Earning a living was, though, only ever part of what he did. Involvement in local bodies was a family tradition he attempted to follow as early as 1953 when he ran for the local hospital board, learning while on tour that he had lost by 14 votes: 'I ran again in 1956, was elected and after then was unopposed through to the end of the 1970s, and was chair or deputy chair for the last ten years.' He also served as a school committee man – becoming first secretary then chair – as a Justice of the Peace, and ran unsuccessfully for Parliament in 1960. In the late 1970s, he was elected, as an independent, for two terms as Mayor of Gisborne: 'I was probably more right-wing than left-wing – I've never been Labour, but I was completely independent as Mayor.' While rugby fame doubtless aided name recognition, he states firmly: 'I never used my All Black status to achieve anything.'

As his wife Elsie puts it, with mildly exasperated affection: 'He's always getting into things. I've been extremely tired, but never bored.' He was also involved in the Queen Elizabeth National Trust for New Zealand's flora and fauna, has received the Queen's Service Order, is an active member of the Order of St John, fishes and sails, although he gave up offshore racing about 15 years ago.

Looking back on 1953 he feels that New Zealand had the worst of the refereeing throughout the tour, but would still have beaten Wales if they had reproduced the form shown against Llanelli. Instead, their performance, and the game, were disappointing: 'There's no doubt Cardiff was a better game,' he says.

His fellow lock Nelson Dalzell died in Christchurch in April 1989, four days after his 68th birthday. He retired, having played all five Tests, after the end of the tour, devoting himself to his farm at Culverden. He married Shirley Elsom, sister of Allan and a noted tennis player. Their daughter Jo-Anne was to marry Graeme Higginson, a lock-forward who made his All Black Test debut in the Welsh Rugby Union's centenary match in 1980 and went on to win six caps. Dalzell was also a successful owner and breeder of trotting horses, several with names including 'Moose' after George Elsom, father of Allan and Shirley, observed of the first of the line: 'That's not a horse, it's a moose.' He evidently enjoyed his tour in 1953. The farm was never forgotten – McLean recorded 'his moment of greatest delight on the tour seemed to be the day he received the cable that his wool had sold at 84 pence a pound'. Asked for his opinion when Scott and Jarden debated whether international rugby could be fun – Scott, intriguingly in view of subsequently expressed views, saying that it could be – Dalzell, in McLean's words, 'Cocked a very blue, beady eye at the three of us. "If it wasn't," he said, "I wouldn't be here."'

Bill Clark lives in his native village of Mapua, near Nelson, and turned 74 in December 2003. He still runs a payroll bureau for local companies, in particular orchards who have a lot of seasonal employees: 'One of them has four full-time staff, but at harvest time it can go up to 70 or 80.' The work is now computerised: 'I never see the workers, as I used to', which makes him one of presumably a limited number of septuagenarian rugby internationals with an email address.

He returned to the Nelson area in the early 1980s: 'We're both from the Nelson area and we came back, as much as anything, to get out of rugby. I had been heavily involved in New Zealand Universities rugby and by the early 1980s, although I felt great pride in what we achieved, I was feeling burnt out. You can over-stay your welcome or end in a position where you have to carry on because there is nobody else to do the job.'

He had been involved in administration with the Universities since

1956, when he took part in their defeat of the Springboks – and still remembers the tourists reneging on their promise to attend the after-match function. While he recalls the atmosphere of that year as 'madness', he played a crucial part in the series victory, playing in the last three Tests, and spending parts of them in the backs covering for injuries. Bob Stuart, a member of the 1956 coaching team, says: 'Bill was the key man. He made Peter Jones the great player he was that year. When Peter was recalled, you couldn't rely on him in cover defence, so we had to rely on Bill to get back and do that work.' Unusually for a rugby player of his generation, he eventually became an opponent of contact with apartheid-era South Africa.

In 1957, he opened a petrol station in Lower Hutt, enabling press pictures of him dispensing petrol in his white coat captioned: 'All Black in All White'. He continued playing for Wellington that year and had not ruled out carrying on until the British Lions toured New Zealand in 1959. Then, though, in 1958: 'I had my only ever injury and pulled out of the Wellington team. We had our first child, I was 28 and decided that was it.' His final cap, the fourth Test in 1956, was his ninth.

While comments on the 1953 tour inevitably point to its extreme length, he recalls: 'As one of the single guys, I wouldn't have minded if it had gone on for another two or three months, although the rugby might have been inclined to deteriorate. By the time we got to France, we were probably all a bit played out.'

Kevin Skinner, who turned 76 in December 2003, lives in the Auckland suburb of Henderson. He retired from representative rugby at the end of the 1954 season, but was to return for the last two matches against the 1956 Springboks. These Tests sealed his place in All Black folklore, but have – in South Africa at least – distorted his reputation. He was persuaded out of retirement by the All Black selectors after earlier selections – Mark Irwin, who was so pounded that he suffered crushed ribs, and Frank McAtamney – had been found wanting in the first two Tests. The front rows brawled through the third Test. Skinner, whose boxing background was cited to suggest that he had been chosen to beat up the Boks, played both sides of the scrum and confronted both props during the match, won by New Zealand to give them a 2–1 series lead.

Skinner remembers: 'They talked me into playing again. I was reluctant, but I'd played against Chris Koch and Jaap Bekker in Africa in 1949 and I could see a little bit where we were going wrong. When I got to Christchurch, I asked Tiny White and Tiny Hill what was happening and they said that our guys were being intimidated. They were pleased to see me because they thought that would now change.'

He says: 'I don't think what I did had a big bearing on the match, but certain people in the news media made it out that way. My theory is that the South Africans had been kicking the black man around since 1658 and were used to the idea that nobody would hit them back. After we'd sorted a few things out in the front row, they got on with playing the game a bit better.'

Wins in the last two Tests gave New Zealand its first ever series win over South Africa. The fourth Test was his 20th and last. Later that winter Skinner wrote to the editor of the *Auckland Star* suggesting that the press might like to find some other controversy to argue about. He returned to the relaxed, low-key club rugby that he had been playing since his first representative retirement: 'I bought a business in Atiamuri, a hydro town in the Waikato and played and coached there. It was most enjoyable and I could relax, but we had some good players. Our full-back John Parema was only 17 when I first saw him play and went on to play for the Maori All Blacks.'

He returned to Auckland, where he has lived ever since, in 1960 because one of his daughters was deaf and needed specialised education. He owned and ran a supermarket, followed by coffee lounges and finally fast-food outlets before retiring in the early 1990s. He says: 'I am sure rugby, and people knowing me, did help with business.' He also, though, enjoys the fact that he can walk down the street in his part of Auckland, where Wilson Whineray was once a neighbour, relatively incognito.

Looking back on 1953, he remains the most committed supporter of the more conservative playing style adopted for much of the tour. He says: 'We were a happy team and if there was any dissent, it was not so much within the team as with Terry McLean and Winston McCarthy, who decided after the Combined Services game that we should be playing Guy Bowers. We did look good that day, we were getting plenty of room and the backs were going well. But it was the only time it really happened.'

Ron Hemi died in September 2000, aged 67. While his accountancy career was to disrupt his rugby, with examinations limiting his participation in 1957 and 1958, it was highly successful in the long-term as he became senior partner in the Hamilton firm of Hemi, Edwards, Bartels and Co.

He too was one of the key men in 1956. After playing a prominent role in the Springboks traumatic opening to the tour, when they found themselves trailing an inspired Waikato team 14–0 by half-time and were only able to cut the deficit to 14–10 against opponents who were a man short after the break, he played in three of the four Tests. In the fourth, he created the opening for Jones's famous try, using the skills as a dribbler he honed through half an hour's practice every night, toeing the ball away from Springbok half-back Strydom, chasing down the touchline and kicking 'a sort of right cross' which Jones picked up.

He also played three times against the 1959 British Lions and, still only 26, harboured hopes of beating Tiny White's record of 23 Tests, although he had by then for some years had serious competition from Canterbury hooker Dennis Young. But he ripped rib cartilages in only the third game of the 1960 tour of South Africa, then suffered Achilles problems at the start of the 1961 season and retired. He finished with 16 caps while Young, whom Bob Stuart felt should have been the other hooker on the 1953 tour, went on to win 22.

Ian Clarke, who died in June 1997 aged 66, was to become the most-capped of all the 1953 All Blacks, retiring in 1964 with a total of 24. His younger brother Don, New Zealand's full-back and kicker of mountainous goals, had taken Tiny White's record a year earlier.

Ian's great distinction, one that Hemi might have shared if he had stayed fit, was becoming the first All Black to make two tours of Europe, following 1953 with a second trip a decade later – although he played none of the Tests in 1963–64. He concluded his career playing against the All Blacks for the Barbarians at Cardiff, scoring his team's only points with a drop goal in a 36–3 defeat. His endurance fulfilled the prediction made a decade earlier by McLean, that, 'his cheerful temperament . . . suggested that he might remain at the forefront of the game for a long time.'

He was to be Stuart's immediate successor as All Black captain – albeit a year and a half later, leading the All Blacks in the three 1955

Tests against Australia from the position of number 8. Appointing a 24 year old may have looked like a gesture towards the future, but he proved to be merely one of a carousel of All Black captains in the 1950s, with eight different leaders in twenty-four Tests before the selectors finally settled on Wilson Whineray in 1958.

He sold his dairy farm in the early 1970s and bought a small dry-stock property, later becoming a meat buyer for the Auckland Farmers Freezing Company. After retiring from rugby, he became a first-class referee, while involvement in the New Zealand Rugby Union took him to the presidency in 1993. His *Dictionary of New Zealand Biography* entry recalls his concern with small, struggling unions. His sudden death came the day after he watched the first All Black Test at Hamilton – a victory over Argentina – reward for a long personal campaign.

The player whose life changed most after the 1953 tour, and who made the strongest links with Wales, was the man Ian Clarke beat for a Test place on 19 December 1953, Snow White. Snow, of whom McLean recorded in 1953 that he had long forgotten his given name of Hallard, turned 75 in March 2004 and lives in the Auckland suburb of Glenfield.

He went on the tour listed as a painter and paperhanger, but began a successful business career on his own account not long after his return – at different times running businesses in trucking, liquor and industrial spraypainting, for years holding major contracts with the Auckland Harbour Board.

He also became a leading administrator, like Clarke becoming President of the New Zealand Rugby Union in 1991 – a fate that might not have been predicted for him in the 1950s when relations with the powers-that-be disrupted his playing career. He remains convinced that a minor incident on the 1953 tour got him a bad name: 'There was a lot of innuendo I never had a chance to answer.' In spite of playing 14 seasons for Auckland and making a record 196 appearances, he won only 4 All Black caps – 3 of them on tour against Ireland, England and France.

He could have been forgiven for retaining only bad memories of Wales. He dislocated his shoulder in the defeat against Cardiff: 'I went down on the ball, Tiny landed on me and it went pop, the only real injury I ever had.' He watched the Test from the grandstand with the other reserves and subsequently played against the combined teams – Abertillery-Ebbw Vale and Pontypool-Cross Keys, missing the more prestigious club contests before playing against the Barbarians at Cardiff. He feels that more and better use might have been made of Guy Bowers.

Yet, starting with his immediate Cardiff opponent Stan Bowes, he made a series of Welsh friendships: 'Stan came out and stayed with me in New Zealand and we stayed great friends. Eventually, I was a pallbearer at his funeral. I've also kept in touch with Bleddyn and with Jack Matthews. Bleddyn has been out and stayed here, as has Ken Jones. I've been back to Cardiff four or five times and it is like going home.' In 1969, as a rising administrator, he asked for and got the role of liaison officer for the first Wales team to tour New Zealand – and from that came lasting friendships with Brian Price and Denzil Williams.

He speaks for nearly a century of friendship between Wales and New Zealand when he says: 'I've got friends in the other home countries, but for me there has always been an affinity with Wales and Welsh people. There are some people you just click with.'

CHAPTER 8

WHERE THEY WENT:

(II) Wales

Normality resumed more rapidly for the Welsh. A victory against the All Blacks is an immense event in any rugby career, but a single day in Cardiff which began and ended in one's own bed has a different impact to a trip round the world taking nearly half a year. Nor did winning make them any less transient a team than their victims. In retrospect, victory over New Zealand was the final triumph of the team that had dominated British rugby in the early 1950s.

None of the 15 who played against New Zealand shared John Tanner's fate of never playing another international. But for the injuries to Gareth Griffiths and Bleddyn Williams, they would have played en bloc against England four weeks later – a week after the All Blacks defeated Ireland. Instead, a new centre-pairing of Alun Thomas, who had played in Cardiff's win over New Zealand, and Gareth Griffiths' St Luke's teammate Glyn John, forgiven for having played rugby league because he had done so before he was 18 and had repaid the signing on fee, appeared at Twickenham.

History repeated itself when a Welshman played on with a dislocated shoulder. Gerwyn Williams remembers: 'I tackled their wing, Woodward, who weighed about 15 st., the same way I had tackled Fitzpatrick in the New Zealand game, but this time Bleddyn wasn't there to help. I knew the shoulder had gone as soon as it happened', he still winces at the memory, 'and Woodward scored. The doctor did not want me to go back on to the field, but Rex Willis had been very badly concussed and if I hadn't gone back, we would have been down to 13 men. We were struggling badly, with Cliff having to play scrum-half. Taking the high ball was a bit of a problem, as I couldn't move anything. I played the whole second half and retired from rugby at the end of the match.'

Gwyn Rowlands scored Wales's try, but it is not an entirely happy memory: 'I fell over in the corner, but I'm very dubious that I touched it down. With television replays today, I doubt that it would have been given. I told Ivor Jones, the touch judge, that I wasn't sure I'd scored and he told me not to say anything. If I had, I've little doubt the referee would have given a scrum. It was my only try for Wales, but I've always felt rather guilty about it. That said, the referee had an off day and disallowed a perfectly good try for us by Rees Stephens, while they should probably have had another try, but Sid Judd kicked the ball out of Woodward's hands as he went to touch down. It was all rather chaotic. Cliff was in trouble with the front row, who said he was putting the ball in on the wrong side. I started the game on the wing, but spent some time at centre when Glyn John went to outside-half, then at full-back. I was criticised after the game for being out of position, which seemed rather unkind.'

Gerwyn Williams was not the only victim of the 9–6 defeat. John Gwilliam, Roy John and Dai Davies were dropped from the pack and, with 59 caps between them, had all played for Wales for the last time. Gwilliam says: 'It was the end of an era, but we'd had a good run.'

There could be few complaints about the quality of the succeeding generation. John's place went to Rhys Williams of Llanelli while Davies was succeeded at hooker by Bryn Meredith of Newport, who had appeared in neither of the pre-Christmas trials and propped for his club against the All Blacks only a few weeks before his Wales debut. Between them they would accumulate fifty-seven caps and five Lions tours.

Wales continued to be the strongest of the home nations, winning the remaining three matches in 1954 to share the title with England and France. They also managed four different captains in five matches during the season – Bleddyn Williams giving way to Rees Stephens, who was succeeded in turn by Rex Willis and Ken Jones. Three wins out of four was their lot again in 1955 and 1956, producing first a championship shared with the French, then an outright title. There were, though, no more Triple Crowns until 1965, with captain and scrum-half Clive Rowlands kicking his team to success and opponents to distraction, and no Grand Slam until 1971.

By then, of course, the men of 1953 were long gone. None lasted quite as long as Ian Clarke, although as many as five were in the Wales team as late as the defeats by England and Scotland in 1957. Two were still around to face the next touring team, Australia, in 1958, but nobody quite made it to the 1960s as an international. Five of the team who beat New Zealand went on the 1955 Lions tour of South Africa, all playing some part in a Test series in which the Lions played some of the most brilliant rugby seen from a British team and drew the series 2–2: at that time their best-ever result against the Springboks or All Blacks.

Their subsequent careers are in intriguing contrast to their New Zealand counterparts. If one postwar Welsh archetype was the miner's son who achieved upward mobility through teaching, another – sometimes the same person – was the teacher who moved on into another career. Of the five teachers originally selected to play against New Zealand the two public school masters continued in the profession, while the three who taught in state schools all went on to business careers. The board director of a Financial Times Stock Exchange 100 company is neatly balanced by the team's full-time trade union official.

The other striking trend is the move into media work. Sometimes seen as a modern phenomenon, the ex-player writer was in fact well established by 1953, with veterans like Gabe, Dai Gent and the 1920s England player L.J. Corbett among those who reported on the All Blacks. Three of the team who beat New Zealand were to enjoy long careers as rugby writers for national newspapers, although none was ever wholly reliant on journalism for a living, while a fourth was to become a major figure at the BBC. Only one of this Wales team was to play a significant role in rugby administration, and he was following a family tradition.

Nine are still alive in the summer of 2004 – six living in Wales and three in England. Bleddyn Williams turned 81 in February 2004 and lives in the Cardiff suburb of Llanishen. He was to win only two more caps, finishing with a total of 22 that staggers his contemporaries when they consider the totals accumulated by modern players. 'Stoker' Williams says, 'Bleddyn would have had 80 caps nowadays.' While injury ruled him out against England, the selectors chose not to recall him when he was fit to play against Ireland and France, and his return was delayed until the final match of the season, a 15–3 win over Scotland chiefly remembered as the last international (save a visit by Tonga in 1997) at Swansea. At the start of the following season, he was back as captain – Wales's fifth leader in six matches – against England at Cardiff. Wales scraped home by 3–0 in the snow and mud that so often bedevilled this fixture in January, and made Wales active campaigners for the rotation of Five Nations fixtures. Even so, Williams – who admitted in his autobiography that he had not played well, but argued that the conditions were not really playable – was dropped again. The conclusion to his club career, on the same ground a few months later, was happier as he was chaired off after 283 games and 185 tries for Cardiff.

He was the first of the team to turn to journalism, joining the *Sunday People* and writing on rugby for 32 years: 'I always enjoyed it, although once the paper went tabloid the lack of space could be frustrating,' he says. Both as a writer and a broadcaster, he expected succeeding generations to uphold the standards he had set himself. Part of the international match day routine for Welsh rugby fans during the 1970s was the post mortem conducted on Radio Wales by Bleddyn Williams and Clem Thomas in which the afternoon's performance was subjected to forensic criticism and, even if the match had been won (it normally had been), numerous points for improvement identified. Days when they found little to criticise were rare.

He remembers: 'I never minded press criticism provided I felt it was objective, so my view was that you should tell the listeners what you felt about the game and why. Players like David Watkins and Barry John told me that they appreciated what I wrote and said and that they had learnt from it. Players did not generally object. They knew that Clem and I had played ourselves and that we understood the game.'

Journalism supplemented a career in business. He moved on from the Penarth coach firm to spend 20 years with GKN Steel and concluded his working life as Marketing Manager for Wales for the building company George Wimpey. His immense rugby fame – in a society where, perhaps in compensation for the paucity of surnames, the supreme celebrity is to be known simply by your christian name, nobody has been in any doubt for the last half-century who 'Bleddyn' is – did help his business career: 'It gets you through the door and it did me no harm that I continued to broadcast a lot. It meant that I was still noticed,' he says.

His fame has endured. He is the one pre-television age player routinely chosen when either public or press are asked to nominate all-time Wales XVs. Of comparable staying power is a friendship with Dr Jack Matthews, partner in a spectacularly effective complementary centre combination for Cardiff, Wales and the Lions – the two invariably to be seen together at Wales matches or in the bar at the Cardiff Athletic Club. He has shown a similar ability to retain friendships in New Zealand – citing such names as J.B. Smith, Fred Allen and Ron Hemi. He says: 'I've had a marvellous welcome every time I've been there, starting with the 1950 Lions tour.' He points to going to New Zealand for the 1987 World Cup as one of his happiest journalistic memories. Cardiff's remarkable victory – and the tradition of annual anniversary reunions maintained to this day (perhaps still more remarkable is that Bob Stuart as captain of the losing tourists often calls from New Zealand to pass on best wishes) – perhaps inevitably bulks a little larger in his memories: 'A better game, one that we won rather than their losing,' but the feat of captaining club and country to beat the All Blacks within the space of a month remains, among Welshmen, his alone.

He was the first postwar British player to publish a book of memoirs, *Rugger My Life* (1956), only the second Welsh player following Rowe Harding to do so. He commented on page 37 that the actor Richard Burton had possibilities as a player. Burton would later write: 'one of the curious phenomena of my library is that when you take out Bleddyn's autobiography from the shelves it automatically opens at the page mentioned above'.

Burton's school friend Gerwyn Williams turned 80 in April 2004 and lives in the Suffolk wool town of Clare. He felt he had no alternative to end his career as abruptly as he did after his injury against

England: 'I was 29 and by that time my career as a teacher was more important to me than playing rugby. I had a family to worry about and there was the psychological fact that while when you first play it is all new and exciting, and you are caught up in the sounds of the crowd and the emotions of the game, by the third or fourth year that part of it has gone.'

Nor were there ever any regrets: 'I enjoyed coaching more than I did playing,' he explains. He also became well known for his three coaching books: *Tackle Rugby This Way* (1957), *Modern Rugby* (1964) and *Schoolboy Rugby* (1966). He remains unclear about the fate of a Spanish translation of the frequently reissued and updated *Tackle Rugby*, intended for the Argentinian market, but with the unfortunate publication date of 1982. The books were not, he admits, the product of any deep-seated literary urge: 'I hated writing, but I was in my early 30s, still had not got a car and could see no other way of earning the money, so I made myself go into our dining room and write.'

Tackle Rugby's success inspired a series on other activities, while he was also asked to present rugby coaching programmes in *Seeing Sport*, a series run by newly established independent television: 'I was paid the huge sum of £25 for a 25-minute programme. I remember one occasion when I had three groups of boys from my school Whitgift – 11 year olds, 15 year olds and 18 year olds. Each group had to demonstrate passing the ball from scrum-half out to the wing. If a pass had gone down, the sequence of the programme would have been disturbed, but they were marvellous – not a pass went astray.'

He also proved himself an innovator in developing coaching equipment – the carpenter at Whitgift constructed scrummaging machines to his design, which, at £25 each, found a lively market from first-class clubs, and he also devised a tackle bag. He believes he was among the first coaches to question the practice of having the winger throw in at the lineout – his preferred solution was the blind side wing-forward: 'It was silly to have the fastest player on the field throwing in, and if the blind side threw in, he was on the right side if a ruck formed. I cannot see nowadays why it has to be the hooker. If one of the props can throw in better, why not him instead?'

His school teams experimented with putting 11 or 13 men into the scrum near the opponents' line – a tactic used against Wales by the

Canadians in the 1987 World Cup, so it may not be coincidental that Whitgift used it on a trip to British Columbia in the early 1970s. The success of his Whitgift teams – they beat Llandovery College 30–0 not long before Carwyn James, who coached their opponents, was appointed coach of the 1971 British Lions – and the Old Boys teams who reached the Twickenham stage of the Middlesex Sevens seven years running, was noticed. He was asked to coach London Welsh in the Sevens and became the first coach of Cambridge University: 'Oxford wrote to the RFU to complain. I went up for two years, at my own expense, and had some excellent players – Gerald Davies and two England half-backs Jacko Page and Roger Shackleton. But I wasn't allowed to go to the dinner after the Varsity match because I wasn't a graduate of Oxford or Cambridge.'

The only real disappointment, though, was that he was never asked to coach in Wales: 'I had plenty of invitations from elsewhere, but nothing from Wales. I had the same feeling that I had as a player – that if you weren't in Wales, you were an outsider and very easily forgotten.' He was delighted by Wales's brief late 1990s spell in exile at Wembley – infinitely more accessible from Suffolk.

He taught maths as well as PE: 'It was a good combination, and inevitably as I got older I did more maths and less PE', and was delighted to find that at least one pupil had registered his eminence as a player: 'A class were asked to name three famous mathematicians. One boy said, "Euclid, Pythagoras and Mr Williams" and when asked why me explained that I had played rugby for Wales. It was rather nice to be classed with Euclid and Pythagoras.'

Ken Jones, who turned 82 in December 2003, still lives in Newport. He is in poor health following a stroke, and was the one surviving player physically unable to be interviewed. In spite of being the veteran of the team who beat New Zealand, only two of his teammates had more caps still to come. He equalled Dicky Owen's all-time Wales record in the final match of the 1954 season and went on to become briefly the world's most-capped rugby player (the record was taken by Jack Kyle within a year), taking his total to 44 with his final appearance against Scotland at Murrayfield in 1957. He remained the most-capped Welshman for 20 years before being overtaken by Gareth Edwards, while his record for a winger survived until overtaken by Ieuan Evans in 1995.

In one sense, though, 19 December 1953 was the end for Ken Jones. While he played 13 more internationals, the try made by the Bounce of the Century was his 16th and last for Wales. Their inability to get the ball to him – something to which he was well accustomed from playing for Newport, for whom he scored only twenty-seven tries in a five-year spell – became something of a national joke. The essayist A.A. Thomson suggested that he might carry plates reading 'running in, please pass'.

Gareth Griffiths was, however, to find that this semi-unemployment was not wholly unwelcome. Aware of the way in which Wales were wasting such an immense asset, he resolved, as the centre playing alongside Jones against Scotland at Swansea in 1954, to make sure that he saw plenty of the ball: 'It was a nice day and we had plenty of ball in the first 20 minutes. I made sure it got to Ken early, but he wasn't making much impression on the Scots. Eventually he said to me, "For **** sake Gareth, either kick it or have a go yourself."'

His speed remained undiminished – in 1954, he won a bronze medal for Wales at the Commonwealth Games in Vancouver, running the fastest 220 yards of his life at the age of 32. Four years later, when the games came to Cardiff and the athletics finals were run at the Arms Park, he was both Welsh team manager and the central figure of the opening ceremony as the chosen carrier of ceremonial baton into the stadium: 'Forward pass, Ken,' shouted a spectator as he handed it over.

He also combined the main career trends of the team – leaving teaching and going into journalism. While his main work was the tyre business he ran in Newport for many years, he was also a rugby writer for the *Sunday Express*. Gareth Edwards described him in the late 1980s: 'From whichever angle you view him, the athleticism is still there: the lean frame, the tapering build, the long legs.' He went with Bleddyn Williams to attend one of the reunions held in New Zealand by the 1953 All Blacks. Bob Stuart still talks appreciatively of his description of his famous try at Auckland in 1950: 'Sixty yards of green field ahead of me and not a single black shirt in view.'

Gareth Griffiths, the one player who might have given Ken Jones a decent race on the track, turned 72 in November 2003 and lives in Penarth, a few miles outside Cardiff. After being a regular in 1953 and 1954 – and scoring a try in the Barbarians farewell against the All

Blacks which he later nominated as his personal favourite from a career that brought seventy-four tries for Cardiff and five for Wales – he fell victim to the vagaries of the Welsh selection. He was recalled for the final two matches of the 1955 season and did well enough to win selection as an early replacement on the Lions tour of South Africa. There he played well enough to be selected for three of the four Test matches, came home and was ignored for the whole of 1956 before winning a last recall for the first two matches of the 1957 season. The Lions tour remains an outstanding memory: 'It was a marvellous holiday, four months away from June to September. The British Embassy staged some of the best parties I've ever been to. It was a great education at the same time. Remember I was still only 24 years old.'

He had done his teaching practice at Tonypandy Primary School, where his impressionable pupils included Dai Smith, later joint-author of the WRU's official history. Smith recalled: 'His freehand chalk sketch of a map of Canada, with lakes and rivers effortlessly drawn on the board, impressed me even more than receiving a pass from him on the Mid-Rhondda Athletic Ground.'

Canada was to make an even greater impression on Griffiths: 'I went with the Barbarians to Canada in 1957 and was duty officer the day we visited the factory of Canada Air, then the biggest overseas maker of aeroplanes for Britain. The personnel manager was very nervous about having these rowdy rugby players visiting his factory, but it went so well, with the players meeting the people who worked there – these were the days when you could emigrate to Canada or Australia on a £10 passage, so there were plenty of expatriates, quite a few of them Welsh – that he invited me back for lunch the following day. I went back, met him and talked and came away thinking, "He's got a good job." I hadn't heard of personnel managers before – in the Rhondda the colliery managers did everything. I came back to Britain and started going to classes at the tech.'

Three years later he was working for the British Steel Corporation at Llanwern, then moved to join the Thomson organisation – first with the *Western Mail and Echo* in Cardiff, then from 1967 Times Newspapers in London: 'I was the first personnel manager after Thomson bought the *Sunday Times* and had to try to merge two very different institutions. Harold Evans, who was editing the *Sunday Times*, was a great friend. William Rees-Mogg of *The Times* was not!'

After joining Warner Lambert USA in 1969, much of his work in a series of companies, culminating in main board membership of FTSE 100 company Amersham, was abroad: 'I worked as a manager in Mexico, Brazil and France – not for very long periods, but they tended to put me in where someone had died or there was another unexpected reason for a gap. I think it was because I built up trust – without that you're dead in the personnel game.'

It meant that he drifted away from rugby: 'At Amersham, I often went to Japan, leaving on Saturday morning for a series of meetings starting on the Monday, and would return the following Saturday. There were a lot of trips like that and when you are away so often it is hard to keep in touch. I'm not a good spectator anyway.' His presence at the 1953 Cardiff team's annual anniversary reunion was often via a message phoned over several time zones.

He does, though, think that rugby, and in particular touring, helped his career. Part of the 'great education' of the Lions tour to South Africa was days as duty officer: 'I had to get the team to the airport on a Sunday morning, after we'd beaten the Springboks on the Saturday and hadn't been to bed. I had to shower, put a suit on and make sure everybody got to the airport. That sort of thing was good experience and I'm sure I was a better manager for it.'

He returned to Wales in 1993 and finished his working life with two years as executive director of the Institute of Welsh Affairs, a think-tank. He is a board member of the Civic Trust for Wales and a trustee of the Welsh Rugby Union's charitable fund, still highly active and often away. He downplays any suggestions that his return to the field against the All Blacks was heroic, or even especially brave, but did tell Gerald Davies: 'It was a day when I may have changed from being a boy to something approaching manhood.'

Gwyn Rowlands, who as an international debutant also underwent a rite of passage against the All Blacks, turned 75 in December 2003 and lives in his native Berkhamsted, where he returned in 1958 to join his father in general medical practice. He was a collateral victim of Gerwyn Williams' injury against England. He says: 'I had no illusions that I was in that side for anything other than the place kicking, or at least that some ability to kick goals certainly influenced that selection.' Aside from earning Rowlands some rather harsh criticism for his spell as emergency full-back, Williams' injury opened the way for Viv Evans of Neath – another from the Book of Eccentric Selection in that he was 34 and had not figured in any of the trials – a highly competent kicker. Rowlands was picked to play against Scotland at Swansea and then, when it was snowed off, dropped for the following match against Ireland: 'They picked Ray Williams of Llanelli. Thirty or forty years later I found myself sitting next to Ray and he thanked me for the letter I had sent wishing him luck.' Recalled purely as a wing against France – Evans was kicking everything and would total twenty-five points from his three caps – he had, on his own admission, a poor game. A further single-game recall against France in 1956 was similarly unhappy and his international career ended with four caps.

Rowlands strongly suspected that the selectors were embarrassed by his near-England experience of 1949 and would rather not have picked him. The New Zealand journalist John Hayhurst recorded that the All Blacks rated him very highly as a winger. Another player might have been angry, but Rowlands – like Tanner, his nearest professional equivalent in the All Black team – was relaxed about it: 'I was always a bit of a fatalist. If it is to be, it will be. It gives you a degree of immunity when things like this happen.'

His happiest rugby experience was not even in the first-class game: 'It was the season [1954–55] when Sid Judd was captain of Cardiff. He fell ill and the captain of the Rags was promoted to the first team. I had been away as a ship's surgeon and they asked me if I would take over the Rags. It was the happiest six months of rugby I ever had. There were three or four internationals in the team and plenty of experience. We played Valley sides and normally had superiority in the pack, so we could throw the ball around with gay abandon.' Among the Rags was the irrepressible Stan Bowes, also encountered during the working week as he was a storeman at Whitchurch Hospital. Rowlands smiles at the memory of Bowes being quizzed about his qualifications to play for Welsh Academicals and answering: 'I was at the College of Knowledge.'

When working as an obstetrician meant he could not guarantee to be available every weekend, he joined Glamorgan Wanderers, who were delighted to have him as an occasional player. After returning to Berkhamsted, he joined the nearby Camelots club: 'I carried on for a couple of seasons, but never had the time to train properly – and you need more training not less as you get older. Injuries take longer to heal if you are not fit – and some opponents were always out to get you if they found you were an international.' He took up golf, and has been captain and president of his club.

He stayed in general practice until the early 1970s: 'It was pretty stressful for me and for my wife, and I had a minor heart attack in 1971. I joined the Wellcome Trust – who were in Berkhamsted then – as an medical advisor. I stayed for 18 years, until they merged with Glaxo, and enjoyed it. They had operations in India, Pakistan and East Africa, and I had carte blanche to go to conferences anywhere.' A subsequent year screening immigrants at Heathrow was rather less pleasant.

He continues to travel regularly to Cardiff for internationals and further afield to see his family. Two of his three daughters live in Perth, Western Australia. The older, Jane, was born in Cardiff. 'My wife is Welsh, we were living there and after what had happened to me I was determined there should be no doubt over her nationality.' She played lacrosse for Wales and was so enthused by Perth when she visited as manager of the Great Britain team that she chose to emigrate and is now a school principal there.

He retains warm memories of his international debut: 'I was lucky, I was in form and in the right place at the right time.' There are more tangible souvenirs as well: 'My father put all the telegrams in an album. I didn't swap my jersey as I wanted to keep it, and the All Blacks were very kind – they gave me a jersey anyway, but I can't remember whose it was.'

If Gwyn Rowlands' career peaked in 1953, that of Cliff Morgan, who turned 73 in April 2003 and lives in Marylebone, London, had greater heights to come. He was a fixture for Wales and Cardiff until 1958, finishing with 29 caps – a record for a Wales outside-half finally eclipsed 38 years later by Neil Jenkins. In consequence, Carwyn James, whose brilliance as a player was complemented by arguably the sharpest Welsh rugby intellect of the century, was confined to only two caps. Instead of bemoaning the misfortune of timing that made them contemporaries, James conceded that the selectors got it right, saying: 'I had to think carefully about what I did on the field. Cliff was different. He did everything naturally and quickly, instinctively and expertly. He was a much better player than I was.'

Yet perhaps better than any of Morgan's performances for Wales was a brilliant sequence of displays on the British Lions tour of South Africa in 1955. He played in all four Tests and was captain in the third as the Lions drew a spectacular series 2–2. Conditions in South Africa were perfect for his type of running rugby, although he characteristically attempts to deflect credit elsewhere: 'We played beautiful rugby because of Jeff Butterfield at centre. We didn't have a coach or doctor – but on the last Lions tour there were 18 people in Lions blazers in addition to the players.' Off the pitch, he was, as J.B.G. Thomas put it, 'the radioactive particle around which the whole social side of the tour revolved'.

He retired in 1958 with two unfulfilled ambitions: 'I would love to have played rugby in New Zealand, and to have played rugby league for Wigan – to prove that I could have done it.' New Zealand at least was within reach, with a Lions tour for which he would have been a near-certainty – possibly as captain – due in 1959. Wavell Wakefield, the great England forward of the 1920s – by 1958 MP for the London district where Morgan now lives – wrote to attempt to dissuade him from retiring, but, as he has recalled, 'We had got to the point where I could not afford to carry on playing.'

Two years later he joined the BBC as sports organiser for Wales. He has said, 'I owe everything to rugby. It gives you a sense of proportion, of understanding people, of fair play and of discipline – which is the most important thing in broadcasting, in rugby and in life generally.' A BBC career lasting nearly 40 years was most closely identified with sport. His voice, not long recovered following a devastating stroke in 1971, provided the evocative soundtrack for Gareth Edwards' extraordinary try for the Barbarians against the All Blacks at Cardiff in 1973. For 11 years to 1998, he was host of the warmly nostalgic *Sport on Four*. You do not, however, attain a job like editor of *Grandstand* (1963–6) or Head of Outside Broadcasts (1976–87), never mind the editorship of a serious current affairs programme like *This Week* (1966–9) unless your skills go considerably beyond darting runs at the Arms Park, a beguiling voice and a poet's ear for the right word. His autobiography *Beyond the Fields of Play* (1996), co-written with Geoffrey Nicholson, underlines that depth and range.

While his last senior game was played for the Barbarians in South

Africa in 1958, there were subsequent charity matches. He has warm memories of going to Upper Cwmtwrch to play outside local hero Clive Rowlands, who was comparable in wit and warmth, but with a rather different playing style: 'I borrowed a pair of boots from Clive and said to him afterwards, "I wanted to run, but the boots wanted to kick!"'

He has retained extensive links with old teammates and opponents: 'It isn't worth it if you don't keep up. Sitting in the club with Bleddyn, Jack and Gareth or any of the other boys you laugh and talk and remember. That togetherness is very important. It carried us through when we were one man short and we said, "OK, so we've got to play without him." And when Gareth came back we said, "Are you OK – don't worry, we'll look after you", although we couldn't look after anybody.'

Beating the All Blacks ranks among his two most important memories from playing international rugby: 'The other was the Lions test against the Springboks at Ellis Park when we won 23–22. There were 95,000 there and it was quite unbelievable.'

Morgan's 'better half', Rex Willis, died in January 2000 at the age of 75. He played two more seasons, retiring at the end of 1955 with 21 caps. One of Wales's four captains in 1954, he led them again against Scotland in 1955. He played for Cardiff during the next two seasons, gradually giving way to Lloyd Williams, younger brother of Bleddyn. After retiring from the game, Willis ran the family cinema business and continued to turn up to big matches in a sports car. News of his death was broken to former Cardiff teammates attending the funeral of John Nelson, another of the 1953 team. Gwyn Rowlands remembers: 'There was a stunned silence and then a voice from the back of the room: "We are all in God's departure lounge."'

Courtenay Meredith turned 77 in September 2003 and lives in Porthcawl. He continued to strike terror into opposing front rows, captaining Neath in 1955–56 and playing for Wales until 1957. He won his 14th and last cap in the defeat by Scotland that was also Ken Jones's last game. In the 1955 Lions tour of South Africa, he linked with Bryn Meredith and Stoker Williams in an all-Welsh front row that played all four Tests and out-scrummaged the Springboks, previously regarded as almost invincible up front, in the third Test victory at Pretoria. Off the field, he continued his career as a production engineer with British Steel, running a rolling mill at the Abbey Works.

He has withdrawn from rugby, declining invitations to reunions and social functions, and was the one player to decline – although taking the trouble to write a courteous note – to be interviewed for this book. In his letter, he recalled 'all members of the 53 Welsh side were well motivated, technically competent in their positions, physically fit and spatially aware on the pitch. Charming, amusing and witty off it.' He is a member of Royal Porthcawl Golf Club, where, Tony Lewis has written: 'It is impossible to convey to members . . . that the slim, gentle fellow in spectacles, sipping a small whisky across the room, is the same fellow who ground down Springbok prop forwards. The body weight has gone. I tell them to look into the eyes.'

Dai Davies, one of the trio of veteran forwards discarded after the England game, died aged 78 in Taunton, his home for more than half a century, in November 2003. He acknowledged the quality of his successor Bryn Meredith, but said: 'I used to be able to sort him out.' His life in the police continued much as before – on the beat in Taunton, with the occasion excursion to Weston-Super-Mare when holiday crowds created pressures on the police there – playing for and later supporting the police team: 'I always followed them and after I stopped playing became more or less the coach.'

Never promoted, he said with some pride: 'I was just an ordinary bobby on the beat.' He retired from the police in the mid-1970s following heart trouble, and subsequently worked in the local motor tax office, the county archives and the road transport department. While proud of his Welshness, he watched the current England team with more than academic interest. He knew assistant coach Andy Robinson, whose mother lived nearby in Taunton, from his early childhood. The physical resilience of his days as pitman, hooker and beat bobby remained – he survived being struck by a car on a visit to the Rhondda when well into his 70s. The condition of the car is not recorded. He remembered the 1953 All Blacks well: 'They were big, strong and hard, and Ron Hemi was a hard boy.'

Stoker Williams turned 74 in November 2003 and lives, as he has done all his life, in Gowerton. His current home, much of which he built himself after he was dropped by Wales in 1956, is about 100 yards from where he lived as a child. His 22 caps were won consecutively and at the end of the 1955 Lions tour of South Africa, when he played in all four Tests and led the pack in the Test victory at Pretoria, J.B.G. Thomas speculated that he might break the Scot John Bannerman's then-record of 37 consecutive caps as a forward.

Shortly after the new season – in which he was captaining Swansea – began, he went down with appendicitis (as had club, country and Lions-teammate Clem Thomas while in South Africa). He remembers: 'I came back too soon, played badly against Ireland and was dropped. It was my fault for rushing back.' His replacement was Rex Richards, the Maesteg high-diver who later worked as a Hollywood stunt man and appeared in *Wild Women of Wonga*, a perennial on lists of the worst films ever made, who was winning his only cap.

Williams was never capped again: 'I probably could have been picked again, but I was asked to play for Glamorgan against Monmouthshire at Pontypool – county games were often used as trials. The opposing prop was Ray Prosser. I rang Ray and said, "I'm not coming up to Pontypool on a Tuesday night to knock hell out of you," but if I'd played I might have got back into the Wales team.' He played for Swansea until 1960, retired and joined the committee: 'The year after, they persuaded me to come out of retirement to play against the South Africans. I retired again and then decided to stay away from St Helens – I knew that if I was there they'd ask me to play again and I'd had enough.'

He stayed away for around 20 years, but is now a stalwart of the former players' association – an unlucky coincidence of timing meant that their 2002 dinner was on the same night, before Wales played the All Blacks at Cardiff, that surviving members of the victors of 1953 were honoured by the Welsh Rugby Writers: 'They'd never forgive me in Swansea if they found out that I'd missed our do to go to a dinner in Cardiff,' he said. He is a regular at All Whites matches and a robust critic: 'I pay to go into matches and the players are professionals, so I'm entitled to criticise,' he says.

In his working life, he left the Gowerton works when they closed in 1959 and moved to the Abbey Works. Three years later he was elected full-time convenor of the Boilermakers Union (now part of the General, Municipal and Boilermakers Union) and stayed in the job for 30 years. He remains an active trade unionist and branch official, going every week to regional meetings in the GMB building in Cardiff and was awarded the British Empire Medal for services to trade unionism. He is also a governor of the infants school that he left nearly 60 years ago. His son teaches physics at Edinburgh University.

He has limited detailed memories of the All Black match: 'Just following the ball at 100 miles per hour. You don't remember much beyond that.' He has, though, no doubt where it stands in his memories: 'The greatest thing was to go on a Lions tour. But beating New Zealand is right up with it, as was captaining Swansea.'

Roy John died suddenly in September 1981, aged 55. Like Ian Clarke, he died shortly after watching a match – in his case Neath v. Glamorgan Wanderers at The Gnoll. Like Dai Davies, he was dropped after the defeat by England early in 1954, ending a run of 19 consecutive caps. While he played several more years for Neath, his chances of an international recall were limited both by the form of Rhys Williams and the ban on blocking in the lineout, introduced by the International Board in 1954. While his extraordinary jumping ability was his main weapon in the lineout, he had been aided, as a comparatively slight forward, by blockers. Towards the end of his life he was quoted as arguing that blockers had preventing barging by opponents: 'When the International Board ruled otherwise, barging came into its own and there is more of it today than there ever was before.' He was still working in the contract section at BP Llandarcy when he died.

His friend and fellow-lock Rees Stephens died in February 1998 aged 75. Regarded as a veteran in 1953, Stephens, like Ken Jones, kept his Wales place for longer than most of his younger teammates, winning another 13 caps. He was to win more caps after his 30th birthday than before, his 32nd and last – then a record for a Welsh forward – a few days before his 35th birthday at the end of the 1957 Five Nations season. He became captain in 1955 and was acclaimed as 'ce vieux renard Rees Stephens' after his best-ever display for his country deprived the French of their first outright championship and Grand Slam in 1955.

In spite of playing under John Gwilliam and Bleddyn Williams, Stoker Williams considers Stephens the best captain he ever played for: 'A great captain. He'd never ask you to do anything he wouldn't do himself,' says Stoker. He might have led the 1955 Lions to South Africa but for another piece of selectorial strangeness: a ban on players over the age of 30 which also ruled out Bleddyn Williams and Ken Jones.

While still an active player, he had started rugby at Neath YMCA, creating the basis for the Neath Athletic club he chaired for more than 40 years. After his retirement, he became a member of the Welsh Rugby Committee and a selector. *The Times*, in an obituary notice more worthy of his achievements than the five paragraphs that were all the Swansea *Evening Post* devoted to an authentic local hero, recorded that unlike many selectors he enjoyed the company of players, but that as an administrator 'he tended to stay away from the limelight' and so did not follow his father as President of the WRU. He had run a number of businesses in Neath and the Neath Valley, including a hotel and a café. In the 1955 Neath floods, he was praised for organising a party from the YMCA to open a mobile canteen at night.

Sid Judd, the man who scored tries for both Cardiff and Wales against the All Blacks and gave Cliff Morgan 'an impression of indestructibility', proved all too destructible, dying of leukaemia in February 1959 at the age of 30. He played five more games for Wales, the last the 14–8 defeat by Scotland in 1955 that ended the Scots' four-year losing run. In the same season, he led a Cardiff team that started with a 22-match unbeaten run, but was struck down by the illness that ended his rugby and eventually his life. When no longer well enough to play, he joined the Cardiff committee and served as a club selector.

John Gwilliam turned 81 in February 2004, five days after Bleddyn Williams, and lives at Llanfairfechan on the North Wales coast. He too was left out for good after the England match, and was effectively lost to rugby in Wales. He explains: 'I was never much of a committee man, although perhaps I should have been.' He published a coaching book in 1958 and became headmaster of Birkenhead school in 1963, a post he held until his retirement 25 years later. He and his wife Pegi, a great-niece of David Lloyd George, returned to Wales after he retired.

Like Gerwyn Williams he is cut off by sheer distance from the mainstream of the Welsh game, although he did attend the Welsh Rugby Writers dinner in honour of the 1953 teams in November 2002, combining it with the launch of *The Gwilliam Seasons*, a book by David Parry-Jones explicitly intended to ensure that the players of this era and in particular their captain are not forgotten. He enjoys modern rugby, although, like most players of his era, he finds the running commentary provided by the referees both mystifying and intrusive. While remembering his delight at victory in 1953, he says that the All Blacks left much less of an impression both as a team and individuals than the 1951 Springboks. 'Hennie Muller, dear, dear,' he says – remembered awe at the South African's genius combined with that engaging chuckle.

When Clem Thomas died in September 1996, aged 67, it was his cross-kick from 1953 that most obituarists and headline-writers chose to highlight from a life of ceaseless activity. He was the last of the men of 1953 to play international rugby, bowing out at the end of the 1959 Five Nations season with 26 caps – a record for a Welsh flanker, taken in 1966 by Haydn Morgan, a teammate in his two seasons as captain. He went with the Lions to South Africa in 1955, went down with appendicitis but recovered to play in the final two Tests. Ken Jones recalled him as 'one of the greatest flank forwards of the postwar era'.

He continued to run the family butchers' business. Other enterprises included the famous No Sign Bar in Wind Street, Swansea – a business happily combining his conviviality with expertise in and enthusiasm for good food and drink. He was a Liberal candidate for Gower at the 1974 General Election and for Wales Mid in the 1979 European election.

It was, though, as a rugby journalist and broadcaster – working for more than 30 years for *The Observer* from 1959 and as regular international-night sparring partner of Bleddyn Williams during the 1970s Golden Age and the harder years that followed – that he continued to make most impact. A trenchant, often ferocious critic of the Welsh Rugby Union, his hinterland of other interests and expertise enabled him to look beyond the merely on-field issues to wider implications. It was this that made him a campaigner for the siting of what became the Millennium Stadium at Bridgend, where it could act as a focus for the revival of depressed deindustrialising regions, and a vocal opponent of contact with South Africa when the Welsh Rugby Union was still all too happy to play games with apartheid.

He was occasionally impatient of the routine disciplines of journalism. One particular personal memory is of hearing him in conversation with a harassed sub-editor on the *Observer* sports desk one Saturday in the late 1980s. 'But Clem, you've written 650 words and we only wanted 450,' said the sub. 'I know,' said Clem, 'but it was such a great game.' Though not wholly appreciated by a sub-editor with a deadline and 200 words too many, that enthusiasm was always a trademark along with a generosity and warmth I greatly appreciated as a novice writer, flattered that someone of Clem's standing should take the trouble to get to know and encourage me.

He was completing the proofs of his history of the British Lions when he died. It is a matter of great regret that someone whose experience and knowledge of the game was quite so broadranging – Clem seems never to have maintained anything so journalistically mundane as a contacts book, he just knew everybody in the game and where to find them when he needed to – never wrote his memoirs. He will, though, be permanently commemorated in the *New Dictionary of National Biography* and a biography by the Swansea-based historian Peter Stead.

As Peter Stead has pointed out, France was a running theme in his life, with his first and last internationals in Paris and a second home in the Medoc where he made such an impression that he appears as a character in the novel *Adios* by Kleber Haedens (1974). A heart attack at an international match in Paris in 1993 was a warning that even his formidable constitution might baulk at a hectic lifestyle. There was no perceptible subsequent slowing down. That might have been prudent, but it would not have been Clem.

Glyn Davies, the man who should have played against the All Blacks, turned 76 in November 2003 and lives in Fairwarp in East Sussex. He did eventually get his cap, but not without a few more adventures on the way – pneumonia ruled him out of a possible cap for Wales against Ireland. Then in 1955 he was picked to play against England, and the game was postponed due to bad weather: 'I got a call from the BBC to ask me to go on *Sportsview*. When I got there, Rex Alston asked me, "Glyn, will you ever get a cap?" I was beginning to wonder myself.'

It happened the following week, in an icy Arms Park swamp all too typical of the era. Brian Sparks, the other man unlucky not to play in 1953, was the other flanker, while Bleddyn Williams was playing his final match as centre and captain. Davies remembers: 'I did not do well at all.' The first cap was also the last, enabling him to claim when speaking at rugby club dinners that, 'Ken Jones and I had 45 caps between us' and when asked, 'How long did you play for Wales?' to answer, 'About 80 minutes.'

He is philosophical about this. If that single cap is slightly clouded by the possibility that it was awarded for doing the right thing in 1953, what cannot be taken away is that he was one of Wales's chosen 15 to play the All Blacks – the time, more than any other, when the only consideration would be fielding the strongest possible team.

He left teaching in 1956 to join Roneo as a management trainee: 'They told me I'd be staying in the Home Counties. The next thing I knew I was being told that I was starting work on the following Monday in Swansea – two days put up in the Mackworth Arms and then I was on my own. It wasn't where I'd have chosen to go, but I joined Swansea and had a wonderful time in teams led by Stoker Williams and Clem Thomas.' Living in Killay, he also played his brief part in launching Dunvant on the path from the junior ranks to the Premier Division.

Returning to England in the early 1960s, he joined the Chiltern club: 'I was on the touchline watching and a fellow came by and said, "You're a big fellow – do you play?" I explained that I'd played in Wales and he said, "OK, can you play for our seconds next week?" He didn't ask my name but told me to turn up with my boots at 2.30 next Saturday. I thought, as a joke, that I'd wear my Barbarians blazer. The same fellow greeted me, "Ah, there you are. That looks like a Barbarians blazer. Bloody hell *it is* a Barbarians blazer!" I was in the first team the week after.'

He played into his 40s, retiring after a youthful teammate said 'thank you, sir' after he'd won a lineout. A developing business career with 3M took him to South America and the West Indies, and to playing for another country: 'In 1961, I was in Port of Spain, Trinidad, and bumped into someone I'd played with in Sussex. He was a former paratrooper whose family owned banana plantations. He asked me if I could play rugby that evening, which is how I came to play for Trinidad against British Guiana. It was only half an hour each way, but they called it a Test match.' After running operations in Portugal and Nigeria, he ended up on the board of 3M.

The tangible souvenir of the day he nearly played for Wales against the All Blacks has gone: 'At the dinner they very kindly presented me with a miniature ball with the signatures of all the players. Unfortunately, with time the signatures faded away.' But he still remembers long conversations with Bob Scott and Bob Stuart, wonders whether he should not have listened more carefully to Doidge's advocacy of a life in New Zealand, and manages to make a joke out of what at the time was a devastating disappointment: 'I can always claim to have played a vital part in helping Wales beat the All Blacks. When people ask how, I say, "By dropping out!"'

Among the other dramatis personae of 19 December 1953 Peter Cooper, the white-clad referee whose decision to penalise Bill Clark still rankles with the All Blacks, should be more fondly remembered in Wales, and not only because of that penalty. Seven of the twelve international matches he refereed between 1952 and 1957 – a frequency of appointment which shows how well he was regarded – involved Wales. All were won, including the 1957 match in Paris that was his and Rees Stephens' last international. He died suddenly ten weeks later, at the age of forty-two, while on holiday in Falmouth.

His fellow medical man Nathan Rocyn-Jones, who put Gareth Griffiths' shoulder back, went one better than Rees Stephens in that he did emulate his father as president of the WRU, presiding over the union in 1964–65. As incoming president he had proclaimed that the game should be played for enjoyment and that too much emphasis could be placed on technique and tactics – an attitude echoing his own days as a once-capped full-back in the 1920s when Welsh rugby was bereft of both – and fell out with a selection panel that included both Cliff Jones and Rees Stephens. He ended the year congratulating Clive Rowlands' team on a Triple Crown won by the grimmest realpolitik; while 1964 is also remembered as the year when the WRU, impelled by a 24–3 hammering in South Africa, began to embrace rather than resist coaching. He retired to Preston and died in 1984 aged 81.

Journalist J.B.G. Thomas – Bryn to his friends – like McLean launched himself into publishing in 1954 with *On Tour*, a history of touring teams in Britain. It was the first of 30 books he was to write, keeping him just ahead of McLean in productivity if not literary style. In 1955, he too 'broke out of the ruck' when the *Western Mail* sent him on the Lions tour, a trip which produced *Lions on Trek*, the first of his many tour accounts. He retired as assistant editor and sports editor of the *Western Mail* in 1982. His knowledge of rugby was unquestionable and he was hugely productive – Cliff Morgan points out that it was not unusual for him to write 2,500–3,000 words a day. Taking a more charitable view than most journalists of not only the good intentions but also the good sense of rugby officialdom, he was wont – in an echo of the *March of Time* newsreels of his teenage years – to end his books with a proclamation that 'The Game Goes On!' He died in April 1997.

Last but not least among the actors on that day was the venue, Cardiff Arms Park. Whether it too survives in 2004 when the Millennium Stadium occupies much of the same space, but with the pitch turned at an angle of 90 degrees and not a single structure surviving from 1953, is a matter of interpretation. Its demise could even be argued to have come earlier than the total rebuilding of the late 1990s to create the Millennium Stadium – the Arms Park became the National Stadium in 1970, with the completion of the giant new North Stand totally transforming the ground.

The reconstruction of the 1953 ground had begun earlier, with the completion in 1956 of the 12,800 capacity South Stand, built for the 1958 Empire Games. Much more radical change came from the late 1960s. Glamorgan's cricketers left for Sophia Gardens, vacating space rapidly occupied by Cardiff's tidy new ground, which backed on to the new North Stand. The greyhounds went as well, a lease scheduled to last until 1977 bought out early by the WRU. Between 1968 and 1984 the ground was comprehensively remodelled at a cost of £9 million. The double-decker structure of the North Stand was extended around the West end of the ground, backing on to the River Taff, in 1977, and then along the South side – replacing the stand built for the Commonwealth Games less than 30 years earlier, in 1984. Four years earlier, the East Terrace, the last part left uncovered and wholly devoted to standing, had been remodelled. The old wooden scoreboard that had recorded the victories of 1953 and of the 1970s gave way to an electronic display whose tidings were often less welcome.

All of this, in turn, was swept away in 1997 and replaced – after a two-year hiatus for construction during which Wales decamped to Wembley, contriving while there an improbable last-minute victory over England that was simultaneously a home and an away win – by the £121 million, 72,500-seater, sliding-roofed Millennium Stadium, venue for the 1999 World Cup final.

New Zealand paid a visit while Wales were lodging at Wembley and saw the new ground for the first time during the World Cup, two days earlier than they had hoped. Traumatised by France's extraordinary performance in the semi-finals the previous Sunday, they had to play South Africa in a desultory third-place play-off rather than the final they had hoped for and expected.

It was November 2002 before the All Blacks played Wales at the Millennium Stadium. By then the special relationship had been transformed almost as completely as the ground.

CHAPTER 9

FLYING KIWI, SINKING DRAGON:

The End of the Special Relationship?

In 1953, the New Zealand Rugby Union's reaction to defeat was to invite Wales to visit them on tour. None of the British nations had ever gone by itself to another major rugby-playing country. The invitation was vetoed by the International Board, anxious both to protect the British Lions and to ensure that tours did not become too frequent. Instead France – invited to South Africa in 1958, New Zealand in 1961 and a revelation in both – would be the beneficiary of the southern hemisphere unions' desire to diversify their international diet.

Fifty years later, in 2003, New Zealand entertained Wales for the third time. In the mid-1950s a Welsh Test would have filled any ground in New Zealand and incited passions comparable to those stirred by the visit of the 1956 Springboks. In 2003, it was consigned to Hamilton, a well-equipped venue in a rugby-minded town, but still an extremely occasional Test ground. The crowd of 25,200 was not a sell-out.

A week earlier, the All Blacks had played England in Wellington. All 43,000 tickets had been sold within an hour of going on sale. England won 15–13. Wales, playing a slightly weaker All Black team (although weakness is a relative concept when it involves giving a game to reserves of the quality of open-side flanker Marty Holah) went down 55–3. Such a result would once have been regarded as cataclysmic. A 24–3 loss to South Africa nearly 40 years earlier led to an inquiry and a revolution in coaching structures. This result was received with something close to a shrug and relief that it was not even worse. It was simply what we had come to expect during the third phase of the New Zealand–Wales rugby relationship.

The century almost completed since that epic first contest in 1905 divides neatly into half- and quarter-century segments. The first phase ended with Wales's victory in 1953. There were only four Test matches, all in Wales, in that first half-century. Wales won three of them. It was never easy. Each of them might easily have gone the other way, while the one blow-out was New Zealand's victory in 1924. Nevertheless, New Zealand was left in the position of a tennis player who wins one set 6–0 and loses the other three on tie-breaks – not manifestly inferior, but still the loser. Hence its deep desire in 1953 to get Wales back to its place.

Phase two was to last another quarter-century to 1978. Contact was more frequent. There were six Tests, two in New Zealand, plus a match in 1974 which the Welsh Rugby Union found some abstruse reason for declaring unofficial, but still fielded its best available team. Playing in a Wales–New Zealand match ceased to be a once-in-a-lifetime experience. The 1953 tourist Ian Clarke did not win selection for any of the Tests when he returned to Britain in 1963, but three players from the 1963 match – Norman Gale of Wales, Malcolm Dick and Colin Meads of New Zealand – played again in 1967. Ten of that All Black side survived to welcome Wales, which fielded four survivors of its own, to New Zealand in 1969. Dick, Meads and Gale all made their third and fourth appearances. Tours became shorter. Ian Kirkpatrick's 1972–73 All Blacks were the last to experience the traditional full-dress marathon, thirty-two matches spread across four months. Their successors of 1978, last to play all four nations, played eighteen.

This was an era of grinding but rather static New Zealand power, broken only by the brilliance of the 1967 team – coached by Kiwi Fred Allen, who succeeded in reproducing much of the spirit of the fondly remembered forces team. The 'unsmiling giant' image of the era, epitomised by Meads, still tends to inform British perceptions of New Zealand rugby.

New Zealand won every match, narrowly in Wales but massively at home in 1969 when the visitors were afflicted by the virulent combination of perhaps the strongest All Black pack in an era of remarkable strength, contentious home-town refereeing and their own union's secondary identity as the Travel Agents from Hell, cheerfully consigning their players to an unbroken 52-hour journey followed by matches against Taranaki within four days of arrival and New Zealand four days after that.

New Zealanders could have been forgiven for wondering what all the fuss was about as the Welsh went down 19–0 and 33–12 in the two Tests. They were to find out two years later when the British Lions visited. True, it was a Lions and not a Wales side. Players like Irish centre Mike Gibson and lock Willie John McBride made enormous contributions as they became the first Lions team to win a series in New Zealand. Wales, though, was the dominant factor. John Dawes was the first Welshman to captain a Lions team, players like half-backs Gareth Edwards and Barry John, full-back J.P.R. Williams, number 8 Mervyn Davies and wing Gerald Davies – whose conversion from centre to wing had been perhaps the only benefit from the 1969 tour – were the stars of the tour and, perhaps most important of all, the coach was a Welshman, Carwyn James. The 1973 Barbarians–All Blacks match was a glorious coda, the best part of two years on, to their efforts.

At the same time as impressing with their attacking brilliance and will to victory, they brought back impressions of New Zealand rugby as a game of joyless, charmless physicality. James, who toured Britain with a newsreel film of tour highlights, lecturing and answering questions on its lessons, told the story of meeting a teenage boy who was watching youngsters of his age play: 'I asked him why he wasn't playing. He explained that he'd like to play, but he couldn't. He had already been concussed three times.'

This was Wales's second (or third if the early 1950s are to be admitted) Golden Age, producing six championships, six Triple Crowns and four Grand Slams in 11 seasons between 1969 and 1979. They were unbeaten in Five Nations matches at Cardiff from 1968 to 1982. Only France offered a consistent challenge – and they won only three times in eleven meetings.

Still more impressive than their results was the way they played the game, with a style and panache likely to draw a reminiscent smile from any middle-aged rugby fan, irrespective of nationality. This most beguiling of all British rugby teams were the immediate beneficiaries of the liberating rule changes of the late 1950s and 1960s – players born in the late 1940s who had learnt the game when restricted by congested midfields, a strict knock-on law and unlimited touch-kicking, but were then offered the opportunity to express their talents in the open spaces rugby's legislators had created.

They had been liberated in another sense – Barry John, Gareth Edwards and Gerald Davies were all the sons of miners and were able to escape the pit by going into teaching. National health, national insurance and student grants gave the mining districts both unprecedented security and an escape route. West Indian intellectual C.L.R. James may have decried the safety-first mentality of 'Welfare State cricketers', but the Welfare State rugby player was a being of unprecedented brilliance.

Yet Wales could not beat New Zealand. The 1960s All Blacks won at the Arms Park with a little to spare, 6–0 in the tryless clash of 1963 followed by a 13–6 win in 1967 that was devoid of the passion or the excitement of its predecessors, although the 1963 team went down 3–0 at Newport, felled by a drop-goal from John Uzzell, near-suicidal back-row spoiling and All Black hooker John Major's loss of eight strikes against the head.

The matches of the 1970s were to be tighter, but New Zealand still won. Llanelli, who completed the set of Big Four club victories in 1972, winning 9–3 on an afternoon immortalised in song by Max Boyce, a comedian whose immense success in the 1970s was an expression of Welsh rugby's cultural confidence, were the only Welsh team to beat the supreme enemy. It could, perhaps should, have been different. The memory remains of a series of blatant obstructions by the All Blacks in the closing stages of their 19–16 win in 1972, a match now chiefly remembered for its aftermath – the sending home and subsequent disappearance of prop Keith Murdoch, scorer of New Zealand's try, following a violent early-hours incident at the team hotel. In 1978 came Andy Haden's pre-planned dive out of the final lineout and double international Brian McKechnie's last-minute penalty for a 13–12 New Zealand win. The penalty was actually awarded against Wales lock Geoff Wheel for a foul on All Black Frank Oliver – referee Roger Quittenton was (and doubtless still is) adamant that Wheel blocked his view of Haden and that he could only make a decision on what he could see – but it is Haden's act of cynicism that is remembered. The 1953 All Blacks are not unreasonably wont to see 1978 as payback for their experience – a superior team deprived of victory because of a contentious penalty.

Wales took that defeat with rather less grace than Bob Stuart had done 25 years earlier. Quittenton's Welsh wife was eventually moved, à la Kevin Skinner in 1956, to write to the *Western Mail* and suggest that her compatriots give her husband a break. These were tetchy, ill-tempered years. In 1972, McLean felt there was something of 1956 New Zealand in the Welsh air, while conceding that a notably charmless team of All Blacks did little to foster better relations. A month after the 1978 Test, prop forward John Ashworth used his boot to perform informal surgery on the face of Wales captain Dr J.P.R. Williams, whose club Bridgend had been awarded the fixture to mark their centenary year. Three days later, the All Blacks chose to employ Ashworth as a substitute in the finale against the Barbarians at Cardiff. A tour which should have been remembered for the All Blacks at last managing a 'Grand Slam' of the home nations ended in a crescendo of booing.

As McLean had noted back in 1953, this is a family relationship – and the worst rows, notoriously, occur in families. Deep-rooted fraternal affection still remained, while Cardiff Arms Park filled the role of the old family home. New Zealand historian Len Richardson remembers pitching up at the Arms Park on his first visit to Cardiff and being puzzled that a member of the ground staff immediately identified him as a New Zealander. The groundsman explained that his deduction had nothing to do with recognising the accent, but from noting that Richardson still had a suitcase in his hand. New Zealanders, he said, were often so keen to see the ground that they came there even before they had checked into their hotels (an impulse admittedly facilitated by the stadium's proximity to Cardiff station). New Zealand journalist Warwick Roger came to Britain in the 1970s on a press fellowship and recalls: 'I was inexorably drawn to Cardiff Arms Park. Something in my blood and an awareness of the tradition just drew me there.'

In spite of ill-temper there was no sense that the balance of the relationship was likely to change. Chris Laidlaw, an All Black scrum-half of immense intelligence and perception, wrote in 1973 that: 'The

Welsh Rugby club is perhaps the most graphic example of a sporting institution providing the central focus of community life anywhere in the world' and that for this reason 'devotion to the game is deeper and will last longer' than in New Zealand.

There was no other possible choice of opponent for the Centenary international in 1980. The All Blacks were invited, because, said WRU President Cliff Jones, outside-half in the 1935 victory, 'They are nearer to us in approach than any other country. We welcome them as friends first and rivals second.' New Zealand commentator Keith Quinn was to write of a repairing of relations, attributed by him to the influence of Jones and of Graham Mourie, an outstanding All Black captain on and off the field. The one possible breach of the peace, when lock Graeme Higginson, son-in-law of 1953 tourist Nelson Dalzell, looked likely to be sent off at Llanelli, was averted by appeals not only from Mourie but also three Llanelli players.

The only problem was the rugby. The balance of power had shifted drastically and (as of 2004 at least) definitively. First intimations of this were felt at Swansea the week before the international. This was personally memorable – a first view of the All Blacks in the flesh. Swansea were without doubt the best team in Wales, in the midst of a period the club historians would describe as 'the nearest, in terms of achievement, to the days of the "Golden Era" before the First World War'. To dream of a rerun of 1935 was not so fanciful. The rerun we got was of 1924, as New Zealand won 32–0. To watch them, from a defender's eye perspective on the small bank at the Mumbles End, was to have few illusions as to what would happen to Wales the week after. New Zealand won 23–3, scoring four tries including a 70-yard combined effort finished by Hika Reid that bore comparison with any ever scored at the ground. Huw Bowen, then an Aberystwyth student and now an economic historian at Leicester University, says: 'I can still close my eyes and see Murray Mexted doing things you didn't know were possible for a back-row forward, like turning up outside the outside centre'. It could, wrote Quinn, with the air of a man who has seen a once-in-a-lifetime possibility lost, easily have been 35–3 or even 40–3.

He could not know that he had seen the launch of the third phase, in which such scorelines would become the norm. McKechnie's kick of

1978, assumed at the time to be merely the deferment of gratification, marked the last time Wales got within striking distance of the All Blacks.

There have been nine meetings since. New Zealand have scored 416 points to Wales's 98. Even the memorable 2003 World Cup match in Sydney, easily Wales's best performance against the All Blacks since 1978, was eventually lost by a margin of 16 points. Otherwise, the smallest margin of victory has been 25 points, the All Blacks winning 34–9 at Cardiff in 1989 and again at Johannesburg in the 1995 World Cup.

Before those matches had come three meetings in little more than a year. In 1987, they clashed in the semi-final of the first World Cup. Wales had done remarkably well to reach the last four and had lost several first-choice forwards. New Zealand's pack combined traditional All Black remorselessness with terrifying speed, dexterity and dynamism. Scrum-half Robert Jones, the Welshman who most impressed New Zealanders, remembers: 'It is an extraordinary experience to play against a team which is so much better than you. Within a couple of minutes we were in awe of them. They were so dominant in every phase of the game . . . they never let up.'

New Zealand won 49–6. Watching on television with a New Zealand friend I became aware even before half-time that he was embarrassed by their superiority and looking desperately for kind things to say about Wales – although the normal spirit of mickey-taking was restored in the final minutes when a Wales lock who happened to be called Huw Richards contrived to be simultaneously sent off and carried off. There was at least a happy coda to this as Wales played Australia at Rotorua in the third-place play-off and were roared to a late 18–17 victory by a New Zealand crowd impelled equally by old friendship and a desire to put one over on the Aussies, whose coach Alan Jones had become a particular hate figure. This, though, was the last time until the 2003 World Cup meeting that Welsh rugby induced something of the old admiration, rather than the embarrassed pity evident in my friend the previous weekend, in New Zealanders.

Wales returned a year later, clutching a Triple Crown, and were mown down by a combination of the Travel Agents from Hell, who agreed yet another suicidal schedule, and an All Black team who were thoroughly comfortable with their role as the game's first official world champions and in consequence even more scarily formidable. New Zealand became the first team to top the half-century against another of the traditional powers, winning 52–3 at Christchurch and then, just to prove it was not a fluke, did it again two weeks later, winning 54–9 in Auckland. Instead of admitting its complicity in this shambles, the Welsh Rugby Union chose to blame the coaches. Derek Quinnell and Tony Gray were sacked and the one Wales team since the late 1970s to offer a whiff of better days, through a back division featuring the half-back combination of Robert Jones and Jonathan Davies, the contrasting centre virtues of Mark Ring and Bleddyn Bowen, the finishing power of Ieuan Evans and Adrian Hadley plus the all-round footballing skills of Tony Clement, broke up.

Following the comparative moderation of the two 34–9s came the 1997 All Blacks, whose 42–7 win at Wembley seemed downright merciful after the 81–3 hammering handed out to Llanelli in the last-ever meeting between the All Blacks and a Welsh club. Llanelli coach Gareth Jenkins, an astute realist, admitted afterwards that there was no possible answer to the All Blacks and that he had been reduced to awestruck admiration.

Perhaps most mortifying of all was what looks at first sight like one of Wales's better results, the 43–17 defeat at Cardiff in the autumn of 2002. Wales scored two tries, played with immense spirit and were within a score until a few minutes from time, after which a surge of All Black tries gave the final score an unfairly lopsided look. The praise loaded on Wales in some quarters was not wholly unreasonable – judgment has to be based on realistic expectation and by their own recent standards they had played well. Yet New Zealand had come on tour without a single first-choice forward and precious few regular backs. This was not even the strongest combination they had on tour – that had played the previous week against England, holding them to 31–28, and All Black coach John Mitchell used the Wales match to delve even deeper into his reserve strength. Worse still was that the moments of intuitive individual brilliance that were once a Welsh speciality were now confined to their opponents. Even in the 1980s Wales had a few players, notably Robert Jones, Jonathan Davies and Ieuan Evans, whose instinctive talent was such that any team in the world would have wanted them. The manner in which the sidestepping of Shane Williams confounded All Black defenders in the World Cup match at Sydney at least suggested that these attributes were not wholly lost, even if Williams' exclusion from the team for most of the previous three years suggested that they no longer inspired the confidence they once had.

The coaches who saw the drawbacks of his diminutive stature more clearly than the benefits of his attacking gifts were New Zealanders, Graham Henry and Steve Hansen. While this showed a lack of sympathy with and understanding of the traditional strengths of the Welsh game, the choice of coaches from New Zealand, rather than any other country, was evidence that the special relationship still holds. It was also no coincidence that Wales was the only other major union to back New Zealand when it was stripped of its status as co-host for the 2003 World Cup. That friendship will, however, be jeopardised if the New Zealand Rugby Union persists in its ludicrous action to stop Neath – which can point out that it was there first – using its 'All Black' nickname. If they persist, the people of Neath should perhaps follow the example of the New Zealand town of Otorohanga, so angered by the Harrods store's similar bullying of a Wellington laundry run by two brothers who happened to be called Harrod, that it changed its name to Harrodsville and every business in the town became Harrods for a day in the mid-1980s.

The great danger, though, is the simple imbalance of power. This distresses New Zealanders almost as much as it does the Welsh. Years ago, John Gaustad, New Zealand founder and ex-proprietor of London's *Sportspages* bookshop, was heard to express a desire for 'Wales to be worth beating again'. John Tanner says that hearing of Wales's results over the last few years has been like hearing that your younger brother has got into trouble. The frisson of beating old rivals depends on the possibility that they might beat you. If victory is inevitable, it rapidly ceases to be any fun. It takes two for a relationship, and Wales simply is not keeping its end up.

New Zealand will not readily junk the relationship. One reason for its enduring success as a rugby nation is an unmatched awareness of its heritage and what it means. One suspects that more New Zealanders are aware not only of current Canterbury Crusaders coach Robbie Deans but also of his great-great-uncle and namesake who so nearly scored in

1905 than there were Welshmen aware of Teddy Morgan, who did score in that match, even 50 years ago when Morgan was still alive and talking about it. Awareness is being further deepened by anniversary celebrations, with the 2003 All Blacks centenary to be followed by the 100th anniversary of the Originals in 2005.

There comes a point, though, where old relationships can become embarrassing. New Zealand relief, almost as much as Welsh delight, characterised reactions to Wales's unexpected performance in the World Cup meeting. One good display will not of itself end fears that in 25 more years New Zealand will not want to play Wales anywhere. It will be a while before it is clear whether Sydney was a harbinger of the future or a belated outcrop of the past, but that Wales could look the old enemy in the eye for the first time in two decades was hugely encouraging. Unless their divergence can be arrested, will New Zealand still want to play Wales anywhere when another 25 years have passed?

The question to ask is not only why Wales has declined, but why New Zealand has not. McLean's observation in 1953 that, 'There is a mana about New Zealand's name in rugby which exceeds all the rest . . . the very name All Black catches the imagination' – it was noted that while the 1951 Springboks were unquestionably a better team, and crowds for most spectator sports had declined a little over the interviewing two years, the All Blacks still pulled in larger crowds – holds equally true in 2004. No matter that England are the current champions or that Australia have won two World Cups since New Zealand won its one. Just as Brazilian soccer retained its singular magic even when Argentina, Italy and Germany were monopolising the World Cup, so All Black mana has survived the 13 years since they ceased to be world champions.

One of rugby's more engaging qualities is the way it inverts the geopolitical world order – USA, Germany and Japan are likeable also-rans while New Zealand, pacific in both senses of the world, is its ruthless imperial superpower. Wales increasingly looks like post-imperial Spain, a former great power with some fine souvenirs of past greatness but limited prospects of regaining its former status.

Wales has undergone profound social and economic change since 1953, losing the heavy industries on which it relied. With them has gone the world of chapel and choir that produced the likes of Cliff Morgan. New Zealand, though, has also changed considerably. In particular, it experienced the deep shock, cultural as much as economic, of Britain joining the Common Market in 1973, not only restricting access to its largest export market but through rejection forcing a rethink of its self-conception as a Better Britain beyond the seas.

It has continued to grow: its population reaching three million in 1974 and four million in 2003. The composition of that population has changed. British descent still predominates, but no longer as overwhelmingly as it did. Belich records that where there were only 8,000 Pacific Islanders in New Zealand in 1956, there were 200,000, heavily concentrated in Auckland, 40 years later. There are more Samoans in New Zealand than in Samoa.

All of this has been accompanied by political change, with New Zealand retaining its taste for innovation. David Lange's Labour government of the 1980s was notable not least for the almost heroic levels of misunderstanding it inspired in a British media and political class which saw everything through the prism of its own preoccupations.

Right-wingers bent on painting British Labour's nuclear disarmament policy as a sell-out to the Russians failed to understand that for New Zealand, being nuclear-free was populist and nationalist, the self-assertion of a small country against an overbearing neighbour (Australia) and its associated superpower (USA). Left-wingers applauded the nuclear-free policy but took a long time to understand that Lange's government was also subjecting New Zealanders to privatisation and welfare reform on a scale to make Margaret Thatcher's eyes pop. Subsequently, New Zealand has experimented with electoral reform and an unprecedented degree of feminisation – with women holding not only the Premiership, through first Jenny Shipley and then Helen Clark, but also other major roles such as Chief Justice.

Rugby has maintained its cultural centrality. It is no fluke that one of the most significant pieces of New Zealand play-writing – former All Black trialist Greg McGee's *Foreskin's Lament* – should have chosen the game as its metaphor for the state of the nation. No sport, let alone one which matters so much, can insulate itself from social and political forces. The eponymous lament spoke of 'The Bokkies in '73 – the ones that didn't come, that never more will come'. McGee, with Bill Clark and a minority of other rugby figures, stood on one side of the brutal divide opened up by the New Zealand Rugby Union's insistence on maintaining links with South Africa, culminating in the savage (by New Zealand standards at least) scenes accompanying the 1981 Springbok tour.

My first visit to New Zealand was in 1987, combining covering the World Cup with writing about higher education. I was advised, when visiting universities, not to mention the rugby. The divisions of 1981 were apparent, but proved to be healing. The 'Baby Blacks' of 1986, a new generation of players like Sean Fitzpatrick, David Kirk and John Kirwan who seized their chance while most of the first-choice All Black XV was on a well-paid unofficial tour of South Africa, had given the game a fresh and acceptable face. They began a process continued by the sheer excitement of hosting and winning the first World Cup a year later. University teachers and administrators, including one pro vice-chancellor who had played for Otago, proved after all keen to discuss the game and the World Cup.

Rugby remains, in New Zealand as elsewhere, a conservative game. It has, however, been capable of accommodating change. The modern All Blacks offer formidable evidence of economist John Kenneth Galbraith's contention that immigration is almost invariably beneficial – a source of talent and dynamism. The team fits New Zealand's newer, more realistic identity as a multiracial Pacific nation, with islanders like Jonah Lomu taking an increasingly prominent place alongside Pakeha and Maori. No longer is it an exclusively male game – and the national women's team, the Black Ferns, dominate their World Cups even more completely than the All Blacks did the male edition of 1987.

Rugby too had a spell of idolising business and its values, particularly when John Hart was All Black coach. Graham Henry was understandably irked when the NZRU cited Hart's business record – running a small but high-powered team at Fletcher Challenge – as a reason for appointing him, apparently taking the view that Henry's experience of running a large school in a tough district of Auckland did not constitute serious management credentials.

Hart's demise following the French uprising in the 1999 World Cup semi-final signalled a shift back to more traditional values and an awareness of the importance of the All Blacks' cultural role. Impending centenaries have created a greater awareness of the past, comparable to that in Australian cricket under the leadership of Steve Waugh. Every player has been made conscious of his role as inheritor of a great tradition by being given a number corresponding to his place on the roll of capped players.

All is not wholly idyllic. New Zealand race relations were never as uncontested as Better Britain propagandists would have had it – the extent of Waitangi Tribunal claims speaks of considerable unresolved discontents and injustices. The furious reaction when Chris Laidlaw, in a thoughtful article rapidly transformed by thoughtless presentation and shock-horror reporting of it, pointed to a swing back to Pakeha players in 2002 showed that these issues remain deeply sensitive – as well as delighting South African reporters in town for the All Blacks–Springboks match who were confronted by a story they found all too recognisable.

Something has been lost with the focusing of rugby talent on the main population centres under professionalism. To watch a hugely promising youngster like Jeremy Manning, still not 17, playing first five-eighth with the cool control of a veteran in Marlborough's Ranfurly Shield challenge against holders Canterbury in 2002 was to reflect that if he is half as talented as he appears he will rapidly follow Leon MacDonald and Hayden Pedersen to professional contracts in Christchurch. Earlier generations like Brian Ford and Alan Sutherland could stay in Blenheim, play for Marlborough and still win both the Shield and All Black caps. Provinces like Marlborough and Hawke's Bay – which still ranks fourth for Shield matches won, ahead of both Wellington and Otago – are reduced to also-ran status, feeders to the big five.

New Zealand rugby, though, has ridden change effectively. Wales has not. The decline of performance in a nation's culturally most significant popular activity is invariably a complex phenomenon, not remotely explicable in the single-factor terms often proffered in debate.

A number of factors are, though, worth considering. In relation to New Zealand, if not to European rivals, population should be noted. While New Zealand's population has doubled since 1953, Wales's has grown by around 10 per cent. A quarter smaller than Wales 50 years ago, New Zealand is now roughly one-third larger. The two lines crossed in the mid-1960s – or just after New Zealand began its winning run in the fixture. Wales has had no energising parallel to the Samoan influx.

Among the most popular explanation for Welsh decline is educational reform and the demise of the grammar schools. Almost every Welsh survivor of 1953 – including Stoker Williams, a firm proponent of comprehensivisation, cites this as a factor. Any view from such quarters deserves the deepest possible respect. If comprehensives were, however, so deleterious to rugby, then England, which underwent a similar transformation at much the same time would hardly be enjoying the most prosperous period in its history. The deepest decline in Welsh standards has also been among the tight-forwards – where the grammar school boys were always least likely to be found.

Terry McLean dated the demise of Wales to the day of the 1980 Llanelli–All Blacks match: 'On the way back to Cardiff in the car with David Parry-Jones and Phil Bennett, we heard the news of huge closures in the steel industry. That was the day when Welsh rugby died.' There is a striking parallel with the decline of Scottish football, which also had its essential base in large-unit, heavily-unionised primary industries and, even in periods when the national team was weak, was singularly productive of individuals of creative genius. It too now produces disciplined, hard-working professionals but has lost the knack of generating true originals.

One must also look beyond coal and steel. The public services, in particular teaching and the police, were as important to Welsh rugby as heavy industry. Most took a fearful battering in the 1980s – the exception, the police, were just extremely busy – and teachers had all but disappeared from first-class rugby by the end of the decade. Welsh rugby might reasonably be seen as a victim of Thatcherism, presumably unintended even if Denis Thatcher was an enthusiastic supporter of England rugby.

Nor was English rugby any help. A question that any thoughtful Welsh fan could not help asking during the 1970s was, 'What will happen if the English ever get their act together?' In the 1990s, we found out. England and France have an enormous advantage in playing numbers and wealth, so if reasonably well organised are likely to be stronger than Wales.

Further contributory factors included the increasing frequency of international rugby. Wales lost their first four matches against South Africa, but they were spaced over forty-five years. After the 1995 World

Cup, they played the same opponents four times in forty-three months. Inferiority is rubbed in that much more frequently nowadays, while the sheer size of modern scores further underlines poor performances. And while a great history is normally a source of strength, it can become an immense burden to a struggling team. McLean wrote of the 1953 All Blacks that they were 'burdened from the beginning with the feats of their predecessors'. Welsh teams since 1980 could say much the same.

This concatenation of forces might have overwhelmed the most enlightened, far-sighted and competent governing body. The Welsh Rugby Union, being none of these things, did not have a prayer. The union, of course, is not exclusively to blame. McLean also noted, unbelievingly, the nexus of petty parochial hatreds afflicting Wales even in a time of comparative prosperity in 1953.

Wales undoubtedly did become complacent in the great days of the 1970s, confident that the system which generated matchless talent for the national game and won such international admiration that National Coaching Organiser Ray Williams was despatched on an aid mission to the hapless Australians in 1973, would continue to deliver. In 1964, the union's reaction to a traumatic tour of South Africa, culminating in a 24–3 Test match defeat at Durban was to convene the inquiry that laid the ground for the successes of the next 15 years. In 1988, after an even greater debacle in New Zealand, it refused to listen to the players – Jonathan Davies offered to prepare a report – and sacked the management team that had delivered a thrilling Triple Crown only a few months earlier.

It then went on to get into an unholy tangle over South Africa. It is regrettable that so many leading Welsh players should have accepted the large sums of money offered to play in the South African Rugby Union's centenary matches in 1989, breaching both the rules on professionalism and attempts to isolate apartheid. But when leading members of their union were actively conniving at their participation, they are hardly to be blamed.

Worst of all was its performance in the immediate aftermath of professionalism in the late 1990s. This was admittedly a time when any ruling body might have struggled. The game underwent a transformation paralleling that of post-Soviet Russia, moving from stifling regulation to a total absence of it almost overnight. Clubs were driven by panic at the thought of being left behind in a market totally destabilised by the aggressive recruiting of English clubs – a phenomenon for which Newcastle owner John Hall must take most blame. Millions had suddenly to be found to pay players. Cardiff, the best-resourced of the Welsh clubs, appeared uninterested in playing in Wales at all.

No union handled it especially well. But where other unions, notably Ireland, kept their focus on building the game in their countries the WRU's energies went into a different kind of construction – the Millennium Stadium, built for the 1999 World Cup. Wales was nominal host but the event made only limited impact because of the blackmailing built into the bidding process, with the other European unions demanding a slice of the action in return for their support. Wales hosted only nine of the forty-one matches. The semi-finals, which proved to be the most compelling games in the tournament, were both at Twickenham.

To do this the WRU demolished the stadium completed to such hosannas little more than a decade before and replaced it with the 72,500-seater, retractable-roofed Millennium Stadium. It can be argued that the National Lottery might have found a better use for £47 million than a building project, replacing a still new facility in the richest area of Wales. It is certainly the case that the WRU might have found a better use for £70 million, most of it borrowed.

It has undoubtedly been of immense benefit to the Football Association, offered a venue for the FA Cup final while they, in recompense, make the WRU look comparatively competent with their handling of the much more expensive and even less necessary new Wembley. For Welsh rugby it has been an unmitigated disaster, a prestige project which has saddled the WRU with crippling interest payments. Not so much Millennium as Millstone, or Mausoleum, a burial place for the ambitions of Welsh rugby.

Shock-horror headlines greeted the possibility that, to recoup some of the losses, the WRU might have to attach a sponsor's name to the stadium. Yet that particular pass had already been sold when the Union, following the example of other nations, agreed to deface the red shirt that has epitomised Welsh aspirations for more than a century with a sponsor's logo considerably larger than the union's own insignia.

Welsh hopes in this era were too often pinned on a concept that predated rugby – an Arthurian deus ex machina sent to lead us back to glory. First Jonathan Davies, then Graham Henry and Iestyn Harris were all cast in this impossible role. None succeeded, as no mortal being could, even if Graham Henry's initial impact led some to believe that King Arthur had been reincarnated as an Auckland schoolmaster. Merely gifted humanity having failed, the WRU has resorted to genetic engineering in the shape of the new regional structure. The clubs had, admittedly, been their own worst enemies, but the new structures – retaining Cardiff, the greatest underachievers of the lot, and Llanelli as the core of 'regions' while Bridgend-Pontypridd, Swansea-Neath and Ebbw Vale-Newport shotgun marriages supply the other three entities – give greater power to the one body still more discredited, the WRU. Maybe they will supply an answer, although the evidence of a first season concluding with the summary execution of the Bridgend-Pontypridd franchise – a decision whose logic, one particularly incisive letter to *Wales on Sunday* pointed out, could equally be used to close down Welsh rugby as a whole – was scarcely encouraging.

Hope springs eternal, and every flash of promise – such as the Grand Slam won by the Under-21 team in 2003, and the spectacular performance by one of its stars, flanker Jonathan Thomas, against the All Blacks at the World Cup – is seized upon as a sign that the bad times may be finite. Rugby still matters in Wales. This can, when refracted through the infantile nationalism of parts of the Welsh media, take on a slightly hysterical form. Victory over England at Wembley in 1999, a somewhat fortunate reprise of what used to be an annual event, was treated as though it were the second coming. The Welsh Rugby Union marketing department, invoking Wales's fading religiosity through the one hymn still regularly sung by international crowds, chose to present Graham Henry as 'The Great Redeemer'. Huge crowds queued for copies of Henry's autobiography. Henry, who did not ask for any of this treatment even if he was quick to turn it to his financial advantage, admitted to being taken aback.

Even so, a passion for good rugby remains. Wales provided more than half of the fans who followed the British Lions to Australia in 2001, even though the team was predominantly English. The chance to see their, and Britain's, best players for once with a real chance of beating the best of the southern hemisphere drew them in their thousands. New Zealand in 2005 may be equally irresistible, even if Welsh representation is minimal.

Maybe recovery is just around the corner. At the same time, though, there is the unnerving spectacle of major sporting cultures that have fallen and show no signs of ever rising again. Hungarian football bestrode the world in 1953, with Puskas and associates demolishing England's historic unbeaten home record against European teams by 6–3 on the same day that the All Blacks were beating Glasgow and Edinburgh 23–3 at Old Anniesland, but is now reduced to the rank of a fourth-rate power. France still stages the world's greatest cycle race, but has not produced a winner in nearly 20 years and has become glumly accustomed to watching Americans, Spaniards and Danes atop the podium in the Champs-Elysées. Belgium, once a comparable cycling power, is even more reduced. Most worrying of all are those most comparable to Welsh rugby – not only Scottish football but also West Indian cricket, player of a parallel role as a unifying popular force in the absence of more conventional national signifiers.

New Zealand is not wholly without its worries. The clear-sighted Bob Scott is not alone in fearing that in an era when professional and financial imperatives override more traditional loyalties, New Zealand may struggle to compete with larger, richer nations like Australia, France and England. Already it has to tolerate midwinter internationals being played at night – when conditions at somewhere like Christchurch can be an all too vivid reminder that the city was Captain Scott's starting point – for the benefit of Australian television audiences. Yet another World Cup failure in 2003 – particularly bitter since it was inflicted by Australia – raised questions about the standards of New Zealand forward play, although these concerns were to some extent stilled by the All Black demolition of world champions England in their first match under former Wales coach Graham Henry.

Among a wide range of distressing spectacles presented by the battle to stage the 2007 World Cup – not least among them, that of Wales's vote being nakedly on offer to the highest bidder – was the New Zealand Rugby Union's clearly expressed concern that the competition might grow beyond its ability ever to stage it again. If rugby becomes so money-driven that it cannot go to the country where, more than anywhere else in the world, the Cup would engage and enthuse the whole society, then something vital will have been lost from the game.

We cannot live on memories, but they are essential to knowing who we are and where we came from. The stories of 1905, 1935 and 1953 were essential elements in the narrative that made Welsh rugby such an expression of national consciousness. James Thurber once wrote that millions of middle-aged Americans went to sleep mentally striking out the New York Yankees. Any number of their Welsh equivalents still doubtless daydream of sidestepping past a succession of black-shirted opponents on an unstoppable run towards the tryline at Eden Park or the Millennium Stadium.

There is, of course, no going back to 1953, nor would it be desirable, whatever the ostensible charms of a world in which Wales could beat New Zealand and feel slightly disappointed that it had not been done with greater style. That coal has gone is ultimately the fulfilment of the ambitions of those miner fathers – Gerwyn Williams', Gerald Davies' – that their sons should not have to spend their working lives in an environment of darkness, dirt and danger. As Max Boyce, whose success, like that of many comedians, was founded on astute observation, once sang of closing pits: 'Don't you worry, buttie bach, we're really very glad.' No more can New Zealanders return to a world dominated by farming, guaranteed British purchasing and 'a rather flat mental and social landscape', its introspection enforced by physical isolation. To go back would be to forego one of the great beneficial changes of the past 50 years – the recasting of New Zealanders as the world's great travellers, their 'overseas experience' enriching not only their lives but also that of their own nation and those that they visit. One shudders to think, for instance, how London would fare without its corps of transient New Zealand teachers whose democratic spirit and ability to cope fit them ideally for the demands of big-city schools.

Nor would New Zealanders wish to return to a time when an All Black team could play five Test matches on tour without their backs scoring a single try – scores by Clark (2), Stuart and Dalzell were the sum total outcome of 400 minutes of rugby when they had possession more often than not. In part of course this can be blamed on 'safety-first'. New Zealand midfield backs of the 1950s seem to have been the major exception to the rule that all things must pass. Far more, though, could be blamed on a game hamstrung by endless stoppages and heavy traffic in midfield, with the ball on the ground much of the time. True, every score mattered – which is not always the case in modern tryfests – but far too many of them came from scrambles and errors rather than being created through open play.

Certainly there is no going back to a world before professionalism. If there is regret that the modern professional is unavoidably a less rounded, interesting individual than his predecessor who found time for the game in between the demands of farming, teaching or making steel, this is an inevitable consequence of the trends of modern sport. Going openly professional also had the immense virtue of purging union of its weight of hypocrisy about league, putting an end to incidents like the monstrous treatment of the hapless George Parsons.

Would we really want a return to a world in which the All Blacks came only every ten years? Cliff Morgan is absolutely right to assert that the infrequency of their visits built up expectation and excitement, demanding that every tour be memorable. Yet it seems unfair that a distinguished career might encompass only a single shot at a meaningful tour abroad, a chance that might be lost through bad timing, ill-luck, injury or selectorial whim. It is a fair bet that players like Morrie O'Connell and George Nola would have appreciated more than one chance per decade. We probably have, however, swung too far the other way – a consistent note in the reaction of players from both sides in 1953 is one of mild derision at the huge totals of caps their successors of 2003 can accumulate, in some cases by dint of a succession of replacement appearances lasting only a few minutes per match.

Australia and South Africa have lost something of their magic by reappearing in Britain with a regularity that makes their players as familiar as those of France or Ireland. New Zealand retains greater mystique, in part because of simple All Black mana, but also because it has rationed visits.

The problem, of course, is that rugby union has so few major countries, depriving it of both variety and unpredictability. This is why its World Cup is less satisfactory than football's and why fans in the years between World Cups are doomed endlessly to see the same few visitors who can guarantee to fill Twickenham or the Millennium Stadium. It is why rugby needs to cherish and encourage its developing nations, so that Argentina, Georgia or Samoa might one day diversify that list of usual suspects. One respect in which the NZRU has been conspicuously unenlightened is its treatment of the Pacific islands. When George Simpkins, coach of the Fijian team who scared the French witless before losing the World Cup quarter-final at Eden Park in 1987, was asked by New Zealand journalists, 'What can we do to help you?' his answer was simple: 'Come and play us.' Fiji is still waiting. Some British criticism of the substantial Pacific Island contingent in All Black teams is ill-founded. New Zealand has rugby players of Samoan and Tongan extraction for the same reason that the England football team fields players who would also qualify for Jamaica – it reflects the reality of a multi-racial society. But at the same time, New Zealand has chosen to treat the islands as a nursery, cherry-picking talent rather than developing them. It should have been their protector in 1995 when Rupert Murdoch, the South Africans and Australians determined to exclude the islands from the new Super-12 competition. It was not. This is one area where Wales can claim a better record – having invited the Fijians to visit as early as 1964, gone on tour of the islands and become the first International Board nation to play the Samoans (generosity rather ungratefully repaid at the 1991 and 1999 World Cups) in 1986 – although the record of the British nations in relation to Continental Europe, left almost entirely to the French, has been pretty miserable.

As well as developing new nations, the game needs to preserve those it has. The game needs Wales, but does Wales need rugby? Gwyn Thomas, a great humorous writer of serious purpose, complained that, 'This game, with its magnets of remembrance, has drained off much of the ardour which might have gone into a more sedulous cultivation of the arts'. Maybe so, but has rugby's decline over the past two decades really been to the benefit of poetry, painting or music in Wales?

There probably are better things for a nation to be identified with than rugby football, but there are also undoubtedly much worse ones. The world is increasingly conscious of spectator sport and a game like rugby offers nations of three million the chance of a prominence they could not possibly hope to enjoy in football, eternally in the grip of the big battalions. (Wales-sized Uruguay's two World Cup triumphs were more than half a century ago, in the two weakest competitions ever held.)

If plotting a revival were so easy, it would have been achieved long before now. It was hard, even before Shane Williams started sidestepping at Sydney, to escape the thought that Wales needs to start placing greater emphasis on the intuitive, instinctive skills that were once its great forte. They still exist at schoolboy level. An English Schools coach recently confided to a Welsh friend that while his teams were strong, fit and well-organised, they still had difficulty with Welsh youngsters' capacity for the unexpected. Wales continues to have the better of age-group clashes.

This need not be at the expense of hard-headed practicality or analytical intelligence. Welsh teams, as McLean pointed out in criticising the attitude of the 1969 touring team to rucking, always were tough and hard-headed. This is not an either/or proposition. Welsh rugby at its best – played by men like Gwyn Nicholls and Dickie Owen, Bleddyn Williams and John Gwilliam, Carwyn James, Clive Rowlands and Gerald Davies – always was a mix of the pragmatic, the thoughtful and the intuitive. Whether we consider the planning of Morgan's try in 1905, the tactical switch that brought Wooller into play in 1935, Bleddyn Williams' calculation of how to negate the All Black back row, or Ken Jones's intuitive judgment of a capriciously bouncing ball in 1953, it is clear that all of these aspects have been brought into play whenever New Zealand has been beaten. Brilliance by itself is not enough, but no more is power or tactical calculation.

All will be needed if the relationship with New Zealand is ever to be restored. It will not be easy. The gap has grown so wide, leaving Wales in the role of the old school friend who has fallen on hard times – dishevelled, the worse for wear, and the subject of pity rather than respect. Victories that once occasioned New Zealanders genuine joy now inspire only embarrassment and fears for the victim's survival.

New Zealand has shown real patience. Nowhere outside Wales is a Welsh revival more truly and urgently desired. It cannot, though, be expected to wait forever. It is possibly too much, Sydney notwithstanding, to hope for a Welsh victory in the immediate future, but if the special relationship is to survive into its second century, it is vital that Wales should be worth beating.

SOURCES AND FURTHER READING

PRIMARY SOURCES

Interviews: Terry McLean (26.7.01, 27.7.02), Brian Fitzpatrick (27.7.01, 27.7.02), John Tanner (28.7.01), Richard White (9.7.02), Allan Elsom (12.7.02), Bill McCaw (12.7.02), Peter Eastgate (14.7.02), Bill Clark (16.7.02), Bob Stuart (19.7.02), Bob Scott (24.7.02), Keith Davis (25.7.02), Kevin Skinner (26.7.02), Snow White (29.7.02), Warwick Roger (29.7.02), Stoker Williams (21.11.02), Gareth Griffiths (22.11.02, 9.12.02), Gerwyn Williams (6.12.02), Bleddyn Williams (9.12.02), Gwyn Rowlands (13.12.02), Cliff Morgan (19.12.02), John Gwilliam (23.12.02), David Davies (20.1.03), Glyn Davies (27.1.03), Ron Waldron (by phone 5.6.03) Letters/emails from Bill Clark, Courtenay Meredith, Gwyn Rowlands, Bob Scott, Bob Stuart, Richard White

Sound recordings: New Zealand Sound Archives/Nga Taongo Korero D1158, match commentary 19.12.53; D1140, interview with Laurie Haig 1976. Fragments held by British National Sound Archive, British Library

Film of Match: Fragment supplied by BBC archives, '1953' tape made for Welsh Rugby Writers Dinner 22.11.02

Match programme: Wales v. New Zealand 19.12.53

Contemporary Reports: Bill Clark scrapbook, New Zealand Rugby Museum, Palmerston North. *The Western Mail, South Wales Evening*

Post, New Zealand Herald, Christchurch Press, The Dominion

BOOKS
Accounts of the 1953–54 All Blacks tour:
Hayhurst, John, *The Fourth All Blacks 1953–1954*, Longmans, 1954
McCarthy, Winston, *Round The World With The All Blacks 1953–54*, Sporting Publications, 1954
McLean, Terry, *Bob Stuart's All Blacks*, Reed, 1954

Books by or about people who played in the Wales v. New Zealand match:
Jarden, Ron, *Rugby on Attack*, Whitcombe and Tombs, 1961
Morgan, Cliff, *Cliff Morgan – The Autobiography, Beyond the Fields of Play*, Hodder and Stoughton, 1997
Parry-Jones, David, *The Gwilliam Seasons*, Seren, 2002
Scott, Bob and McLean, Terry, *Bob Scott on Rugby*, Kaye, 1955
Scott, Bob and McLean, Terry, *The Bob Scott Story*, Reed, 1956
Williams, Bleddyn, *Rugger My Life*, Stanley Paul, 1956

Contemporary Reference:
Playfair Rugby Football Annual 1952-3-4-5
Rugby Almanack of New Zealand 1954
Whitaker's Almanac 1953

Wales v. New Zealand:
Billot, John, *The All Blacks in Wales*, Ron Jones Publications, 1972
Dixon, George, *The Triumphant Tour of the New Zealand Footballers 1905*, David Ling, reprint 1999
McLean, Terry, *Red Dragons of Rugby*, Reed, 1969
Ryan, Greg, *Forerunners of the All Blacks*, Canterbury University Press, 1993
Wooller, Wilfred and Owen, David (eds), *Fifty Years of the All Blacks*, Phoenix House, 1954

Welsh rugby:
Evans, Alan, *Taming The Tourists*, Vertical, 2003
Evans, Alan and Gardiner, Duncan, *Cardiff Rugby Football Club 1876–1939*, Tempus, 1999
Evans, Alan and Gardiner, Duncan, *Cardiff Rugby Football Club 1940–2000*, Tempus, 2001

Farmer, David, *The All Whites, The Life and Times of Swansea RFC*, DFPS, 1995

Jackson, Peter, *Lions of Wales*, Mainstream, 1998

Jenkins, John M., Preece, Duncan and Auty, Timothy, *Who's Who of Welsh International Rugby Players*, Bridge, 1991

Morgan, John, *John Morgan on Wales*, Christopher Davies, 1993

Parry-Jones, David, *Prince Gwyn*, Seren, 1999

Parry-Jones, David (ed.), *Taff's Acre*, Collins Willow, 1984

Richards, Huw, Stead, Peter and Williams, Gareth (eds), *Heart and Soul*, University of Wales Press (UWP), 1998

Richards, Huw, Stead, Peter and Williams, Gareth (eds), *More Heart and Soul*, UWP, 1999

Smith, David and Williams, Gareth, *Fields of Praise*, Welsh Rugby Union, 1981

Thomas, Wayne, *A Century of Welsh International Rugby Players*, Western Mail, 1980

Thomas, Wayne, *A Farewell to Arms*, Western Mail, 1997

Williams, Gareth, *1905 and All That*, Gomer, 1991

New Zealand rugby:

Chester, R.H. and McMillan, N.A.C., *Centenary*, Blandford Press, 1984

Clarke, Don and Booth, Pat, *The Boot*, Reed, 1966

Howitt, Bob, *New Zealand Rugby Greats Vols 1, 2 and 3*, Hodder Moa, Beckett, 1997

Jones, Peter, (as told to Norman Harris) *It's Me, Tiger*, Reed, 1965

Knight, Lindsay, *They Led the All Blacks*, Rugby Press, 1991

Laidlaw, Chris, *Mud In Your Eye*, Reed, 1973

McCarthy, Winston, *Rugby in My Time*, Reed, 1958

McCarthy, Winston, *Haka, the All Blacks Story*, Pelham, 1968

McCarthy, Winston, *Listen It's A Goal*, Pelham, 1973

McLean, Terry, *Great Days in New Zealand Rugby*, Reed, 1959

McLean, Terry and Nepia, George, *I, George Nepia*, London League Publications, revised reprint 2002

MacKenzie, Morrie, *All Blacks in Chains*, Truth, 1960

MacKenzie, Morrie, *Black, Black, Black!*, Minerva, 1969

McKenzie, Norman, *On With The Game*, Reed, 1961

Palenski, Ron, *The Jersey*, Hodder Moa, Beckett, 2001

Palenski, Ron (ed.), *Between The Posts*, Hodder and Stoughton, 1989

Slatter, Gordon, *On The Ball*, Whitcombe and Tombs, 1970

Warwick, Roger, *Old Heroes*, Hodder and Stoughton, 1991

Rugby – general:
Davies, Gerald, *Tries*, Harrap, 1984
Edwards, Gareth, *100 Great Rugby Players*, MacDonald, Queen Anne Press, 1987
Hands, David, *The Five Nations Story*, Tempus, 2000
Holmes, Bob and Thau, Chris (eds), *My Greatest Game*, Mainstream, 1994
Morgan, W. John and Nicholson, Geoffrey, *Report on Rugby*, Heinemann, 1959
Nauright, John and Chandler, Timothy L. (eds), *Making Men*, Frank Cass, 1996
Reason, John and James, Carwyn, *The World of Rugby*, BBC, 1979
Stewart, J.J., *Rugby, Developments in the Field of Play*, Massey University, 1997
Thomas, J.B.G., *The Lions on Trek*, Stanley Paul, 1956

History – Wales:
Morgan, Kenneth O., *Wales 1880–1980*, Oxford University Press (OUP), 1981
Smith, Dai, *Aneurin Bevan and The World of South Wales*, UWP, 1993
Williams, Gwyn, *When Was Wales?*, Penguin Books, 1985

History – New Zealand:
Belich, James, *Paradise Reforged*, Penguin (NZ), 2001
Phillips, Jock, *A Man's Country*, Penguin (NZ), 1987
Rice, Geoffrey W. (ed.), *Oxford History of New Zealand*, OUP, 1993
Sinclair, Keith, *A History of New Zealand*, Penguin, 1980 edition
Sinclair, Keith, *A Destiny Apart*, Allen and Unwin (NZ), 1986

WEBSITES
New Zealand Rugby Museum rugbymuseum.co.nz.
Dictionary of New Zealand Biography dnzb.govt.nz

INDEX

INDEX